WHEN SHALL THEIR GL

Battle Honours

On 16 September 1957, Her Majesty the Queen approved the award of the following battle honours to the Commando Association in recognition of the services of the commandos in the Second World War:

VAAGSO, NORWAY 1941, ST NAZAIRE, DIEPPE, NORMANDY LANDING, DIVES CROSSING, FLUSHING, WESTKAPELLE, RHINE, LEESE, ALLER, NORTH-WEST EUROPE 1942, '44–45, LITANI, SYRIA 1941, STEAMROLLER FARM, SEDJENANE I, DJEBEL CHOUCHA, NORTH AFRICA 1941–43, LANDING IN SICILY, PURSUIT TO MESSINA, SICILY 1943, LANDING AT PORTO SAN VENERE, TERMOLI, SALERNO, MONTE ORNITO, ANZIO, VALLI DI COMACCHIO, ARGENTA GAP, ITALY 1943–45, GREECE 1944–45, CRETE, MADAGASCAR, ADRIATIC, MIDDLE EAST 1941, '42, '44, ALETHANGYAW, MYEBON, KANGAW, BURMA 1943–45.

THE COMMANDO ASSOCIATION BATTLE HONOURS FLAG
DEDICATED ON 15 APRIL 1961
AND LAID UP IN ST GEORGE'S CHAPEL, WESTMINSTER ABBEY
DURING A SPECIAL SERVICE ON 1 MAY 1971
IN THE GRACIOUS PRESENCE OF HER MAJESTY
QUEEN ELIZABETH THE QUEEN MOTHER

WHEN SHALL THEIR GLORY FADE?

THE STORIES OF THE THIRTY-EIGHT BATTLE HONOURS OF THE ARMY COMMANDOS 1940–1945

JAMES DUNNING

Foreword by Countess Mountbatten of Burma

Frontline Books, London

When Shall Their Glory Fade?
The Stories of the Thirty-Eight Battle Honours of the Army Commandos 1940–1945

This edition published in 2011 by Frontline Books,
an imprint of Pen & Sword Books Ltd,
47 Church Street, Barnsley, S. Yorkshire, S70 2AS

ISBN 978-1-84832-597-5

A CIP data record for this title is available from the British Library

Typeset by M.A.T.S. Typesetters, Leigh-on-Sea, Essex in 11.5/13 Centaur

Printed in the UK by CPI Antony Rowe

CONTENTS

ILLUSTRATIONS

(plates to be found between pages 144 and 145)

Plate 8: No. 2 Commando officers at Gibraltar prior to their going on active service in Sicily, Italy and the Adriatic; loading equipment prior to crossing Lake Comacchio

Plate 9: The Sarande operation, Albania, July 1944; Commandos of Lovat's Brigade move off from their Normandy landing beach to join up with their parachute comrades at Pegasus Bridge

Plate 10: Captain Charles Head, Brigadier John Durnford-Slater and Colonel Peter Young at Normandy; graves of some of No. 4 Commando in their first defensive position at Hauger in Normandy

Plate 11: FLUSHING – some of the German prisoners being collected by No 4 Commando; the crossing of the Rhine

Plate 12: A special bodyguard from Nos. 4 and 6 Commandos organised to protect Field Marshal Montgomery; FLUSHING – Commandos of No. 2 Troop, No. 4 Cdo, take over a captured German position

Plate 13: No. 3 Commando Brigade wading ashore at Myebon; Tag Barnes

Plate 14: Victoria Cross Commandos

Plate 15: Henry Brown; Commando Basic Training Centre at Achnacarry

Plate 16: Veterans of No. 4 Commando reunited at St Marguerite; Countess Mountbatten with Lord Lovat and his D-Day piper Bill Millin

LIST OF MAPS

FOREWORD

Countess Mountbatten of Burma, CBE, CD, JP, DL,
Patron of the Commando Association 1981–2005

I was very pleased to have been asked to write a Foreword for this book by Major James Dunning (himself a founder member sergeant in 1940) on the famous Commandos. He attempts to tell the human stories behind the heroic exploits that earned them thirty-eight battle honours. These stories are often told by the men themselves of their very tough training and the terribly difficult climatic conditions they endured during their extraordinary exploits, ranging from Norway and Europe to Burma in the Far East.

My father, Lord Mountbatten, was Chief of Combined Operations with overall responsibility when they were formed as a spearhead for taking the war back to the enemy after the evacuation at Dunkirk.

Men joined the Commandos from every regiment in the British Army and also the Royal Marines. It tells us much about their quality and heroism that no fewer than eight of them earned Victoria Cross, our highest and most prestigious military award.

I myself, as a nineteen-year-old wartime Wren in the Womens Royal Naval Service served for fifteen months in a Combined Operations base near Southampton, where I had close contact with Commandos right over 'D-Day of the invasion – a time I shall never forget.

My father had an enormous admiration and affection for these marvellous brave men and became their first patron until his assassination in 1979. Two years later I was asked to succeed him in that post, which I have always felt to be a great honour.

Commandos had a fabulous and exciting reputation over the whole country, a special memory for older people that will never be forgotten. I truly believe the answer to the question posed by the title of this book 'When shall their glory fade' is quite simply – 'NEVER.'

Patricia Mountbatten of Burma

INTRODUCTION

STEP INSIDE WESTMINSTER ABBEY, using the west door, and there in St George's Chapel, hanging on the wall, is the battle honours flag of the Army Commandos Association.

The flag is emblazoned with over thirty battle honours commemorating the campaigns, raids, battles, and notable engagements fought by the Army Commandos from 1940–1945. However, it must be pointed out that nine are for campaigns in which the Commandos fought many actions that did not qualify for specific battle honours and so the twenty-nine raids and battles that were recognised as battle honours represent only a fraction of the many actions fought by the Commandos during the war – but they are the most noteworthy.

A cursory glance at the formidable list of place names on the flag will reveal that they are not restricted to one or two theatres of war but are world-wide – the Commandos fought with distinction in Norway, France, Belgium, Holland, Germany, North Africa, Sicily, Italy, the Adriatic Islands, Crete, Syria, Yugoslavia, Madagascar, and Burma.

The tradition of awarding battle honours to regiments goes back over three hundred years when the first was awarded to 2nd Regiment of Foot for their service in Tangiers from 1662 to 1682. From the eighteenth century onwards, when regimental colours were no longer used as rallying points in battle, they were retained for ceremonial occasions and, of course, they helped to preserve regimental histories. Today regiments still proudly march through their 'freedom' towns with 'colours flying and drums beating'.

The Commando battle honours flag is unique. Following the end of the Second World War the Army Commandos were disbanded, although their traditions and fighting spirit have been maintained by the Royal Marines. However, in 1957 it came to the notice of the Commando Association that the Ministry of Defence was considering the question of awarding battle honours to regiments for distinguished actions and enquiries were made to see whether it would be possible for the association to apply for those honours on behalf of all the Army Commandos who had fought in the actions selected for recognition. (It must be pointed out at this stage that only army units were eligible for award of battle honours and the Royal Marines, who came under the Royal Navy, were not eligible; nevertheless I have endeavoured to record their involvement in the relevant actions when they fought alongside their Army Commando comrades).

Permission was given and later that year, in a special army order, it was announced that Her Majesty Queen Elizabeth II had graciously approved the award of the thirty-eight battle honours to the Commando Association and steps were taken to produce a worthy flag and also consider a suitable place to display it permanently. The association committee, under the chairmanship of Colonel Charles Newman, VC, (leader of the St Nazaire raid) commissioned Hobson and Sons of London, specialist makers of regimental colours, to design and make the flag, which they did for the sum of £250.

In April 1961, in the presence of a congregation of over a thousand people – ex-commandos, their families, the relatives of fallen commandos, and distinguished guests – the dean of the abbey dedicated the flag and it was subsequently placed alongside the Commando Memorial in the cloisters of the abbey. Incidentally, Sir Winston Churchill had previously unveiled this statue, along with those of the parachute soldier and the submariner in February 1948 and it was then, in his tribute to those men, that he posed the question, 'When shall their glory fade?'

It soon became apparent that the site of the flag in the cloisters was not ideal and alternatives were considered; happily this problem was solved when the dean and chapter of the abbey advised the association that they were in a position to hang the flag in its present position. To commemorate this honour a special service was organised; in the presence of HM Queen Elizabeth the Queen Mother and a congregation of nearly two thousand people, including many distinguished guests, a moving service of thanksgiving for the laying up of the flag was held on I May 1971.

So much then for the background of this unique flag, the only military flag of its kind in the abbey – now for a word or two about this book.

From the outset I wanted to recall the stories behind these Commando battle honours, some of which are already well known and have been the subjects of many books. So my aim was not to provide an official record nor detailed history but rather to tell the stories with as many personal accounts as possible from commandos who were actually there.

Unfortunately time over the elapsing sixty-odd years has taken its toll on commando veterans and to gather their stories has restricted the sources mainly to previous books – many out of print – and other recorded accounts. Nevertheless a number of comrades who had not previously told their tales were found and together these background anecdotes have been woven into the narrative that follows.

I also wanted to briefly outline the origins of the Commandos and what type of men volunteered for 'special service', then to point out that these volunteers were ordinary men from different regiments, army services and corps of the British Army. They were not supermen, but ordinary chaps who were highly trained, self-disciplined and resolute with high morale, and led by officers who had the respect of their men. It was the combination of all these factors that created the indomitable fighting spirit with which the name 'Commando' became synonymous and so enabled them to win those thirty-eight battle honours. It is to these men that this book is dedicated.

JAMES DUNNING

CHAPTER 1

CHURCHILL CALLS FOR VOLUNTEERS

BEFORE THE SECOND WORLD WAR Britain had no special forces at all so it is interesting to trace the origins and formation of today's Commandos, the Parachute Regiment, the Special Air Service (SAS), and the Special Boat Service (SBS) because they are all interrelated.

The Commandos – the first of our present-day special forces – were formed during the grim days of 1940 when Britain's fortunes were at their lowest ebb and the priority was on the defence of these islands and not offensive action across the Channel.

During the month of June Hitler followed up his conquests of Poland and Norway by defeating the armies of France, Britain, and the Lowland countries; the German army, by advancing on to the Channel ports, had forced the withdrawal of the British Expeditionary Force (BEF) from Europe through Dunkirk. The subsequent evacuation was hailed as a miracle, but in reality it amounted to a military tragedy because, although the bulk of the BEF was safely evacuated back to England, it incurred the loss of considerable amounts of arms, weapons, and vehicles of all sorts, plus huge supplies of ammunition, stores, and equipment needed for the defence of Britain.

As a result the Germans, now masters of Europe from Norway in the north almost to the Pyrenees in the south, were planning (Operation *Sea Lion*) to mount an invasion of Britain. A start had already been made with a series of daylight raids by the Luftwaffe on airfields and other targets in the south of England.

Winston Churchill had only taken over as prime minister and minister of defence in May and so his first few weeks in office were witness to the series of military defeats outlined above, added to which were losses at sea of ships and vital supplies of raw materials, fuel, and food imports that were essential for a successful outcome of the war. This situation had been made worse by Italy's entry into the war on the side of Nazi Germany, making the sea route through the Mediterranean to the Middle East too precarious to use regularly even though the alternative 'round-about' route via the Cape was expensive in time and resources. Furthermore Mussolini's participation meant that our forces in the Middle East, totalling some fifty thousand, now faced an enemy in North Africa of almost half a million.

But back to the immediate situation in Britain and the imminent threat of invasion. Although the defences on land were in a precarious state there were a couple of factors that offered some crumbs of consolation. Firstly, the English Channel provided a formidable water obstacle and thus a degree of protection; secondly, the Royal Navy and the RAF, our first lines of defence, were both in better shape to face an invader than the army, which was preoccupied with re-organisation and anti-invasion preparations following the evacuation from Dunkirk.

Against this historic background the obvious priority for the whole nation – whether they were in the armed forces, merchant navy, civil defence, or were workers in the factories or on the land, even housewives – was clear and indisputable, namely the defence of Britain. In his memoirs Winston Churchill recalls the spirit and mood of the whole nation: 'This was a time when all Britain worked and strove to the utmost limit and was as united as never before . . . the sense of fear seemed entirely lacking in the people . . . Nothing moves an Englishman so much as the threat of invasion, the reality unknown for a thousand years . . .'[1]

It was against this background of fear – air raids, tanks and infantry landing on our beaches, parachutists descending from the skies, and Fifth Columnists sabotaging our essential services and communications – that Churchill took the bold decision to look beyond this bleak immediate situation and proposed the raising of an elite military force to take some initiative and carry the fight to the enemy, albeit on a limited scale. As an ex-soldier and military historian he knew and had experienced the effects and losses incurred on the British Army by the Boers' irregular forces (then known as 'Commandos') at the end of the nineteenth and beginning of the twentieth centuries. In fact Churchill, as a war reporter, had been captured and made a prisoner when Boer commandos ambushed an armoured train at Estcourt in November 1899, but about a month later he managed to escape from the prison camp. As a coda to this story it is interesting to recall that no sooner was Churchill's escape discovered than a reward of £25 was offered for his recapture – dead or alive!

Notwithstanding this, Churchill always maintained great respect for those Boer commandos and later counted their leaders among his friends and allies, so it is little wonder, therefore, when it later became necessary to give his special forces a title that he chose that of his old adversaries – 'Commandos'. I must admit, however, as a founder member of No 4 Commando, I – along with my comrades – was most surprised to learn that our new unit was named after ex-enemies of the British Army!

With this experience in mind Churchill argued that in the short term his special forces would be available for counter-attacks against any invaders – 'to spring at the throat of any small landings or descents'. However, he proposed that their main purpose would be to wage a continuous campaign of 'butcher-and-bolt' raids on the Nazis' extended European coastline, thus imposing – in his words – 'a reign of terror' on the enemy prior to an eventual invasion and the liberation of occupied Europe. For even in those dark days Churchill was confident of victory and the ultimate overthrow of Hitler's Nazi regime.

Mention must be made here of the fact that some attempt to create a formation of special forces had been made earlier in 1940 when 'independent companies' were raised. However, before they had had time to train and settle down as units they were dispatched to Norway when the Germans invaded that country. Once there the independent companies were deployed in an orthodox infantry-of-the-line role and saw little action before being withdrawn. Back in Britain they were deployed on anti-invasion duties, although one independent company, commanded by Major Ronnie Tod (who went on to attain a distinguished Commando record) did take part in two early, but disappointing, minor raids. Later in the autumn of 1940 volunteers from the independent companies were integrated into Commando units with notable success, as will be told later.

In spite of the existence of these independent companies, however, Churchill wanted his own corps of shock troops; accordingly, in a typical Churchillian memo to his Chiefs of Staff, he spelt out his ideas regarding the size and roles of this new force. There was some initial negative reaction to this proposal, as many senior officers at the War Office were opposed to the special-forces concept. Nevertheless, Churchill was persistent, he got his way and action was quickly taken to implement his proposals.

Fortunately there was a very capable staff officer at the War Office, Lieutenant Colonel Dudley Clarke, who had made a study of guerilla warfare —in his capacity as military assistant to the Chief of the Imperial General Staff he was able to convert Churchill's ideas into reality.

As a result things moved very quickly and towards the end of June notices appeared in unit orders across the country for volunteers for 'special service duties'. There were not many details, but what there were provided a fair idea of what might be involved. In my case I recollect something along the following lines: 'able to swim, not prone to sea-sickness, prepared to parachute or travel in a submarine, able to drive a car or ride a motor cycle . . .'

A previous book of mine, It Had To Be Tough, is devoted entirely to the origins and special training of the Commando units in the Second World War, but it will suffice here to provide an outline of the main factors involved in the formation of the Commandos, the types of officers and other ranks who originally volunteered, and some details of the innovative training introduced and developed by these original commandos, which became universally known – and still is – as 'Commando training'.

There were three important basic factors inherent in the formation and development of the Commandos from that June 1940 and onwards. Firstly, all who served in the Army Commandos were volunteers: all officers and other ranks were seconded from their parent regiment or corps until final disbandment in October 1945. This voluntary element was most important.

Secondly, the commanding officer of a Commando unit had the power to return to their original unit any officer or other rank who for any reason whatsoever failed to meet the standards demanded, be that in training or matters of discipline. This procedure was known as 'RTU' – Returned To Unit. There was no right of appeal against the CO's decision to RTU any individual, but by the same token any volunteer could, in turn, request to leave his Commando. In my five years in the Commandos I cannot remember any man having been retained against his wishes, though I do recall some who requested to return to their regiment or corps, especially during the frustrating period from late 1940 to early 1941, and their wishes were granted. There were a number of RTUs for those who failed to make the grade in training, were found to be lacking in self-discipline, or were unreliable as 'team members' in the Commando. The number of RTUs decreased dramatically in 1942 following the establishment of the Commando Basic Training Centre at Achnacarry in Scotland, where all potential commandos were sent to 'graduate' and earn their green beret. There they were 'weeded' out, a process that had hitherto been carried out in each Commando when the volunteers joined direct from their parent units.

The third basic factor was an unusual one. It concerned the administration of each Commando unit, whereby every individual, officer or other rank, was responsible for his own quartering and feeding. There were operational and administrative reasons for this unique arrangement.

From the outset the advantages of this arrangement were apparent, especially with regards to training. It enabled the Commando units to overcome at a stroke the inherent problems that all army units stationed in barracks or camps faced: the reduced number of men available for daily training because of the draining effects of carrying out the domestic chores and duties necessary to sustain and guard a unit in any type of static accommodation. It was estimated that at any one time about 20 per cent of a unit was employed on these querulous duties, with obvious effects on the numbers available for training.

It was therefore planned to overcome all these problems with the simple solution of giving each commando a ration card and a subsistence allowance and making him responsible for his own feeding and accommodation, thereby eliminating the need for all those domestic chores and duties necessary to maintain army life in barracks. Furthermore it meant that practically all ranks in the Commando were available every day for training. There were other bonuses too: this arrangement promoted self reliance, each man was responsible for getting on parade at the right place in the right dress, properly equipped and at the right time, even if that place was miles away from the Commando base – as it often would be, to test the initiative and resourcefulness of the Commando soldiers.

How did this arrangement work in practice?

Armed with the necessary wartime ration card – no food without that little piece of paper – and cash for 'board and lodgings', each man organised his own billet. The cash allowance was thirteen shillings and four pence (66p in today's coinage) per day for all officers irrespective of rank – the same for the colonel as the newly commissioned subaltern – whilst for the other ranks the daily rate was six shillings and eight pence (33p), again a flat rate for all – privates, NCOs and even the regimental sergeant major.

Each man, although he often teamed up with a mate or even joined in with a couple more, sought out his own accommodation, usually being helped by the local authority or police who had lists of recommended 'B and B' places or families prepared to take in a couple of soldiers. Generally there was no shortages of suitable places, especially as most of the towns selected as Commando bases were on the coast in seaside resorts and in the austere wartime years holidays were, for most folk, a thing of the past and so the landladies of many 'B and B' houses were glad to take in soldiers as paying guests. The officers with their higher allowance were also welcomed in the hotels, which were often without any other guests.

All other ranks paid 'thirty bob' (£1.50) per week for their board and lodging, which included three meals per day. This might sound a pitiful amount to pay but one must remember that in those days £5 per week was a good wage for the average working man.

I well remember my first civvy billet in Weymouth, a little house, 'two up, two down', but we did have a bathroom – not all billets did in those days. Our landlady was a typical pre-war B-and-B landlady, a formidable matriarch. She stood no nonsense, but was an excellent cook and fed us well. We had to keep our room tidy, boots off at the front door with no mud or dirt inside the house. She, like most of the other landladies, was a little taken aback when we explained at the outset that we had to keep our personal weapons – rifles or revolvers – with us in the billet, and was further aghast when we were later 'standing-to' for the threatened invasion and had to keep our ammunition and grenades in the house too. It is inconceivable to think of such an arrangement, with weapons and ammunition on such a scale, in civilian homes today.

However, as a result of this billeting arrangement most of us who served in the Commandos from the beginning enjoyed living with families in many parts of Britain. In fact the list of locations where commandos were billeted reads like a Tourist Board publication list. There were the seaside resorts of Sidmouth, Falmouth, Dartmouth, St Ives, Paignton, Brighton, Bexhill, Worthing, and Bridlington in England, Ayr, Largs, Girvan, Troon, and the Isle of Arran in Scotland; whilst for climbing and mountain-warfare training there were billets on the Isle of Skye and the Cairngorms in Scotland and Snowdonia in Wales to mention just those that readily spring to mind.

This billeting arrangement only applied when the Commandos were based in Britain on normal training. At all other times, when we were in 'quarantine' for security reasons pending an operation, on board one of HMS ships, or attending courses in established service barracks and the like, we lived and were accommodated in the normal military way.

So much for the unique billeting system which carried on until the end of the war – now for a brief description of the method used for selecting the five hundred volunteers for each Commando.

One restriction was imposed on the recruiting from the onset: namely that no single parent unit should be diverted from its priority and paramount task of the defence against the potential invasion. To meet this condition, volunteers were sought from units stationed throughout the country – England, Scotland, Wales, and Northern Ireland – and not from just one region.

Furthermore volunteers were not restricted from the 'teeth arms' such as infantry, armoured, artillery, and engineer units, but also from the service corps; indeed several of the original outstanding commandos came from the latter.

Following the publication of the notice in unit orders, as mentioned above, the lists of all volunteers were forwarded to the local regional headquarters; there the first choice was to select commanding officers for each Commando – the officer chosen was then immediately promoted to lieutenant colonel.

The selected commanding officers, armed with the lists of officer volunteers, then went off to interview and select the ten troop leaders (captains), who in turn travelled around the region to select their two section officers and the subsequent forty-odd other ranks to complete the full troop strength of fifty. The great advantage of this seemingly unwieldy method of recruiting was that the colonel and his troop leaders themselves chose the men they wanted to lead into battle; they had only themselves to blame if they had made a bad decision, although they also had the RTU system to fall back on if a commando volunteer was not up to standard.

I was serving as a sergeant in a training unit of the Royal Armoured Corps at Bulford in Wiltshire when I volunteered; I was interviewed there by Captain L. C. Young of the Bedfordshire and Hertfordshire Regiment, who was the chosen troop leader of F Troop, No 4 Commando. It was a cordial interview and the sort of questions asked were similar to those posed in the original unit notice. I was also asked questions about my background: all very general but I was left in no doubt that I was volunteering for operations that would be dangerous, but exciting. There was no testing of any military skills: it seemed that 'if your face fitted' and you appeared to have the right attitude for the operations envisaged then you were in. The inference was that subsequent training would prepare one for the operations envisaged. It is also fair to add that none of us knew at that stage what those operations might be.

Ten days after that interview I was a section sergeant in F Troop of No 4 Commando in Weymouth, established in that billet just off the sea front. And then the training began. But before recalling the initial training it is pertinent to mention some of the comments made by three outstanding commando leaders on the subject of interviews.

First, the original CO of No 8 Commando, Lieutenant Colonel Robert Laycock, who later commanded a Commando Brigade and then took over from Admiral Lord Louis Mountbatten as Chief of Combined Operations. His yardstick was succinct and to the point: 'Chose your other ranks more carefully than you choose your wife and tolerate no creepers.'

Peter Young, who started in No 3 Commando as a troop leader, took part in the raids on Lofoten, Vaagso, and Dieppe, then campaigned in Sicily and Italy, before being made CO of No 3 for the invasion of north-west Europe after which he gained further promotion to brigadier for commando service in Burma, had this to say on the subject: 'To pick them? You look at them, don't you? You talk to them a bit, make up your mind whether he's a bull-shitter or has something to contribute – you can tell. Young soldiers are good, they have no wives to consider. A good old soldier is a good soldier, but a bad old soldier is worse than useless . . .'[2]

The larger-than-life Commando character, Captain Roger Courtney was thirty-eight years old when he volunteered and already had a most varied and adventurous life. Besides being a professional hunter and gold prospector in east Africa, he had served in the Palestine Police and in his 'spare time' had paddled down the river Nile; he joined No 8 Commando in July 1940, pioneered the raiding techniques using canoes, and ultimately founded the Special Boat Section (SBS) – typically, he had his own ideas about the men he wanted. His first choice was any boy scout, especially ex-rover scouts – they needed no explanation, he maintained, but he also looked out for any army bandsman as they were universally known as good shots on account of their training to play an instrument and march at the same time. He reckoned that this training enabled them to do three things at once, which was particularly applicable to firing a weapon, namely, aligning foresight, backsight, and target all at the same time at any range and with any weapon. Actually I can quote an example to support this theory because when I joined the 12th Royal Lancers, just before the war, the regimental marksman was a corporal in the band.

Finally, no matter what criteria interviewing officers had for selecting their men, all agreed that there was one undesirable type not wanted in the Commandos and that was the swaggering pseudo-tough guy whose bravery was mostly apparent in pubs when under the influence of alcohol.

No one was more adamant on this matter than the old warrior Charles Vaughan. He had fought in the First World War and volunteered for the Commandos in 1940 as an administrative officer, but such was his background and knowledge of basic military skills and man-management (he had been a regimental sergeant major in the Brigade of Guards in the inter-war years before being commissioned as a quartermaster) that he became the obvious choice as commandant of the famous Commando Training Centre at Achnacarry when it was established in 1942. In his opening address to commando recruits at the start of their course he voiced his views, in no uncertain manner, on the so-called 'tough guys', the bully boys who fought in brawls on the streets after the pubs had been turned out. 'Give them two pints of beer and the smell of the barmaid's apron and they'll fight. We don't want them, we don't need them and we won't have them,' he warned all and sundry.

What readers might find extraordinary is that, initially, in 1940 there were no tests of any kind, military, physical, or even medical. Indeed a lot of the original volunteers reckoned later that if there had been tests, say, on the lines of the Achnacarry tests, they would have failed. But what most of the volunteers did share were two important aims – 'to have a go at the Jerries and avenge Dunkirk' and the anticipation that the training they were to receive would surely enable them to succeed – there was no lack of confidence and determination.

Continuing on the subject of recruiting, a word or two about the types and background of the original volunteers. From whence did they come and what manner of soldiers were they?

As mentioned earlier they came from all branches of the army and included old regular soldiers, those who had joined the Territorial Army before the war, as well as youngsters.

Among the old soldiers were a few who had served as very young soldiers in the First World War such as Colonel Charles Vaughan, already mentioned, and the first CO of No 7 Commando, Lieutenant Colonel Dudley Lister, who had won a Military Cross in that war and in the intervening years had been a prominent amateur army boxer representing Great Britain in the 'Golden Gloves' Tournament in New York. He later commanded the unique No 10 Commando.

There were officers and other ranks of the regular army who had served in India, on the North West Frontier, or seen active service in Palestine; these included the likes of Major 'Mad Jack' Churchill and Lieutenant Colonel John Durnford-Slater, both of whom became outstanding Commando leaders, whilst amongst the other ranks was RSM 'Jumbo' Morris of No 4, who later was to be awarded a Military Cross (a rare award for such a rank, but one which he was entitled to as a warrant officer). Another outstanding NCO who must be mentioned is George Herbert of No 3 Commando, who had won a Military Medal (MM) serving with the Northamptonshire Regiment in France in 1940 prior to the Dunkirk evacuation. With No 3 he took part in the Lofoten, Vaagso, and Dieppe raids, adding a Distinguished Conduct Medal (DCM) to his MM before being commissioned and then serving as a section officer in Sicily, Italy, and Normandy, where he was killed leading his section in action in June 1944.

Although the average age of the volunteers must have been in the mid-twenties there were some volunteers who were much younger. One such example was a newly commissioned regular subaltern from the Dorsetshire Regiment,

Tony Lewis, aged just nineteen. He joined No 4 at Weymouth as a section officer in July and later took part in the Commando's first taste of action, the Lofoten Islands raid in March 1941; but like several others, he was disappointed with the lack of real action so decided to return to his old regiment, who were then due to go to the Middle East. It was there that he later met up with No 6 Commando in 1942 and surprisingly applied to rejoin. With them he quickly established a reputation for sound leadership and subsequently rose to second-in-command when that Commando returned from the Middle East to prepare for the Normandy campaign. During the campaign he subsequently took over command, becoming one of the youngest commanding officers in the British Army at the age of just twenty-four – more about him later.

Another feature concerning the types of early volunteers was that the brief details in the initial notices calling for volunteers clearly inferred that it would be adventurous, so among those who joined were mountaineers, rock climbers, and some who, although in the army, had plenty of experience in yachts or other small boats.

Among those who were experienced mountaineers was Captain Geoffrey Rees-Jones of No 5 Commando. Rees-Jones was a keen rock climber – and also a Welsh rugby international – so he soon had his troop rock climbing and abseiling on the rocky coastline of Cornwall. After taking part in the Madagascar landings he became one of the founding instructors of the Commando Mountain Warfare Training Centre, established in the Cairngorms. Incidentally, the second-in-command of that unit was later, after the war, the leader of the first team of climbers to conquer Mount Everest, namely Major John Hunt, later honoured as Lord Hunt of Everest.

In those early days, one can sense the excitement and anticipation of leading their chosen men into action felt by many officers of the Commandos from a letter written at the time by Subaltern Geoffrey Appleyard of the Royal Army Service Corps, a Cambridge graduate and an international skier, who had volunteered for No 7 Commando and later became one of the most outstanding Commando leaders, winning a DSO and MC and bar on clandestine commando raids before being killed in North Africa in 1943.

In a letter, dated 1 August 1940, after he had volunteered and accompanied his troop leader, Captain 'Gus' March-Phillips, to interview the volunteers for his own section, he wrote:

I shall be in command of 23 picked men – all volunteers. We have about 200 men (volunteers) to pick from . . . Everything depends on the men we choose . . . It's rather frightening, this selection of men. This thing can either be a flop or a colossal success, and so much depends on the men – they must be utterly reliable, steady and intelligent. But with the right men what a wonderful fellowship we can have in the unit – just picture it – a command of 23 of my own picked men . . .[3]

One of the major weaknesses of commando training in those early days was that, because of the anticipation – and demand – for immediate raids, there was no structured programme of training and preparation, including combined training with the navy on the right type of landing craft for the job.

This shortcoming became apparent as a result of the first two raids mentioned earlier. In the second raid a detachment of the then newly formed No 3 Commando, plus a group from an independent company, carried out a raid on the Channel Island of Guernsey. Only the men from No 3 got ashore, the others failed to find a suitable landing beach in the dark. The whole operation turned out to be a disappointing failure. Militarily it achieved nothing; Colonel Durnford-Slater of No 3, who was in charge of the raid, had this to say:

The raid was, of course, a ridiculous, almost comic, failure. We had captured no prisoners. We had done no serious damage. We had caused no casualties to the enemy. We had cut through three telegraph cables. A youth in his teens could have done the same. On the credit side, we had gained a little experience and learnt some of the things *not* to do . . .[4]

All concerned with the raid were, understandably, greatly disappointed – none more so than Winston Churchill, who called it a 'a silly fiasco'. As a result the overall structure and policy for amphibious raids was reorganised and Admiral of the Fleet Sir Roger Keyes – hero of the Zeebrugge raid in 1918 that was later rated as a classic commando operation – was brought in by Churchill and took over the command of a new organisation that developed into 'Combined Operations' involving all three services and whose motto summed up it's purpose: 'United We Conquer.'

The initial training we underwent in F Troop, No 4 Commando, was recorded in a troop diary by Captain Young and fortunately it survived the war, ending up in the possession of one of my comrades-in-arms, Sergeant 'Tich' Garnett. It describes in detail the training we carried out in those early days at Weymouth in the summer of 1940. Comparing it with the reports of those in other Commandos, it was much the same as theirs.

The following summary provides an idea of a normal day's programme at that time:

0700 hours	Parade on the beach for early morning PT followed by a swim then back to the billets for breakfast.
0900 hours	Muster Parade with weapons inspection. Weapon training on rifle, Bren LMG, Thompson Sub-Machine Carbine ('Tommy' gun), Boys anti-tank rifle, revolver (Webley .38) and grenades (Mills. 36) Short march 8 to 10 miles, frequently to an area where fieldcraft, stalking, unarmed combat, map reading and compass training, could be carried out.
1230 to 1400 hours	Midday meal in billets, local café or sandwiches provided by landlady.
From 1400 hours	Selection from boating in local boats, mostly rowing, cross-country runs, instruction on demolition; lectures on specific subjects such as, First Aid, German Army, Escape and Evasion and briefings for night training and 'mock raids'. We did two night exercises each week.

It is interesting to see from Geoffrey Appleyard's letters that the training of his B Troop in No 7 Commando was almost identical to that of ours in Weymouth. The fundamental difference was that Appleyard's troop leader had requisitioned a house to accommodate the troop, sleeping eight to a room, and had 'borrowed' two cooks from a regular unit nearby to do their cooking instead of moving into 'civvy billets'.

On the impact of the vigorous training, it is worthwhile recording the early experiences of two officers who became legendary commandos.

The first was a young regular officer in the Scots Greys, Captain Geoffrey Keyes, the son of Sir Roger Keyes; the other young officer was Lieutenant Paddy Mayne. They both volunteered for No 11 (Scottish Commando), which, soon after being formed, moved to the Isle of Arran for training. In a letter home Keyes summed up the training in just twenty words: 'We march and swim and do other violent things. I go to bed at night and sleep like a dog.'[5]

Paddy Mayne, who later became one of the most decorated soldiers of the Second World War, recorded the details of one of his Commando exercises on Arran in more detail. They set off in the early afternoon on an overnight scheme and for the first four miles or so there was only the odd shower. This did not hinder them and they quickly dried out as they carried on, but then for the next thirteen miles it not only poured, but gale-force winds blew in from the sea so that the rain pelted into their faces as they marched. They then had a river crossing, though this did not make them much wetter as they were already soaked to the skin.

They reached their destination at dawn and searched for somewhere to dry out without success, until at last some locals, who originally thought these dishevelled soldiers might have been German parachutists, offered them help and shelter, which they readily accepted before 'brewing up'.

This type of experience – carrying on to one's objective in spite of atrocious weather conditions, as experienced on Arran – must have prepared Keyes, in particular, for his epic raid on Rommel's headquarters, which was carried out under similar weather conditions.

We can all recall similar experiences on exercise in the wilds of Scotland and on the Hebrides. One has to remember that this training was in the days before we had weatherproof clothing: we all wore just standard battle dress with only a gas cape to offer some protection from the rain, and each man was laden down with weapons, ammunition, and other equipment. Another significant feature of Commando training was that during exercises and mock raids every man was expected to be able to look after and fend for himself. There was no 'follow up' of prepared food, as provided in the normal infantry battalions. We had to sleep where we could, in barns or hastily prepared bivouacs, and no man ever went out on any exercise lasting longer than a day without his emergency rations, foremost among which was tea, powdered milk, and sugar for that essential morale-boosting 'brew up'. We also quickly learnt how to survive in the wilds without formal rations by foraging and 'living off the land'. In our troop we did well because we had a self-professed poacher, Trooper Harris, who taught us how to snare rabbits and where to seek out salmon and trout, which we only managed to catch using 36 grenades! I can also remember, while we were on an 'anti-invasion' exercise in Devon, going out in some 'borrowed' boats to catch mackerel off Clovelly using silver paper from a cigarette packet on a hook as 'slivver' bait. We did well in a short time and enjoyed a good supper of fresh fish.

About the same time as the Commandos were raised, a special training centre was started in the Highlands of Scotland to specialise in the art of irregular warfare – officers and NCOs from the Commandos were sent there on courses to return and instruct in various subjects of this type of warfare. There is a fascinating story behind the establishment of the Special Training Centre (STC) at Lochailort, on the road to Mallaig from Fort William – it was founded by a group of officers who had volunteered for a British Army ski battalion, raised to assist the Finns when their country was invaded by the Russians in February 1940. In the event, although the unit was formed and did some training in the French Alps, it was disbanded when the Finns signed a peace treaty with the

Russians shortly afterwards. But that was not the end of the story: after disbandment, a group of the more forceful officers, keen to carry the war to the enemy in the Arctic, managed to persuade the 'powers-that-be' to send them, as a token force, to Norway to link up with some partisans there.

They duly set off with stores and explosives in a submarine from a port in Scotland. After only a few hours, however, they had the misfortune to hit a mine and although the sub was damaged they managed to limp back to port, the operation aborted. Nevertheless the group, under the leadership of Captain Bill Stirling, hatched up the idea of starting a special training centre in the Highlands for raids and guerrilla warfare. He also managed to persuade some other like-minded officers, including his cousin Lord Lovat, to join in the scheme. It says a lot about the 'old boy network' and knowing the right people in the right place that within a few weeks an area around Lochailort had been requisitioned for their new project and a little mixed camp of huts and tents was established.

An impressive team of instructors was recruited, many of whom became well-known leaders of irregular forces, including Lord Lovat, Brigadier 'Mad Mike' Calvert of Chindit's fame, Colonel Spencer Chapman, the Stirling brothers (Bill and David, the latter, of course, becoming the founder of the SAS), Captain Wallbridge (a King's Medalist in shooting), and Captain Peter Fleming (a famous explorer, author, and brother of Ian Fleming, the post-war creator of James Bond) who specialised in signalling techniques. In addition there was the extraordinary couple of seemingly elderly gentlemen, captains Fairbairn and Sykes of Shanghai Police fame, and it was these two who introduced the philosophy and skills of unarmed combat and close-quarter fighting to the Commandos that became key elements in the development of their offensive spirit and later spread throughout the British Army.

I attended one of the demolition courses and my instructor was Captain 'Bobbie' Holmes, RE. In his opening talk he told us that he would teach us to blow up anything 'from a battle ship to a brigadier' and we certainly learnt a lot from him, which we took back to our Commandos, spreading the gospel. Most of the officer and NCO demolitionists who went on the St Nazaire raid in 1942 were 'graduates' of Lochailort demolition courses.

All the training at Lochailort was done under realistic conditions and the concluding schemes at the end of the different courses were carried out as 'operations' – usually involving long approach marches, 'lying up', carrying out the mission, and ending with the trek back to a mock re-embarkation rendezvous. All these exercises involved live firing and real explosions in a landscape that was remote, wild, and uninhabited. This training in itself was an innovation as hitherto all military training involving live firing had been carried out under rigid safety regulations on formal 'rifle ranges'. But now this form of 'battle inoculation', as it became known, was one of the basic experiences of Commando training – and it all started at Lochailort. Later it became the concluding feature of the Achnacarry course, known as the 'Opposed Landing'. No commando trainee ever forgot it, as Lord Mountbatten recalled later: 'I shall never forget the impact Achnacarry made on me when I visited it in 1942 after taking over Combined Operations, and I suspect that neither will those who went through the course, since many told me later that they found the real thing less alarming than the "Opposed Landing".'[6]

Back in the individual Commandos each commanding officer prepared his own unit training programme and the standards to be aimed for. In the preparation of *It Had To Be Tough* I only managed to find one example of a CO's directive on this subject and that was for No 2 Commando, when it was commanded by Lieutenant Colonel Newman and would have been written in October 1940.

Following the appointment of Admiral Keyes in overall command, with the responsibility for co-ordinating training and operations, the provision of suitable landing craft was speeded up and they became available for combined training; we in No 4 Commando were some of the first commandos to undergo training on them.

The purpose-built Landing Craft, Assault (LCA), was an excellent little craft, ideal for the job, and was used throughout the war with great success in all the major invasions; it continued to be used in amphibious operations after the war too.

For our initial training we embarked on one of the several cross-Channel civilian ferries that had been converted to troop-carrying ships (Landing Ships, Infantry – LSI) and adapted for assault landings, with the LCAs slung on davits ready to be lowered mechanically into the water for the run-in to the shore. We joined the LSI, HMS *Glengyle* on the Clyde at the beginning of October and sailed around the coast to start our initial training on Loch Fyne and the area ashore around Inveraray. It was an ideal area for landing exercises as well as tactical exercises ashore; this area was later developed into a major combined operations training centre.

Naturally there were many teething problems during this early joint-training period and the outcome on the troops' mess deck was often chaotic, giving rise to chants of 'Order, Counter-order, Disorder'. Gradually the problems were resolved and the RN/Commando relationship became harmonious and cordial – even if living conditions on the LSIs for the troops left much to be desired.

Living on board a LSI was a new experience for all of us. We were introduced to the routines, methods, and even a new language, that of the Royal Navy –

some of the customs of the senior service dated back to the days of Nelson. The bugle calls of the barracks were replaced by the bo'sun's whistle, followed by a tannoy announcement, always preceded by the call, 'Do you hear there . . .' We slept in hammocks slung on ceiling hooks on the mess deck. Instead of 'Reveille' the tannoy ordered: 'Wakey, wakey, lash up and stow', referring to our hammocks, which had to be stowed away to provide room on the mess deck to live, eat, and prepare for the training ashore.

However, there was one naval tradition that was most welcome and enjoyed whenever we stayed on HMS ships, and that was the daily issue of 'Nelson's blood' – rum. Another naval perk that we enjoyed was the weekly issue of duty-free cigarettes.

By the end of October 1940 all the Commandos were billeted in towns on the west coast of Scotland and there followed a major reorganisation of both the Commandos and the independent companies, inasmuch as they were amalgamated to form one big Special Service Brigade, under the command of Brigadier J. C. Haydon, DSO, consisting of three special service battalions, each consisting of two companies of five hundred men. However this arrangement proved most unwieldy and was short lived, so the Commandos reverted to their original titles and organisations, with volunteers from the independent companies forming Nos 1, 2, and 9 Commandos – the original No 2 (Parachute) Commando having become a separate parachute unit and not part of the Special Service Brigade.

During the winter months the whole Special Service Brigade was concentrated on the Isle of Arran, accommodated in civilian billets. There a new feature of the training developed, namely that of preparing for large-scale Commando operations in addition to the original 'butcher-and-bolt' type.

This development was the result of some ambitious planning under the direction of Admiral Keyes, with the approval and support of Winston Churchill. Admiral Keyes appreciated that larger Commando operations were clearly not feasible in north-west Europe, but there were possibilities in the Mediterranean. So he initially proposed that Pantellaria, a small island off Sicily, should be invaded and captured for use as an alternative or supplementary base to Malta. This proposal was accepted by the Chiefs of Staff and, with the operation codenamed 'Workshop', training on Arran was focused on this projected operation, although the troops had no idea of where or what they were training for.

Then, on the very day that they were due to sail, 14 December 1940, the operation was postponed, causing bitter disappointment. It was not to be the last time that an operation was postponed or even cancelled at the last minute.

(I remember well a raid that we were going to carry out on the coast of Holland in early 1942 – we were not far from the launch area in the North Sea and the operation was cancelled. On that occasion it was because naval reports indicated a strong enemy E-boat presence in the area we were heading for and we had no navy escorts.)

Back on Arran, everyone felt frustrated – here we were nearly six months after joining the Commandos, having trained hard, and still no sign of action. Morale suffered and Christmas on the Isle of Arran was not a happy time for those billeted there.

A month later the Chiefs of Staff decided, as an alternative to the cancelled Operation *Workshop*, that the Commandos would take part in a major operation to capture the island of Rhodes: a commando force consisting of Nos 7, 8, and 11 Commandos, plus Captain Courtney's section of canoeists and a troop from No 3 Commando, under the command of Lieutenant Colonel Laycock, the CO of No 8, would sail to the Middle East to prepare to participate in this projected operation. Accordingly, on 31 January 1941 this force, later to be known as *Layforce*, embarked on the two LSIs, the *Glengyle* and the *Glenroy*, and left for the Middle East.

However, whilst the training for these larger-scale operations was being carried out, some smaller groups – within their Commandos – continued experimenting and training for small-scale raids. One such group, a section of canoeists in No 6 Commando, became known as and operated under the name '101 Troop'. There was also a group in No 7 Commando led by Captain 'Gus' March-Phillips and Lieutenant Geoffrey Appleyard that became the highly acclaimed Small Scale Raiding Force (SSRF). Unfortunately none of these commando sub-units, in spite of carrying out many highly successful clandestine missions, qualified for specific battle honours, their operations being recognised instead under all-embracing campaign battle honours such as NORTH AFRICA 1941. Likewise the highly successful Lofoten Islands raid in March 1941 was another operation that fell into this general category, recognised only under NORWAY 1941. However, the successful Vaagso raid – the first of the 'great raids' – was rightly recognised and as such was the first specific battle honour of the Commandos in the Second World War. With this in mind, some of the successful operations that were not singled out as battle honours and are not emblazoned on the Commando flag will be included in the narrative that follows, under the relevant campaign, starting with the Lofoten raid in the next chapter.

CHAPTER 2

NORWAY 1941
(The Lofoten and Vaagso Raids)

FOLLOWING THE DEPARTURE OF *Layforce* for the Middle East, the rest of the Commandos left the Island of Arran and established themselves in billets mainly in the towns on the west coast of Scotland. We in No 4 Commando returned to our old base in Troon where, after a spot of leave that to some extent offset our disappointment of not being included in *Layforce,* carried on training.

Another event also helped to bolster our morale: namely a visit and rousing talk from 'Sir Roger' (Keyes). Although he was old enough to be our father, or in some cases a grandfather, we all greatly respected and admired him and were most reassured when he forcefully declared that he had no intention of allowing 'his bright sword to rust in the highlands of Scotland!' When he left we all felt better and had renewed hopes of some action soon. We in No 4 and our comrades in No 3, based in Largs, certainly did not have long to wait.

On 20 February we were told that we were going on an exercise in the north-west of Scotland and to warn our landladies that we would be away for a fortnight. However rumours began to circulate that this might be 'a job' when next day we were issued with sea-kitbags and fighting knives prior to our departure from Troon.

What none of us knew at the time was that the commanding officers of Nos 3 and 4 Commandos, lieutenant colonels Durnford-Slater (No 3) and Lister (No

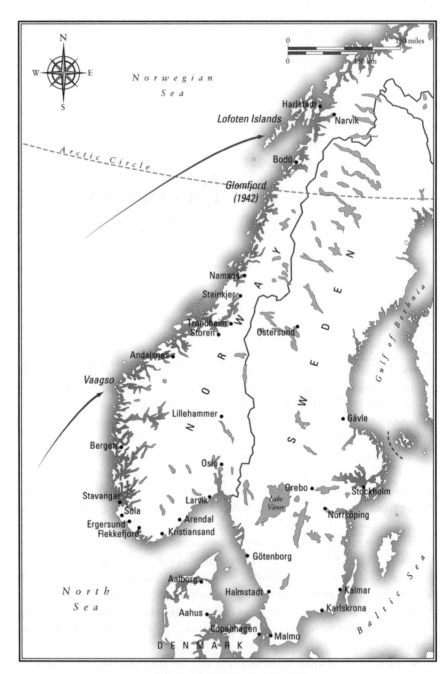

MAP I. Raids on Norway in 1941

4) had already been secretly briefed for a combined commando raid on the harbours of Svolvaer, Brettesnes, Stamsund, and Henningsvaer in the Lofoten Islands of Norway and the proposed raid had been given the codename of 'Claymore'.

It was interesting to learn later that this raid had originally been proposed by the minister of economic warfare in a memo to Winston Churchill – he had suggested sending raiding parties to this region of Norway to destroy herring and cod liver oil factories; destroy ships in the harbours; dispose of any isolated German garrisons; and to kidnap Quislings. Churchill liked the idea and quickly passed it on to Sir Roger who immediately 'took it on board'.

We in No 4 left Troon on 21 February and boarded the LSI *Queen Emma* – a converted North Sea passenger ferry – at the port of Gourock on the Clyde and set sail for Scapa Flow, where only our troop leaders were briefed for the operation. Meanwhile No 3 had boarded the LSI *Princess Beatrix*, which was the sister ship to our 'QE', and sailed for Scapa too.

The main aim of the raid was, as suggested originally, to destroy the fish-oil-processing factories and the storage tanks, plus the fishing vessels and any other German-used ships. The refined fish oil was being exported to Germany and used in the manufacture of nitroglycerine for high explosives as well as for vitamins A and D for use by the German Army. In addition vast supplies of fish, salted and fresh, were being exported to Germany to supplement civilian food supplies. So with these objectives in mind one can appreciate that the main object of the raid was economic rather than military. However, we did not know what opposition we might have to face so obviously had to be prepared for action from garrison troops or from air attacks.

The next seven days were spent at Scapa preparing and rehearsing for the operation. The weather conditions at the time were 'testing' to say the least, but they gave us a taste of things to come for we would be operating in the middle of winter in an area well within the Arctic Circle, where temperatures would be below freezing. On average, snow normally falls there every two days and winter gales occur every ten days – and we did not have any special Arctic clothing. It was a chilly prospect, but more importantly, it was action at last! Apart from the normal tactical training, the firing of all our troop weapons, boat drills, and the operation rehearsals, it is also worth mentioning the instructions and sessions we had on the subject of 'escape and evasion'. Among the items issued to section officers and NCOs were silk maps that were concealed in the collars of battle dress tunics and also special 'fly buttons' to sew on to the appropriate part of the trousers – when needed, they could be detached and, used jointly, acted as a basic little compass. We were also issued, just prior to the raid, with some 'hard rations' to sustain us should we be left behind and had to try and escape.

Finally, we were instructed in the use of codes for use in letters written to our folk back home should we end up in a POW camp. Another feature of this particular raid was the learning of simple Norwegian phrases to warn the local civilians of our intentions to blow up their factories, etc. and to take cover; phrases I still remember to this day – some sixty-eight years on.

On 1 March we left Scapa and our two ships had a formidable naval escort – two capital ships, HMS *Nelson* and HMS *King George V*, plus two cruisers and five destroyers – for most of the seven hundred miles to Vestfjord, which leads to the Lofoten Islands. At this point the two capital ships were to 'stand off', and a submarine, acting as a navigational beacon in the dark, would guide our two commando ships and the destroyers towards the launching areas for the final run-in to the following four objectives: No 3 Commando were to tackle the southern ports of Stamsund and Henningsvaer and No 4 the further objectives of Svolvaer, the capital of the islands, and the neighbouring little island of Brettesnes. I was in the group for the latter mission. Both Commandos had some Norwegian (Liberation) Army troops attached to them to act as guides and interpreters – they also taught us the phrases mentioned above.

Unfortunately as we sailed north the weather, as forecast, turned very nasty and we were quickly made aware of the shortcomings of converting these cross-Channel ferries: with their shallow draught, top-heavy with the landing craft, and without any form of stabilisers they were not suited for stormy seas and a North Atlantic swell. Our ship, the *Queen Emma*, in the words of one of my comrades 'did everything but turn upside down and I am sure everyone was seasick – even the captain'.

We did not suffer alone, for our comrades in the *Queen Emma's* sister ship were in the 'same boat' too. Indeed Colonel Durnford-Slater wrote:

> The voyage started badly for me. I always dreaded seasickness and on the first day managed to lose my breakfast, but Joe Brunton, the ship's captain, took me in hand firmly. Beginning now, he said, every morning at eleven you will consume with me a couple of bottles of beer with some cheese and pickled onions. What could I do but obey? Happily I can report that Joe's remedy effected a complete cure.[1]

We on the troops' mess decks did not have the chance of such remedies and had to make do with wine gums!

The rough weather continued for three days and both commanding officers became very worried that so many of their men were suffering from seasickness, but then – as if by magic – when we sailed into the Arctic waters the weather and the sea changed for the better. It became quite pleasant as the sea calmed and we were all able to get up on deck and recover, so that on the day before the planned operation everyone felt better and ready for the action for which we had volunteered some seven months earlier when we joined the Commandos.

Reveille, or rather 'Wakey, wakey, rise and shine', was at 3 a.m. on 4 March and after a breakfast meal we all got ready for our first operation. Knowing that we were going to face really cold weather everyone wore as much clothing as was practical, 'three of everything' as one commando later wrote. It was still dark as we clambered into our assault landing craft, and were lowered into the still, calm Arctic waters to set off for our various landing places – not beaches, but the quays of the four designated harbours. The look-outs in the bows of the landing craft reported that they could see twinkling lights on the coastline and there did not seem to be any black-out precautions, suggesting that they were not expecting any sort of attack from the sea or the air.

All was quiet except for the sound of the landing craft engines; it was quite eerie, but bitterly cold, and the occasional spray that came over the ramps, at the bows of the landing craft, froze on the decking, some even froze on the steel

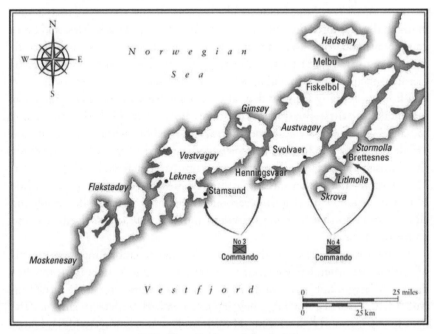

MAP 2. Raid on Lofoten Islands, Norway

helmets of a couple of the commandos who were seated for'ard. We in No 4 landed as planned and on time on the quays of Svolvaer and Brettesnes unopposed – not a single German in sight. It was like one of those many exercises we had been on during the past seven months. Once ashore all the groups set off to carry out their various tasks: soon the sounds of explosions and pillars of smoke announced the demolitions of the oil-refining factories and storage tanks by the commandos and specialist sappers allotted to these tasks. Within an hour or so of the initial landing in Svolvaer all the main buildings in the town, including the police station, the mayor's and the harbour master's offices, the main hotel, and the town hall, had been occupied and searched for any useful intelligence information. A few Quislings had been arrested, whilst in the police station some weapons and ammunition had also been found and taken away.

Mid-morning Colonel Lister received information of a German Luftwaffe wireless station that had been established some miles outside the town and he decided that this was a task for his reserve and so detailed a strong fighting patrol for the job. They were under the command of Captain Lord Lovat who was attached to the Commando for this operation; with the co-operation of the local people some transport was requisitioned and off they went. In his memoirs, *March Past*, Lord Lovat recalls the story of this successful little action in which they captured the Luftwaffe personnel, destroyed the wireless and other equipment, and took away documents. Colonel Lister also sent a party to accompany some naval parties and help in the capture and destruction of German-manned ships, including a large one, the *Bremen*, which was being used as a floating refining factory; they also brought back the German seamen as prisoners. All these missions were successfully accomplished without any casualties – in fact the whole operation was carried out without any casualties to our forces, except for one extremely embarrassed officer who accidentally shot himself in the leg pulling his loaded revolver out from his thigh holster. No 4 Commando's other mission at Brettesnes went according to plan, while No 3 Commando landed at their harbours unopposed, successfully completing all their tasks so that by noon the commandos were ready to re-embark and return to Scapa.

At all the quay-sides where the commandos were re-embarking, large crowds of enthusiastic islanders gathered to fraternise, and in some cases offer hot drinks. A large number of young men, and some women too, had turned up with a few personal belongings, begging to come back with us to continue the fight for their country's liberation. The atmosphere was unforgettable and most moving. Major Kerr, who was in charge of our group on Brettesnes, later wrote:

'As our LCAs left the quay the cheers, such as none of us will ever forget broke out and followed us as we left the harbour. I know I speak for the rest of us when I say it was unforgettable, especially as those factories, which were in the vicinity of the quay, were in ruins.'[2]

The total tally of the successes shared by the two Commandos on the operation was impressive:

Destroyed: Eleven fish-oil factories and storage tanks holding eight hundred thousand gallons.

Ships sunk: Eleven German and German-used ships – total of twenty thousand tons.

Captured: 215 German prisoners, mostly merchant seamen, but also German Army and Air Force personnel, including one army officer and ten Norwegian Quislings.

Volunteers: A total of 314 Lofoten islanders including eight young women.

By early afternoon the entire force was making its way back to Scapa Flow; we expected some German reaction to our operation but none came so the journey was uneventful and the conditions were good too, which was just as well because with five hundred extra passengers on our two boats we were literally 'packed to the gunwhales'.

'A highly successful operation with no casualties' was how the BBC prefaced their bulletin of the raid that evening on the six o'clock news. In the days that followed, the raid was given much publicity and it could not have come at a more opportune time. It provided a tonic for everyone in Britain and especially for those in the towns being nightly bombed in 'The Blitz'.

What was not made public was the fact that among the pieces of technical equipment and documents brought back from the raid were vital links in the intelligence battle being fought at Bletchley to break the Enigma code. They had been taken by a joint Commando/RN party that boarded the armed trawler *Krebs* during the raid.

Although the capture of this important piece of the jigsaw that would help break the code was kept secret for many years – not only during the war, but also after the end of hostilities – when the whole extraordinary story of Enigma was told, historians and researchers alike acknowledged and emphasised the importance of this additional bonus from the Lofoten raid.

Readers may wonder why the Lofoten raid – which was an undoubted success, albeit a bloodless one – does not qualify as a separate battle honour, the answer is simple: unlike the 'great Commando raids' of Vaagso, St Nazaire and

Dieppe, it was not listed as one by the special committee set up to classify the battles, actions, and engagements fought by the land forces of the Commonwealth during the Second World War. Nevertheless it does qualify under the theatre battle honour of NORWAY 1941 as did some later but smaller raids in the region, one of which will be briefly mentioned later.

After the Lofoten raid the Army Commandos, now based in various towns along the west coast of Scotland, continued to train and prepare for various amphibious operations that were planned by Admiral Keyes's staff. One of these was the operation '*Pilgrim*', in which the Commandos were involved as part of a larger force formed and trained to invade the Canary Islands and occupy the ports to prevent the Germans using them as bases for their U-boats. However, like other plans it did not materialise even though an advance party of commandos was dispatched to West Africa to prepare for the operation – it was a frustrating period.

On 27 October 1941 there was a change in the overall command of the Commandos, when the much younger Lord Louis Mountbatten (forty-one years old and only a Royal Navy captain at the time) was chosen to replace the sixty-nine-year-old Admiral Keyes. Mountbatten was considered to be a man of action and ambition, furthermore he was clever and forceful, yet diplomatic; he was also a member of the royal family and so had 'connections'. He had already seen plenty of action at sea and only recently had distinguished himself when in command of HMS *Kelly* in the Mediterranean during the battle for Crete – this particular naval action, incidentally, became the theme for a popular wartime film *In Which We Serve*, produced by Noel Coward.

On appointment, Mountbatten was promoted and was given a fresh directive personally by Winston Churchill at Chequers – according to Bernard Fergusson in his *The Watery Maze: The Story of Combined Operations*, the prime minister's verbal brief started 'something like this': 'I want you to succeed Roger Keyes in charge of Combined Operations. Up to now there have been hardly any Commando Raids. I want you to start a programme of ever-increasing intensity, so as to keep the enemy coastline on the alert from North Cape to the Bay of Biscay . . .'[3]

As a result it was not long before the Commandos were in action on the first of their great raids – Vaagso.

Lieutenant Colonel John Durnford-Slater in his book *Commando* recalls how in November, just about a month after Mountbatten had taken over, he was summoned to the headquarters of Combined Operations in London and on arrival given a full appreciation and intelligence summary of the German garrison, their defences, and an outline plan for a commando raid in the area of Vaagso and Maaloy in Norway. He was told to study this summary before seeing Mountbatten and then be prepared to advise him as to whether No 3 Commando could carry out a successful raid on this target.

The island of Vaagso and the much smaller island of Maaloy lie alongside the Norwegian coast between Bergen and Trondheim at the entrance to a system of fjords where the German Navy had established an anchorage defended by coastal guns and a garrison of some two hundred regular troops stationed on the two islands. There were further coastal guns in the area as well as anti-aircraft guns that covered the entrance to Vaagsfjord. The Germans also had fighter aircraft and naval forces located in the area, but the commando raiders were to have full naval and air support – it was going to be a 'proper combined operation'.

The object of the raid was to attack and destroy a number of military and economic targets in both the town of South Vaagso and on the little island of Maaloy, to sink or capture enemy shipping at anchorage in Vaagsfjord, and to bring back German prisoners and Quislings as well as any volunteers from the Norwegian forces. In addition it was hoped, strategically, that a successful operation of this nature would force the Germans to reinforce their occupying forces in Norway, which, in turn, would help to reduce the pressure on the Russians.

(It was further planned that a diversionary commando raid, Operation *Anklet*, would be mounted on targets in the Lofoten Islands by No 12 Commando, which they subsequently did on 26 December, catching the German garrison by complete surprise. They remained in the Lofotens for two days before withdrawing to return to Scapa.)

Meanwhile, back at Combined Operations headquarters, Colonel Durnford-Slater, having studied the summary, was called for his interview with Mountbatten and the former's account of that meeting is most interesting.[4]

Durnford-Slater recalls that Mountbatten appeared to be a little doubtful about the project. This was understandable as it was to be his first Commando operation and Durnford-Slater had the feeling that Mountbatten wanted to be as sure as possible that his initial operation would be a success. In the discussion that followed Durnford-Slater told Mountbatten that he was confident that his Commando could successfully carry out the operation. When questioned on how he would deal with the serious threat of the coastal batteries on Maaloy, he suggested that they could be dealt with by intense close-range naval gunfire support from the escorting cruiser *Kenya* and her attendant destroyers just prior to the commando landings. He reassured Mountbatten that his men were fully trained to deal with the German garrison and the various other tasks. Finally, Durnford-Slater emphasised to Mountbatten that after all their months of hard training, and with their morale so high, his Commando could do 'a very fine job' and he recorded that Mountbatten was so reassured that he became enthusiastic and 'Operation *Archery*' was on.

For the operation two troops from No 2 Commando, some medical personnel from No 4 Commando and a detachment of the Norwegian Army were attached to No 3. The Norwegian detachment was under the command of Captain Linge, who had been attached previously to No 3 Commando for the first Lofoten raid and had established a sound working relationship with Colonel Durnford-Slater and his men.

In his appreciation of the problems facing him Durnford-Slater decided that he had a total of some seventeen tasks. These included destruction of the coastal battery, barracks, and ammunition store; the searchlight and oil tanks on Maaloy; the enemy strongpoint located at Hollevik to the south of the town; and various objectives in the town of South Vaagso itself, which included two factories, garrison headquarters, the main hotel where soldiers might be billeted, and a garage in which a tank was situated. At the northern end of the main street, which was about three-quarters of a mile in length, there was also a power station, a further factory, the telephone exchange, and more billets for the garrison troops. It was a formidable list.

To deal with these objectives Durnford-Slater decided to divide his force of commandos into five groups, and allocated them the following tasks:

Group 1   to land to the north of the town itself and establish a road block to prevent any enemy reinforcements coming to the aid of the garrison in South Vaagso.

Group 2   to land south of the town at Hollevik to deal with the strongpoint and any other enemy there.

Group 3   consisting of two troops under the command of Major Jack Churchill, to deal with the enemy guns and installations on the island of Maaloy.

Group 4   consisting of four troops, to deal with all the objectives in the town of South Vaagso – this group would be under the direct command of Durnford-Slater himself.

Group 5   consisting of the two troops attached from No 2 Commando, to be held afloat, as the Commando reserve.

No 3 Commando and the attached personnel left their base at Largs and embarked on the two landing ships, HMS *Prince Charles* and HMS *Prince Leopold* at Gourock on the Clyde in mid-December and sailed for Scapa Flow, where

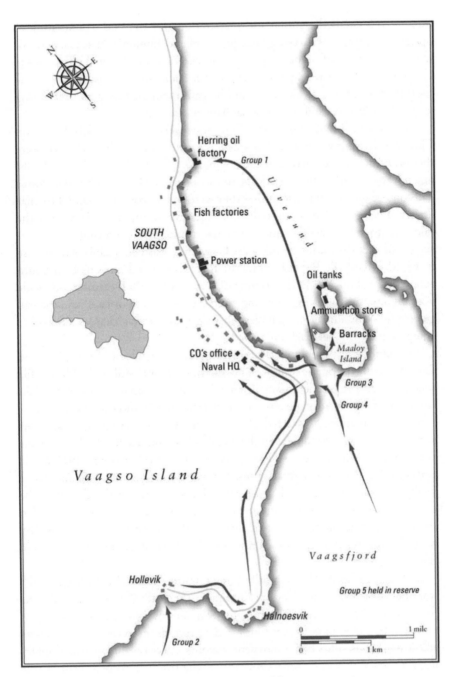

MAP 3. Raid on Vaagso, Norway

they started detailed training and preparations for the raid, culminating in operational rehearsals carrying full equipment and ammunition as planned. All went well in spite of some 'very severe weather' and on the final rehearsal the Commando was visited by their new overall commander, 'Lord Louis', as he soon became known to all ranks, and he gave them a rousing and reassuring 'pep talk', which became a traditional hallmark of his.

Escorted by HMS *Kenya* and four destroyers, the force left Scapa on Christmas Eve but was buffeted by gale force winds and rough seas; so bad were the conditions that on arrival at the staging post, Sollum Voe in the Shetlands, urgent repairs had to be carried out to one of the LSIs. However, the troops had some slight recompense in that they were able to have a decent Christmas dinner. The delay also prompted some rumours on the mess decks that the raid was to be cancelled; one particular rumour was amusing in that it suggested that the raid, scheduled for Christmas, was being cancelled because it would offend the Pope! Finally, the force, ready and anxious to get into action, left Sollum Voe in the evening of Boxing Day (26 December). Reveille was at 4 a.m. the following morning, with breakfast an hour later, and then all got ready – ammunition, grenades (in plenty), explosive charges, and other equipment having been already issued.

At 7 a.m. the leading ship picked up the guiding signal light of the submarine *Tuna*, as planned, for the approach up the fjord. It was still dark. The flotilla sailed on until it reached a small bay where the commandos boarded their landing craft for their final run-in to their respective landing places.

As the commandos started their run-in it was getting light and the spectacular snow-covered hills on the mainland became visible. At this stage the prearranged RAF bombers (Hampdens) came over to bomb the coastal batteries and light anti-aircraft guns. It was now about 8.45 a.m. and No 2 Troop, designated to attack the battery at Hollevik, peeled off and – under the cover of a smoke screen put down by one of the Hampdens – landed successfully, enabling them to quickly deal with the enemy there so that they were able to later join up and re-enforce the main body of the Commando in South Vaagso.

At 8.48 a.m., as the flotilla was heading towards Maaloy, HMS *Kenya* fired a star shell over the tiny island to illuminate the battery positions; this was followed by a full-scale bombardment from the five naval escorts – it was reckoned that they poured over four hundred rounds on to the island defences and installations. This had a most encouraging effect on the men, as Captain Peter Young who was commanding one of the troops recorded: 'Spirits rose almost visibly; Jack Churchill took up his bagpipes and began to play 'The

March of the Cameron Men', standing the while, fully exposed, in the front of the craft and gazing calmly ahead. The men liked that.'[5]

It is relevant to recall the fact that both Major Jack Churchill (fondly christened 'Mad Jack') and Captain Peter Young were both involved in this attack on Maaloy and apparently were determined to beat each other on to the enemy objectives. In the event, Young won; this rivalry in action was typical of these two officers who went on to become legendary commando leaders – more about their exploits later.

As the two troops neared Maaloy, Durnford-Slater put up Verey light signals to stop the naval bombardment, which was proving so effective that the landings on the island were 'dry-shod' and unopposed. The commandos stormed ashore and soon the white Verey light signal of success was fired to announce that the first objectives had been taken – and without any casualties. However, things then changed as the commandos advanced to their next objectives: they met some opposition, but this was quickly overcome and they started to round up prisoners, including the battery commander, 'a stoutish middle-aged officer with an Iron Cross on his chest'. As the enemy resistance came to an end the commandos started on their various demolition tasks, although some of the targets were already alight having been set on fire by the naval cannonade. By 10 a.m. the battle for Maaloy was successfully concluded and the commandos had quite a haul of German prisoners and, apart from some men slightly wounded, had no serious casualties or losses.

It was a different story at South Vaagso where Colonel Durnford-Slater and the main body were meeting stiff opposition. Following the success on Maaloy, he had signalled to Churchill to dispatch Young's troop as reinforcements and had also signalled to Brigadier Haydon to send in the two reserve troops.

At the start of Durnford-Slater's action, as he neared the landing place during the naval bombardment, he had fired the Verey light signals to stop the bombardment. At this stage further smoke was laid down by the Hampdens to cover the main landing. This was most effective although unfortunately one of the Hampdens was hit by anti-aircraft fire as she came in and as a result a phosphorus smoke bomb fell into one of the incoming landing craft, causing an explosion and a fire that inflicted terrible burns on some of the commandos; the wounded men were later shipped back to the parent ship, *Prince Charles*. Fortunately the rest of the colonel's group were unaffected and they too landed dry-shod and unopposed.

The leading troops started to storm down the main street, but already enemy snipers had taken up positions in the houses. The opposition proved to be greater than expected, mainly because, unbeknown to the raiders, some fifty mountain division troops had been sent to the town for Christmas 'rest and recreation', and so increased the size of the garrison. In the first twenty minutes or so the commandos suffered severe losses, the troop leaders of both Nos 3 and 4 troops (captains Giles and Forester) had been killed, and three of the four section officers of these troops had been badly wounded; the Norwegian Captain Linge, who was attached to No 4 Troop had also been killed. Soon, however, the reinforcements began to arrive and they were able to steadily deal with the snipers – in a couple of cases by setting the houses on fire, which, being made wholly of wood, burnt furiously. It is pertinent to record here the courage and resourcefulness of the section NCOs of those leading troops and how they took control and carried on with the attack. One in particular, Corporal White, who was left in command of No 4 Troop, was outstanding and he was subsequently awarded the Distinguished Conduct Medal (DCM) for his gallantry and leadership.

Durnford-Slater's men fought their way slowly, but successfully, up the main street until they finally reached the northern end of the town, where they made contact with the group that had landed there to prevent any German reinforcements coming from the north. By now the short winter hours of daylight were slipping away and at about 2 p.m. Durnford-Slater gave orders for the Commando to withdraw and re-embark in the south of the town where the landing craft were waiting for them.

The withdrawal was phased, one troop at a time, with the last troop covering the rear of the Commando. As they withdrew they passed the burning buildings, which were blazing furiously. Incidentally, most of the action was captured by the small team of newsreel and press photographers who accompanied the commandos and whom Durnford-Slater later praised, saying that he was impressed by their courage and the fact that they never roamed far from the leading soldiers. Some of their shots are among the most graphic of the war.

Whilst the action was taking place on the land the destroyers were busy in the fjord: a total of ten ships of some eighteen thousands tons were sunk. Boarding parties were also able to secure some valuable documents. Similarly, the commandos ashore, before they blew up any of the German-occupied quarters, also searched for any useful intelligence information. Durnford-Slater records that the 'master code for the whole of the German navy' was found. Writing in 1953, before the full story of the breaking of the Enigma code was made public, he was unable to record, or appreciate, the full value of the captured code.

The RAF Hampdens and Beaufighters were also very active overhead during the raid, attacking additional targets in the areas beyond the immediate Vaagso area. Re-embarkation of the commandos aboard the two LSIs was completed by 2.45 p.m.; with ninety-eight prisoners and four Quislings, along with some volunteers for the Norwegian Army of Liberation, the flotilla set sail to return to Scapa where No 3 Commando and the attached men arrived after an uneventful voyage to a rousing welcome. The raid was subsequently given much publicity as good news was scarce at the time.

Although the Vaagso raid was an undoubted success and enhanced the reputation of Churchill's Commandos, like all fighting it came at a cost. No 3 Commando lost two officers and fifteen other ranks; in addition the Norwegian Captain Linge was killed, as were two naval ratings, whilst in the air the RAF reported that seven of their aircraft were lost on the mission. Nevertheless, Vaagso rates as the first of the 'great Commando raids'.

Before leaving these two battle honours of NORWAY 1941 and VAAGSO, one must mention the disappointment of many commando veterans that subsequent raids on Norway in 1942 did not receive recognition – in particular the dramatic and daring raid on the heavy-water plant at Glomfjord (Operation *Musketoon*) in September 1942. The raiding party consisted of twelve men: ten were from No 2 Commando and the other two were Norwegians. They were put ashore from a Free French submarine on 11 September and successfully attacked the Glomfjord hydro-electric power station on 22 September, which in turn put the Haugvik aluminium plant out of action too. Unfortunately, in the operation one Norwegian was killed, four commandos managed to escape, and the remaining seven commandos surrendered to the Germans when it became impossible to fight on or escape. They all expected to be treated humanely as prisoners of war, but it was not to be.

The seven commandos were Captain Graeme Black, a Canadian who had won the Military Cross on the Vaagso raid and his second-in-command, Captain Joseph Houghton, a survivor of St Nazaire Raid and wounded at Glomfjord. The others were Troop Sergeant Major Miller Smith, Sergeant William Chudley, Privates Eric Curtis, Cyril Abram, and Reginald Makeham.

These captive commandos were handed over by their captors in Norway to the German Army in Denmark, and subsequently to the SS. They were taken to Berlin for interrogation after which they were transferred to the Sachsenhausen concentration camp, where, under great secrecy, on 22 October they were taken out and shot. They became the first victims of Hitler's infamous top secret 'Commando Order', which called for the interrogation and summary execution of all men captured on commando missions.

On 6 July 2001, on the site of the concentration camp, a service of dedication for the British Memorial was held. On the memorial are remembered by name not only the seven commandos, but a further thirteen other Royal Navy and army servicemen captured in clandestine operations, who 'were interned in Sachsenhausen and perished here or elsewhere at the hands of their captors'.[6] The full story of the Glomfjord raid is the subject of Stephen Schofield's book *Musketoon*, published in 1964.[7]

Further raids were made on Norway but they did not qualify for battle honours.

CHAPTER 3

MIDDLE EAST 1941–1942
(Crete, Syria, Litani, and Madagascar)

ALTHOUGH THE ORIGINAL REASON for the departure of the three Commandos to the Middle East – Operation *Workshop*, the capture of the island of Pantellaria – had been cancelled prior to sailing, the commandos of *Layforce* had every reason to believe that their departure heralded the welcome prospect of a series of Commando raids on the North Africa coastline and/or on the Axis-held islands in the Mediterranean – but it was not to be, for a number of reasons.

When they did arrive in Egypt in March 1941, having taken the long 'round the Cape' route, the military situation there looked bleak. Our forces were on the defensive, having been driven back from the Western Desert by Rommel's formidable Afrika Corps; nevertheless, it was planned that *Layforce* would participate in the capture of the island of Rhodes and the canoe section, under Captain Courtney, carried out a daring reconnaisance of the island. However, when the Germans invaded Greece in April, the Rhodes operation was cancelled.

As a result the three UK-raised Commandos, now joined by a composite Middle East Commando formed from Nos 50 and 52 Commandos, were regarded by General Headquarters as a reserve force and reinforcements for the Eighth Army. They even lost their proper titles of 'Commandos' and were retitled 'Battalions', with No 7 as A Battalion, No 8 as B Battalion, No 11 as C Battalion and the composite Middle East Commando as D Battalion.

However, in the following narrative relating the actions of the Commandos of *Layforce* I will continue to refer to these units by their original and 'proper' titles of Commandos.

At this stage mention must be made of the background of that composite Middle East Commando. In July 1940 following the raising of the Commandos in Britain, steps were taken to form three Commandos in the Middle East. There was no shortage of volunteers and two were initially formed – Nos 50 and 51, followed by a third, No 52. It is worth mentioning the nature and background of the volunteers for these three Commandos.

In No 50, in addition to those from the British Army, there were not only volunteers from both the South African and Rhodesian armies but also a contingent of some sixty Spanish troops, veterans who had fought against Franco, but had fled Spain when he came to power, and subsequently enlisted in the British Army.

In No 51 Commando, although the majority of the officers were from the British Army, most of the other ranks came from a most unusual unit: No 1 Palestine Company, Auxiliary Military Pioneer Corps. Their commanding officer, Major H. Cator, who had served with the Scots Greys in the First World War, called them his 'Foreign Legion' – with good reason as three-quarters of them were Jews (Poles, Czechs, Russians, Bulgarians, Austrians, Germans, and Spaniards) and the other quarter was made up of Arabs, including Egyptians, Iraqis, Palestinians, and Sudanese. No 52 Commando was, however, raised entirely from volunteers from the British Army, although, in the event, not all were worthy commandos and a number were returned to their units.

In his comprehensive history of these three Middle East Commandos Charles Messenger records their full story, although their lifespan was short – 1940 to 1942. He also explains why these Commandos did not receive the recognition of specific battle honours even though they took part in raids and operations in the Middle East as well as protracted action in the campaigns in Eritrea and Abyssinia. Indeed No 51 Commando played a prominent role in the battle for Karen, in Eritrea, which was rated as the most fiercely fought fight against the Italians in the whole of the East Africa campaign. Their casualties were such that after this campaign they were sent back to Egypt on leave and subsequent disbandment. No 52 was also depleted during their actions in East Africa and when they returned to Egypt they were amalgamated with No 50, who had recently returned from a short tour of garrison duties in Crete. Thus it was that the composite Middle East Commando was available and joined *Layforce*, as the fourth Commando.

From April 1941 to the end of that year the Commandos of *Layforce* took part in a series of operations in North Africa, Crete, and Syria; not all were successful. Generally speaking the failures were due to poor intelligence and other factors outside the control of the Commandos.

Notwithstanding this, for their participation in all operations, even those aborted, the Commandos were awarded the overall theatre battle honour of MIDDLE EAST, but for their outstanding displays of courage and bravery they were granted the specific awards of CRETE and LITANI and it is these two battle honours that will be described in some detail, whilst brief references will be mentioned of commando operations that are included in the overall theatre battle honour MIDDLE EAST.

On 19 April No 7 Commando became the first of *Layforce* to see action, with a raid on Bardia on the North Africa coast. Their objective was to attack the town, which was believed to be held by up to two thousand Italian troops, and also destroy selected targets in the area.

The Commando embarked on HMS *Glengyle* at Alexandria and, escorted by a cruiser and three destroyers from the Royal Navy, set sail. Prior to their departure Captain Courtney and a team from his canoe section had set off in a submarine, tasked with providing navigational lights for the four beaches selected for the Commando's landings. Unfortunately Courtney's men were intially delayed by an attack on the submarine by friendly aircraft and then subsequently had problems launching their folboats (canoes), so they were late by the time the *Glengyle* had arrived off Bardia ready to launch its landing craft with the commandos aboard. The raiders had further bad luck when one of the landing craft failed to make its descent into the water and so could not take any further part in the operation.

The remainder of the Commando landed on the beaches fifteen minutes late – worse still, some were on the wrong beaches, which caused obvious confusion. However, it was not all 'bad news' – after all, they had landed unopposed and were able to set off quickly on their various planned tasks. Furthermore, they found that some of the information on which they had based these tasks was incorrect and so the results were disappointing, although a bridge and some enemy guns were destroyed. During the withdrawal one party of commandos returned to the wrong beach and got left behind; they were later reported as prisoners.

It was a disappointing start; although useful lessons were learnt, a period of frustration followed with further operations being planned and then cancelled. The feelings of the commandos were aptly summed up by those in No 7, who, on disembarking from the *Glengyle* after one cancelled operation left this pertinent graffiti message on a bulkhead: 'Never in the whole history of human endeavour has so few been buggered about by so many . . .'[1]

Mid-May saw *Layforce* split up on the following assignments: No 7 and the Middle East Commando were standing by in general reserve; No 8 was based at Mersa Matruh in North Africa; and No 11 Commando was dispatched to Cyprus to strengthen the garrison there.

The two Commandos in the general reserve did not have long to wait for action for they were to be directly involved in the battle and evacuation of Crete.

The story behind the battle honour award of CRETE is one of great courage and unselfish resolution displayed by commandos, in an operation for which they were neither armed, equipped, nor trained to carry out, namely fighting a rearguard action and then covering the evacuation of a field force. But first, a brief summary of the background to this story.

Following their successful Balkan campaign, which culminated with the conquest of Greece towards the end of April 1941, the Germans turned their attention to the possibility of capturing a Mediterranean island as a base to support their troops in North Africa. The obvious choice was Malta, but they considered this island too well defended and so they decided on the second option, Crete, which was poorly defended. They launched an airborne invasion to capture the island using their formidable Air Corps, supported by a mountain division, motor cycle troops, artillery, and, most importantly, a powerful Luftwaffe fleet of some 600 Junkers transport aircraft, 350 bombers – including 150 Stuka dive bombers – and 200 fighters, all located in Greece just twenty minutes flying time from Crete. Sadly there was no RAF fighter presence on the island as the seventeen Hurricane fighters that had been on the island were withdrawn for the Greek campaign.

On the island the original garrison of one infantry brigade with some artillery support had been increased by troops evacuated from Greece, including survivors from the New Zealand and Australian divisions, but they were short of the basic infantry battalion weapons such as the Vickers machine guns and the three-inch mortars, so essential in defence. The enlarged island garrison (Cretforce) commanded by Major General Bernard Freyberg, who had won the Victoria Cross in the First World War, totalled some thirty thousand troops, but it lacked any air support and had the crippling deficiencies and problems outlined above.

On 21 May the Germans attacked Crete with the first major airborne invasion in modern history. It was preceded by massive attacks on the main airfield of Maleme, in the west of the sausage-shaped island, and on two minor airstrips to the east. Then followed the mass descent of paratroops and the crash landing of gliders carrying airborne troops. At first the defenders not only held their ground but inflicted very heavy casualties and even took prisoners – among whom was Max Schemling, the pre-war heavyweight boxing champion of the world, although, in the event, he did not stay a prisoner for long.

During the next two days (22 and 23 May), under the umbrella of strong Luftwaffe support, German reinforcements of fighting men with their heavy weapons and stores were flown in. At Maleme alone the total numbers rose to just over twenty thousand; as a result, in spite of stubborn resistance and even spirited counter-attacks, the defenders had to start withdrawing on 25 May.

Meanwhile back at General Headquarters in Egypt the initial reaction was to send the reserve commandos of *Layforce* (No 7 and the Middle East Commando) to Crete to recapture the airfield at Maleme, or if this was not practical to carry out harassing raids. On 24 May an advance party of commandos was dispatched to the island with these aims in mind; early next morning they landed at Suda Bay, but already the situation had deteriorated.

The main body of *Layforce* eventually left Alexandria on 26 May. Bill Parker, who had originally joined No 4 but had later transferred to No 7, takes up the story and sets the scene:

> Once more we were transported down to the docks at Alexandria, where instead of boarding our own ship [*Glengyle*] we embarked on a new-looking mine-laying cruiser, HMS *Abdeal*. As soon as we were aboard she upped anchor and we were off, and only then were we told that we were going to Crete to try, if possible, to retake the airstrip at Maleme or fight a rearguard action. The *Abdeal* was reputed to be the fastest mine-laying cruiser in the navy at the time, capable of forty knots. She was loaded to within three feet of the mess deck ceiling with stores and ammunition, all apparently destined for Crete. We were immediately dispersed around the deck on Ack-Ack duty, at least the Bren gunners were. Eric and I found ourselves on the flying bridge section directly behind a pom-pom gun. It didn't seem long before we were called to action stations, the ship was travelling flat out . . . It was a dull day with low cloud and every time the ship changed direction one deck, or other, was awash and trying to get a fix on a target was impossible. One moment we were aiming at the sky the next at the sea . . .[2]

Eventually the commandos arrived at Suda Bay at about midnight, 26–27 May, and Parker recalls that the commandos were ordered to disembark with all speed and soon afterwards the *Abdeal* pulled away and left the harbour. This action

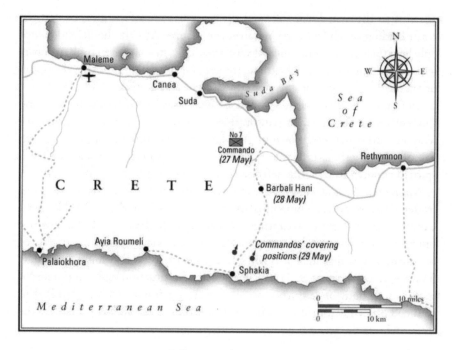

MAP 4. Rearguard action in Crete

was essential to ensure that all ships were clear of the island waters by daylight to avoid enemy air attacks. As a result only a fraction of the Commandos' spare ammunition and stores was unloaded – the rest was on its way back to Egypt.

At the quayside Colonel Laycock, who had travelled on the *Abdeal,* was met by one of the officers from the advance party from No 7, who briefed him on the current situation. It was grim news. Apparently Cretforce was already retreating and making for the little fishing port of Sphakia on the south coast to be evacuated by the navy, and the commandos were to cover this retreat. Furthermore, there was no transport available and, more to the point, little hope of food and ammunition resupplies on the route south to Sphakia. Finally, the *Layforce* commander was to report to General Freyberg at once for further orders.

Whilst Laycock went off to report to the general, his brigade major, Freddie Graham, hastily issued orders for all the commandos to load themselves up with ammunition and other supplies just unloaded from the *Abdeal,* which they readily did. There was even one account of four commandos who had managed to acquire a stretcher and had laden it with boxes of ammunition.

Freyberg confirmed that the commandos were to fight a series of rearguard actions to cover the retreat of Cretforce from the north to the evacuation port at Sphakia. It was an unenviable task for any unit, more so for Laycock's commandos, lightly armed and trained for offensive raiding operations, especially as they had no heavy machine guns or mortars, essential weapons for any infantry troops in defence. They would have to rely on their Brens and rifles, allowing the enemy to come within small-arms range. Nevertheless, in spite of these shortcomings they accepted the situation and started to tackle the undertaking with typical commando spirit and confidence – plus some morbid humour.

Laycock's plan was for the advance party from No 7 Commando to march off and take up a position some three miles east of Suda, where the road to Sphakia in the south forked away from the main coast road that continued to the east of the island. It was a location he disliked but had been ordered to take up; meanwhile the rest of that Commando was to march further down the Sphakia road and take up a further defensive position astride the road. The Middle East Commando was to follow on, marching through the night to take up a position further south and thereafter the two Commandos would disengage as the situation necessitated and withdraw through the other's lines in a series of 'leap frogging' tactical moves down to Sphakia.

The morning of 27 May saw the commandos, having marched through the night, in their defensive positions. Again Parker of No 7 takes up the story:

As dawn approached we came to an olive grove where we had to dig in as we were staying there for the day. Five of us were fortunate to find a trench already dug to a depth of about five feet. It was fine by us, as the ground was mostly rock, so our problem was solved and all we had to do was to prepare parapets for the Bren and other weapons. Meanwhile the rest of the troop sweated 'cobs' trying to dig their trenches in solid rock.

Then we received what we considered rather strange orders, especially as we seemed to be far away from the front, to make no more movement than necessary. We soon discovered the reason for that order, for as soon as it got light the air seemed to be full of Stukas. They came in wave after wave . . .[3]

He went on to describe one attack in detail and how after diving into their trench:

As usual, I ended up on top. In an instant the world seemed to explode as the bomb landed just a few feet in front of the trench, then the next thing I remember is being pulled out of a heap of earth and laid on the ground –

this must have been some time later as there were no aircraft around . . . It was then that I realised what casualties there were and how lucky we were to find that deep trench. The bomb that had buried us killed some of the lads next to us and the padre was still with a wounded one . . .[4]

The *Layforce* war diary for this period reiterates that report of Parker's in no uncertain terms. For 27 May at 8 a.m., it reads:

Enemy air activity began and continued with two brief lulls until dusk. In the forenoon it was mainly concentrated on hills to the left flank of 'A' Bn's [No 7 Commando] position. Throughout the day the Sphakion Road was thronged with retreating men who moved in independent groups, taking cover during attack and pushing on during intermission.[5]

The diary was written up by Evelyn Waugh, the famous novelist, who was then Captain Waugh, intelligence officer of *Layforce*. He had been one of the first volunteers for No 8 Commando back in July 1940 and a fellow volunteer of his at that time was Winston Churchill's son, Randolph Churchill, who was also in *Layforce*, though not in the two Commandos committed in Crete.

During the day, whilst No 7 was holding their line, Lieutenant Colonel Young, commanding officer of the Middle East Commando, was able to reconnoitre a suitable defensive position on the Sphakia road to the south of No 7 Commando's line, but to avoid being spotted from the air his Commando remained under cover all day and only moved to take up their position, which was near the village of Babali Hani, after dusk. The Commando did receive a welcome reinforcement in the shape of a tank that was placed under Young's command – providing magnificent support in the battle that followed next day.

During that first day 'in the line', No 7 Commando, in spite of being heavily attacked by the Luftwaffe, was not directly attacked by ground troops until the evening, when they were subjected to two attacks which they repelled. However, they did suffer several casualties later when they withdrew, as planned, to take up an intermediary position some ten miles further south, passing through the lines of the Middle East Commando en route and, as ordered, detaching a reinforced troop, under the command of Major Wylie, to provide flank protection on the left.

As anticipated, soon after dawn on 28 May the Middle East Commando position was heavily attacked from the air. It was the start of a hard day's fighting for the commandos.

Firstly they were subjected to a heavy concentration of mortar fire against which they could not retaliate; one of the outposts of Young's defensive position reported the approach of some enemy motor-cycle troops who appeared to be acting as scouts.

At about midday a full-scale enemy attack was launched by two battalions of the enemy's 5th Mountain Division, advancing down the axis of the road but also using a ravine that provided a covered approach to the commandos' left flank. However, although lacking medium machine guns, they did manage to repel these attacks with their Brens and rifles plus the support of that solitary tank at short range.

One of the Bren gunners, Arthur Noble, recalled: 'We never had a moment's respite. I had to keep my Bren in constant action. The need to estimate distance had by then gone. I dropped my sights down to zero.

'Boyle [his No 2 on the gun] was carrying on valiantly, filling and changing magazines as they became empty, and changing barrels as they became hot . . .'[6]

By 1330 hours, this first attack having been repulsed, the Germans brought up two further battalions to renew the offensive, concentrating on the vulnerable left flank of the commandos' line. Again they held their ground, but only just. William Seymour, who served in No 52 Middle East Commando, but was unfit at the time of the Crete campaign and so was left behind in Egypt, later wrote in his excellent book, *British Special Forces*: 'It was a close run thing. All spare personnel were rushed to the scene and the Germans were only held when troops from an Australian battalion, who were in reserve, gave timely assistance.'[7]

But the commandos did hold on, indeed they had the better of the encounter and it was estimated that the Germans had some eighty men killed as opposed to just three commandos killed, although the latter did have others wounded.

The commandos' action that day had enabled the main body to filter down the escape road to Sphakia and by early evening both Commandos were ordered to withdraw at dusk and march through the night and continue the next day to take up a position guarding the right flank of the evacuation area about three miles north of the port. This they did, arriving in the area during the afternoon of 29 May, by which time the commandos were utterly exhausted, although with typical commando resourcefulness they did manage to 'requisition' some local vehicles to lift the wounded and also to ferry some of the more exhausted men. They also managed to scrounge and forage for local food to eke out their nigh-exhausted rations.

Regarding food, Captain Arthur Swinburn, of the Middle East Commando had this to say about one meal he had during the withdrawal:

Twenty-seven men into one tin of sausages [one tin contained 13] so each man had half a sausage leaving the 27th man, poor blighter, with the tin, some fat and the smell of what was once there! As the senior in each case had to distribute the ration imagine how unlucky I was! But I did better on potatoes. Nine into a tin of potatoes left one over for me. Army biscuits were distributed – one and a half biscuits per man. This was the first food we had had for a very long time.[8]

Both of the *Layforce* Commandos took up their position for the beachhead defence in the hills overlooking the port. All next day they kept watch whilst the retreating troops of Cretforce passed through in their hundreds on their way to the beaches and evacuation – on the night of 29–30 May some six thousand troops were successfully evacuated, but thereafter the numbers were greatly reduced, mainly because of the damage to the ships wrought by air attacks.

On 31 May Laycock received orders from General Freyberg to the effect that his commandos were to stay to the end. They were to be the last fighting troops to be evacuated and leave on the last boat during the night of 31 May–1 June. When they finally received the order, at about 10 p.m. on 31 May, to make the three-mile descent to the beaches they were frustrated and delayed by the enormous disorganised shamble of troops who congested the road – although the commandos stayed compact in organised formations, they did not arrive at the port until after the last boat had sailed.

Meanwhile Colonel Laycock, who still had two of his Commandos outside Crete, had been ordered earlier on that evening of 31 May to evacuate his staff and return to command the rest of his brigade; they just managed to catch a destroyer at about midnight.

As a result Lieutenant Colonel Young was left as the senior commander of the two Commandos and he was ordered to contact the enemy and negotiate a surrender. It was a humiliating and thankless task, but he gave his commandos the option of trying to escape, though most were too weak and exhausted to contemplate this alternative. Nevertheless, some did take the chance. One group, consisting of fifteen men from No 7 and seven from the other Commando, managed to find a deserted landing craft and, boarding it, made off for North Africa. After a most extraordinary adventure they finally, nine days later, struck land at Sidi Barrani in North Africa. Such was the nature of this incredible escape that it became the basis of an episode in Evelyn Waugh's trilogy, 'The Sword of Honour'. However, others were not so lucky and the majority of the survivors of *Layforce*, including the likes of Bill Parker, ended up in Germany to spend the next four years as POWs.

Finally, William Seymour aptly summed up the commandos' action on Crete with these words:

'And so the best part of the two Commandos went into captivity after a long and courageously contested withdrawal which lacking proper weapons, had begun on a note of uncertainty but had achieved, through its performance, something of an epic quality.'[9]

The bravery of the commandos was duly recognised with awards and decorations for some of the officers and men, including that of the DSO to Colonel Young, plus the battle honour of CRETE.

The next major operation for *Layforce* involved No 11 Commando, which – after a brief stay in Cyprus, where there was much activity preparing defences against a possible German invasion – carried out a major operation in Syria. While in Cyprus, the commandos of No 11 had begun to wonder if they would ever have the chance to take part in offensive commando operations or raids. Their feelings and the atmosphere prevailing in the Commando at the time is apparent in Elizabeth Keyes's biography of her brother Geoffrey, who was in No 11 Commando. He was an avid writer of letters to the family at home, including some to his father, Sir Roger Keyes, and her book 'Geoffrey Keyes,' (see 'Select Bibliography) contains extracts from these letters that, among other things, certainly provide a clear picture of daily life in the Commandos during those early days.

Suddenly and unexpectedly on 3 June the Commando got the rush order to embark that night on two destroyers, *Hotspur* and *Ilex*, both just back from Crete, and set sail for Port Said in Egypt. On arrival there Lieutenant Colonel R. H. H. Pedder, commanding, was sent off to Jerusalem to General 'Jumbo' Wilson's headquarters, where he learned that the Allies were to invade Syria, which was still occupied by the Vichy French. The French had agreed to allow the German Luftwaffe the use of Syrian airfields, thus threatening the Suez Canal and Allied bases and supply routes in Egypt and the Western Desert. It was a situation that the Allies could not ignore. General Wilson, with limited forces, decided to make three thrusts. The 7th Australian Division was to provide the main thrust from Palestine using the coastal road leading from Haifa to Beirut and they were to be supported by two other flanking thrusts by forces based in Iraq in the east.

Lieutenant Colonel Pedder's Commando was to carry out landings in support of the Australians and its mission was centred on the problem presented by the Litani River, which ran east–west with the Masmiye bridge over it. The river also shielded a strong Vichy force located in the area between the Litani

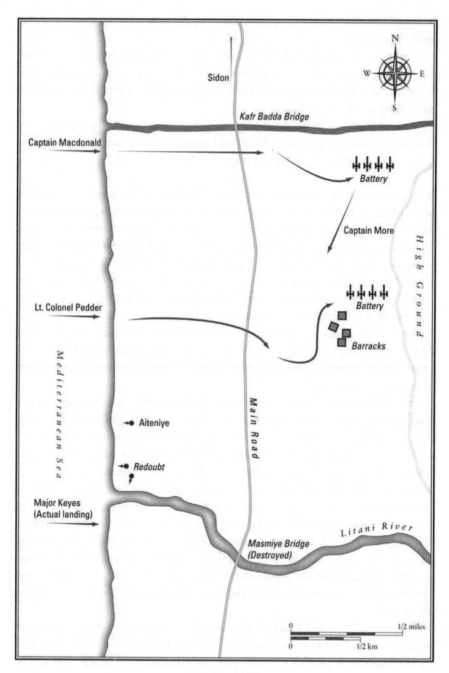

MAP 5. Litani River

river and another, smaller, river with another important bridge at Kafr Badda, about three thousand yards to the north of the Litani.

Colonel Pedder's plan was based on splitting his Commando into three parties, each with their own separate tasks. Their landings were to be on three separate beaches north of the Litani River, enabling them to attack from the flank and also in the rear of some of the enemy positions. The main aim was to prevent the enemy blowing the main Masmiye bridge and also the Kafr Badda bridge in the north, so enabling the Australians to make a rapid advance into Syria. In addition the commandos had other targets with the object of causing as much confusion and chaos amongst the considerable Vichy forces and defences in the area, which included two artillery batteries, a barracks, a redoubt, and various machine gun and mortar positions. With a paucity of intelligence information and aerial photos and little time to prepare it was a formidable commitment, but for No 11 Commando it was action at last!

Leaving Port Said aboard the HMS *Glengyle* on 7 June the Commando arrived off the coast in brilliant moonlight and started to prepare for the landings. Then, much to the bitter disappointment of Colonel Pedder and his men, the captain of the *Glengyle* – acting on the advice of a naval party that had just returned from a reconnaissance of the beaches and reported dangerous surf conditions, making the landings nigh impossible with the possible loss of all the landing craft – decided that he could not take the risk, so the landings for that night were cancelled and the bitterly disappointed commandos were ordered to return to Port Said. However, just as they arrived back they were ordered to return and carry out the operation the following night, 8–9 June. Meanwhile the main force advancing from Palestine into Syria had forced the Vichy French to start withdrawing, but in their retreat they had blown up the Masmiye bridge over the Litani, though the Kafr Badda bridge to the north was still intact.

In the light of these circumstances Colonel Pedder had to hastily revise his plans and the result was that he would land three parties on separate beaches between the Litani and the northern river, with the aim of securing the Kafr Badda bridge and deal with the two gun batteries and other enemy positions on the north side of the Litani – thereby helping the Australians to build a pontoon bridge over the Litani and continue their advance.

The northernmost party, consisting of two troops under the overall command of Captain Macdonald, was to seize and secure the Kafr Badda bridge, deal with a gun battery to the east, and then harass the enemy in the area and deny them access to the bridge area.

The second party, landing in the centre about eight hundred yards to the south of Captain Macdonald's group, and consisting of three troops under the command of Colonel Pedder, was to deal with a battery of 75-mm guns and attack the barracks: these two targets were about one and a half miles inland. Thereafter the party was to act as a reserve able to react to the situation on the ground by causing as much confusion and chaos to the enemy forces as possible and so take pressure off the Australian advance.

The third party, the southernmost one, consisting of three troops under the command of Major Geoffrey Keyes (the second-in-command of No 11) was to land about eight hundred yards north of the Litani and destroy a strong enemy outpost in the Aiteniye area and then carry on to seize an enemy redoubt position covering the mouth of the Litani River.

It was almost dawn on 9 June when the *Glengyle* arrived off the landing beaches; fortunately the swell and surf had subsided so the landings went well and, as practised countless times before in training, the commandos 'cleared the beaches like scolded cats', with just one casualty.

The following account is based on that in Elizabeth Keyes' book, Chapter XX, plus comments/additions from Sir Tommy Macpherson who was in No 10 Troop.

After landing Captain Macdonald's party started on their way over open ground to the Kafr Badda bridge with only a few rifle shots passing over their heads. As they neared the bridge, however, they encountered opposition, not only from enemy outposts but also from armoured cars. Nevertheless, by 6 a.m. they had captured the bridge intact. Captain Macdonald left one of his troops to consolidate on the position whilst he pushed on to the east of the bridge to deal with a battery of four guns, which No 8 Troop succeeded in capturing with 'an embarrassing number of prisoners' — at one point the number of prisoners exceeded their commando captors.

One of the problems during the whole of this action was the lack of intercommunications between the three main commando parties. Initially they had only one wireless set in each of the three main parties and one of these was immobilised on landing. To overcome this problem and find out what was happening in the central area, Captain More took one of the enemy's motor cycles and made off to contact Colonel Pedder who was on his right flank. More could hear a lot of firing in the area where the Colonel's party was operating and was concerned, but he did not get far — he was shot at and had to give up and so returned to rejoin No 10 troop at Kafr Badda.

The colonel's party set off after landing and made steady progress using the cover of a dry river bed, but this was not fast enough for Pedder. He shouted to his men to speed up, so they broke cover and got out on to open ground where the going was much faster, albeit subject to enemy machine-gun fire. Luckily this was mainly ineffective and Lieutenant Bryan with No 1 Troop was able to surprise and capture seven of the enemy before pressing on, beyond the barracks, towards the battery of 75-mm guns. One of the guns was not manned: they found the crew in a trench nearby and successfully dealt with them before taking over their gun. The other guns were manned and had opened fire on the beach area, but in Lieutenant Bryan's section were two artillery men who had the 'know-how' and initiative to turn their captured gun on to the other guns and silence them. This was not the last time that the commandos were able to use captured enemy weapons against their original owners. In fact the use of enemy weapons was a standard subject in the commandos' training at Achnacarry.

Next came the attack on to the barracks; the enemy began to inflict mounting casualties on Pedder's men with machine-gun and sniper fire. The situation was getting serious and, at 8.45 a.m., Pedder decided to withdraw and seek the shelter of a nearby gully. Before they could make the gully, however, Pedder was killed, together with another officer, and Regimental Sergeant Major Trevendale took over command. He led the remnants of Pedder's party along some high ground towards the Litani River in the south, where they took up a position with good all-round fields of fire; they stayed there for several hours, under continuous fire, until the enemy eventually surrounded and captured them.

Major Keyes's party was the third and southernmost one. Although their landing was unopposed they soon discovered they had been landed on the wrong side of the Litani. Instead of being north of the river they were south of it. However, undaunted and with commendable resourcefulness Keyes contacted the Australian sappers who were waiting to support the attack north of the river and persuaded them to lend him seven collapsible boats to help him ferry his men over the river and carry out his original mission. At that point, much to the chagrin of the commandos, the enemy started a 'box' barrage on the Australian and commandos' positions and they all had to go to ground to take cover. After a while, thanks to some counter-battery fire from the Australian artillery and, doubtless, also to the commando actions already outlined, there was a lull in the enemy fire. During this respite Keyes, with the help of the 'Aussies', was able to gradually, although still under intermittent mortar fire, ferry his men across the Litani and eventually capture the redoubt covering the mouth of the river. It was now about 1.30 p.m. With a pontoon bridge established and the redoubt destroyed the Australians were able to continue their advance, only to be held up by the strongpoint at Aiteniye.

Meanwhile, in his baptism of fire Lieutenant Paddy Mayne (who later became the most highly decorated member in the SAS, awarded the DSO and three bars) had collected some fifty prisoners in his skirmishes with the enemy outposts just to the south of the barracks, towards the strongpoint at Aiteniye.

Another officer in No 11 Commando who had his baptism of fire on the Litani operation and later became a highly decorated officer for his exploits with the Special Operations Executive (SOE) was Lieutenant Tommy Macpherson. His troop (No 10) was with Captain Macdonald in that battle for Kafr Badda bridge and later in the action to capture the battery of howitzers. By the late afternoon Macpherson had also captured a haul of Vichy French prisoners, mostly Senegalese and Algerians.

As dusk fell most of the commandos started to withdraw and under the cover of darkness make their way to the Australian lines by keeping to the high ground and finding fordable crossings of the river further inland. Keyes and his party however consolidated and remained in their position at the captured redoubt overnight.

Early next morning the Vichy forces in the area of the Litani surrendered. For No 11 Commando the battle was over. It had been a bitter action and although the Commando had succeeded in fulfilling all its objectives success came at a heavy price – 123 men of all ranks were killed or wounded, including Colonel Pedder. This then is the story behind the battle honours of SYRIA 1941 and LITANI, and is just one of that little-known Syrian campaign, of which the last words are those of John Keegan in his definitive work, *The Second World War*: 'Sour, costly and regrettable though the little Syrian war had been – 3500 Allied soldiers were killed or wounded in its course – the effect of its outcome on British strategy in Africa was wholly beneficial.'[10]

The remnants of No 11 Commando, now under the command of Lieutenant Colonel Geoffrey Keyes, who at twenty-four years old was one of the youngest commanding officers in the British Army, returned to Cyprus again for garrison duties.

Although CRETE and LITANI were the only specific battle honours for the *Layforce* Commandos, as already mentioned they did take part in other operations before they were finally disbanded, as such, in August 1941.

Perhaps some of the most significant of these operations were carried out by No 8 Commando when it was based in Tobruk. Indeed the raids and operations carried out from that besieged base are good examples of the proper use of commandos in defence and are the subject of the book *Tobruk Commando* by Gordon Landsborough, published in 1956. These operations, based on the concepts of 'long-range desert raids', led to the eventual formation of the Special Air Service (SAS) by David Stirling and his fellow officers from the disbanded *Layforce*.

However, the final story of the commandos of *Layforce*, although not a specific battle honour, must be that of the famous raid on 'Rommel's headquarters' in North Africa, in which the first of the eight Victoria Crosses won by commandos was posthumously awarded to Lieutenant Colonel Geoffrey Keyes of No 11 Commando. As such, it features in all the histories and accounts of the Army Commandos of the Second World War, so suffice it here to give but a brief description; a very detailed account of the raid with illustrations is presented in Elizabeth Keyes' book.

The idea and object of the raid were both bold and daring, and in keeping with the original concept of the use of the commandos, but, as so often happened, the intelligence was inaccurate and out-of-date.

The raid was planned to coincide with General Auchenleck's counter-attack, Operation *Crusader*, to drive Rommel's German–Italian army out of Cyrenaica. The objective of the raid was to land a party from No 11 Commando, under Colonel Keyes to attack a complex of Rommel's administrative headquarters behind the enemy lines and within which was believed to be Rommel's own quarters. At the time Rommel was coming to be regarded by the troops as a 'super general', a cunning and crafty adversary. He was nicknamed the 'Desert Fox'[11] and so to raid his headquarters and kill him would have had a tremendous psychological impact on the enemy and bolstered the morale of Allied troops, especially on the eve of the planned counter-attack.

It was obviously considered to be such an important assignment that Colonel Laycock himself was to accompany and direct the operation (codenamed *Flipper*) although Keyes was to lead the actual raid on the headquarters complex.

Briefly the plan was to land the raiding party on the North Africa coast some fifteen miles to the east of the objective in rubber dinghies launched from two submarines three nights before the raid. There they would be met by Captain Haselden, an intelligence expert who had been 'dropped' by a detachment of the Long Range Desert Group reconnaissance unit to meet the raiding party and update them on intelligence details and the layout of the target area. Time was also allowed to enable Keyes to move by night only, lying up by day, and to make a thorough reconnaissance and finalise his attack plan before the raid at midnight on 17–18 November.

Accordingly, Laycock, Keyes, and the rest of the raiders embarked on two submarines at Alexandria on 10 November and arrived off the selected beaches on the night of 14 November, but they had great difficulty trying to land in their rubber dinghies and not all of them made it to the beach. However, those that did hid up in a shrub area and a new plan was hatched to accommodate their reduced numbers. The raiding party was split into two groups: the main one under Keyes and a supporting group under Lieutenant Cooke, whose task was to cut the telephone communication lines from Rommel's headquarters. Unfortunately the weather conditions were foul: torrential rain fell the whole time and made the raiders' advance towards their objective, over rock-strewn tracks and through ankle-deep mud, a test of endurance. Nevertheless, over the course of two days, moving only by night and hiding by day, Keyes was able to approach his objective in time to make a thorough reconnaissance and subsequently get to the perimeter of the objective on the night of the 17th. On the way Cooke's party left Keyes and successfully carried out their own mission, though unfortunately they were later captured.

Keyes's main party got within a few yards of the house, where they cut the perimeter barbed-wire fencing; there was only one sentry on guard – the rest were sheltering from the rain. Keyes silently killed this lone sentry. They reached the front door and kicked it open and burst in, but were confronted by a German. Captain Campbell shot and killed him but the element of surprise was lost. Nevertheless, Keyes and his men started to search the house. The first room was empty, but in the second room they found ten Germans. Keyes emptied his Colt automatic at them and Captain Campbell rolled a primed grenade along the floor, but sadly before Keyes could get out of the room one of the Germans fired at him and mortally wounded him. Captain Campbell, Sergeant Terry, and the other three of the party ran out of the house – tragically, while emerging outside to call in the covering party, Captain Campbell forgot the password and was shot and badly wounded by his own men. Sergeant Terry assumed command and, after destroying the generator to the house, successfully led them back to Laycock's base on the coast. The submarines that were meant to pick them up failed to arrive, however, and there was no option but for the survivors to split up into little groups of twos and threes and try to get back to the British lines separately. In the end, only Laycock and Sergeant Terry succeeded, but it took them forty-one days.

William Seymour aptly summarises the outcome of the raid: 'The mission, in which many deeds of heroism were performed, had failed. It had been carried out with considerable dash and a degree of skill and Colonel Keyes undoubtedly deserved the posthumous Victoria Cross awarded to him.'[12]

Now for an entirely different commando operation and battle honour, namely MADAGASCAR, but first the background.

In the early months of 1942, following their land successes at Singapore and in Malaya, the Japanese began to operate their submarines in the Indian Ocean, thus threatening Allied supply routes to the Middle East, via the Cape, as well

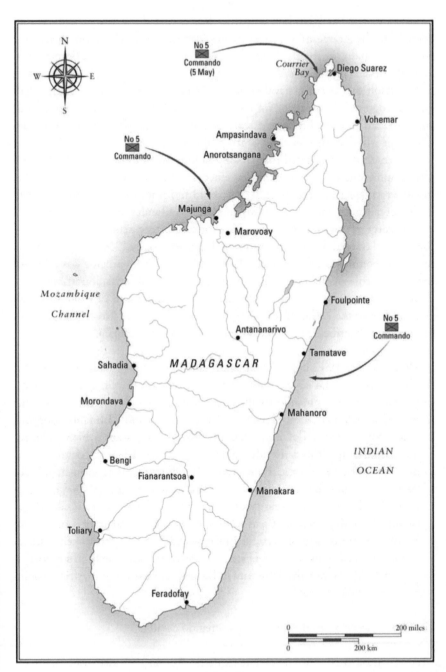

MAP 6. Madagascar

as routes to the Far East. It was further feared that the Vichy French, still in control of the strategically placed island Madagascar, might allow their Axis partner, Japan, to use the excellent naval facilities and resources of Diego Suarez and other ports on the island.

In March the German naval commander-in-chief reported to Hitler that Japan recognised the strategic importance of Madagascar for naval operations and intended to establish bases at various ports on the island. It was a danger that Churchill and his Chiefs of Staff could not ignore.

As a result it was decided that an amphibious operation, Britain's first large-scale amphibious assault since the Dardanelles in the First World War, would be mounted to capture Madagascar. It was a bold and ambitious decision inasmuch as the force would have to sail nearly nine thousand miles direct from Britain.

The force of two infantry brigades with supporting arms and services was formed and trained for the operation (codenamed 'Ironclad'). No 5 Commando, under the command of Lieutenant Colonel W. S. S. Sanguinetti, was selected for the key role in the initial assault of destroying two coastal batteries that dominated the sea approaches to the main port and harbour of Diego Suarez.

In a letter to the author in 1988, the late Geoff Riley (ex No 5 Commando) recalled and described some of his experiences in that campaign:

On 23 March 1942 No 5 Commando sailed from Glasgow in the *Winchester Castle* in one of the largest military convoys to leave Britain at that stage of the war. No 5 Commando totalled some 365 men and we were part of the force that included 29 Independent Infantry Brigade and 13 Infantry Brigade. The convoy consisted of more than fifty Royal Navy ships, which included three battleships, three aircraft carriers, destroyers, frigates, corvettes and minesweepers. We carried Free French Intelligence officers on board, so guessed our destination was a Vichy administered colony. Our briefing explained the absolute necessity of preventing the Japanese from taking the island of Madagascar, as it was known that they had their eyes on Diego Suarez, the third natural harbour in the world. For had they taken it there would be no El Alamein, as the Eighth Army could not have been supported in North Africa, nor the 14 Army in Burma, and even South Africa would have been under threat.[13]

Geoff then went on to describe the commando assault:

At dawn on 5 May we landed at Courrier Bay on the north-west coast of Madagascar, some eleven miles from Diego Suarez. In our assault landing craft we followed the minesweepers down a channel to our landing area. We caught the Vichy garrison completely unawares, because of a triumph of seamanship by the Royal Navy and the Merchant Navy, who avoided coral reefs believed to be impassable to a force of our size. Above us on cliffs fifty feet high was a battery of six-inch guns. We climbed the cliffs and caught the Vichy gunners by surprise. They were asleep.[14]

Riley's commando comrades had a mixed bag of prisoners: French officers and NCOs, plus Malagasy and Senegalese soldiery. However, the action was not concluded, for a group from the garrison, about forty in all, led by NCOs counter-attacked, but they were beaten off and, with their leaders killed, the rest surrendered. The commandos continued with mopping-up operations; meeting little or no opposition they ended up with nearly three hundred prisoners with only light casualties themselves. One of these was the popular Captain 'Chips' Heron, who was wounded by a grenade thrown by someone in the back of the surrendering enemy.

After this success Riley continues: 'In sweltering heat and loaded like pack mules we marched for about ten miles against a hot wind, blowing across from the bay on our left flank, to take part in the final stages of the assault and capture of the port and also the nearby town of Antisrane.'[15]

By nightfall on 6 May all the main objectives had been taken and the enemy force in the area accounted for. The operation had taken less than two days and with Diego Suarez and Antisrane completely under British control, the force commander, Brigadier Festing (later Field Marshal and chief of the Imperial General Staff) hoped that the rest of the Vichy French forces on the island would capitulate, but they did not. So further operations, involving No 5 Commando, were necessary.

With the main port secured Brigadier Festing decided to await reinforcements and supplies before taking further action. Meanwhile a detachment of No 5 Commando took over the guard duties of an old defunct nineteenth-century coastal battery located on the west side of the bay. On 31 May, at about 8.15 p.m., a terrific explosion was heard from the direction of Diego Suarez and the anchorages of our ships in the harbour there. Corporal John Wall, one of the commando guards in the old battery, takes up the story:

Next morning we found the beach strewn with 'flotsam' and concluded that somehow it was connected with the explosions. Then in the distance we saw two natives running towards our camp and when they neared us we saw that one was carrying a carved wooden stick vertically. At the top was attached a clean white envelope addressed (in French) to '*The Captain, Artillery*'. Inside was a note, also in French, which none of us could speak, but together we managed to grasped the meaning . . .[15]

John Wall and his comrades gathered from further gestures and the odd words such as 'nippon' that the message referred to Japanese submariners who were now in the natives' village. So they sent a message to Commando headquarters, based in Antisrane, giving details of the message received and they were told that a commando patrol was being sent to the village where the two submariners were hiding. They were also told that the explosions of the night before were attributable to a midget submarine attack and as a result HMS *Ramilles* had been damaged and an oil tanker, SS *British Loyalty,* had been sunk. John Wall continues:

> The patrol led by Lieutenant Eric Fox later landed at the rocky mouth, where the midget submarine had come to grief; and made for the village where the submariners were known to be hiding, The patrol laid up until next morning and then approached the village, whereupon one of the submariners came out of a native dwelling, saw the advancing patrol and immediately fired his hand gun. The other submariner also joined in firing his weapon, but the patrol then opened fire and killed both men, stripped them of all their possessions, and buried them nearby.

This midget submarine attack clearly provided concrete evidence of the potential danger to our sea convoys travelling to the Middle East and the Far East that might have materialised had not *Ironclad* been mounted.

With elements of the Vichy French forces still holding out, a new plan was prepared for an amphibious assault on one of their strongholds at the port of Majunga on the west coast of the island, facing the Mozambique Channel. This task was delegated to No 5 Commando and after a spell of training and preparation, the unit duly attacked the port. Geoff Riley recalls that one of the landing craft broke down, so instead of landing before dawn they had to land in broad daylight – but with the support of a destroyer's gunfire they were able to land directly on to the quayside. They met only sporadic enemy fire and after some skirmishing they forced the Vichy French to surrender; the port was occupied and the commandos duly returned to their Diego Suarez base.

There they awaited their next mission. During this period John Wall recalls that they existed on meagre rations:

the food was terrible, bread was scarce so I and others used to go into the town to buy local rice cakes. In the evenings I went across to the 'South Lancs' (my old regiment) camp to see many chaps I used to know in Warrington before the war. Their food was plentiful and I was always assured of a well-filled savoury sandwich. Two of my mates in 2 Troop did the same thing.

Another vivid memory of John's in that Madagascar campaign 'that will never be effaced from my memory is being dosed with pure quinine, for it was so bitter. Our officers supervised us carefully to ensure that we swallowed the full dose every morning. Our spoons were used for the dose and they were stripped of their plate after a few days!'

The Commando's next mission was to capture Tamatave, a major port facing the Indian Ocean on the east coast of the island. The plan for this operation was to land the commandos direct from the decks of four destroyers in a 'crash landing' on to the dockside of the port. So with this in mind No 5 embarked on the four destroyers and sailed to Mombasa, in East Africa, to prepare and practise for the planned crash landing at Tamatave. John Wall elaborates: 'The plan was simple, for the destroyers were to head for the dock wall at speed and then turn broadside on to the wall and drop gangplanks to bridge the gap between the ships and the dockside, thus allowing the men of No 5 to run on to the dock and attack the enemy.'

On 18 September the naval force with the commandos aboard the destroyers sailed into the harbour of Tamatave and instead of an immediate assault the enemy were given the opportunity to surrender. John Wall relates: 'an envoy, under the cover of a white flag, was sent in a small craft to the port, but it was fired upon and returned to the HQ ship. Within a short space of time the Royal Navy directed a salvo of gunfire over Tamatave and shortly afterwards the Vichy forces raised the white flag.'

The four destroyers, in turn, steamed at speed to an isolated quay where they landed the commandos who quickly took over the port and occupied other strategic places in the town.

Five days later on 23 September the formal surrender of the Vichy French government took place at Antananarivo, about a hundred miles south-west of Tamatave. But still it was not the end of the campaign for No 5 because scattered detachments of the Vichy French in areas south of the capital refused to surrender, so a volunteer party of commandos, each able to ride a horse, was organised and sent to deal with them. This party, about sixty strong and under the command of Major Bob Laird, were mounted on 'requisitioned' horses and, because the promised saddlery was not forthcoming, they departed on their mission on a mixture of 'make do' saddlery – thus emulating the original mounted commando enemies of the British redcoats of the Boer War – of whom Winston Churchill had some unpleasant memories.

After a series of small skirmishes and ambushes Laird's commandos successfully brought to an end all resistance and rejoined the rest of the Commando. This was the last action of No 5 on the island. Its job over, and not required for further occupational duties, the Commando returned to Britain with the satisfaction of a job well done and with the latter-day award of the battle honour of MADAGASCAR as a permanent tribute to a most unusual little Commando campaign.

CHAPTER 4

ST NAZAIRE

THE RAID ON ST NAZAIRE, often referred to as the 'greatest raid of all', is certainly one of the best-known Commando battle honours. To appreciate the significance, purpose, and outcome of this famous operation it is necessary to mention the background of Operation *Chariot*, as the raid was codenamed.

One of the most worrying and certainly the longest-fought battle in the Second World War was not fought on the land, but on the sea: namely, the 'Battle of the Atlantic', and winning it was vital to the Allies' cause. Vital because Britain had to import the raw materials, fuel, and food to manufacture all the aircraft, ships and weapons needed to successfully wage war and also sustain all those on the 'home front'.

A huge fleet of merchant ships was needed to meet these requirements and from the outbreak of the war – in spite of the convoy systems employed by the Royal Navy, supported by the Coastal Command of the Royal Air Force – the losses in ships and supplies grew at an alarming rate. It was a most worrying situation and Winston Churchill – who was the one who coined the term 'Battle of the Atlantic' – considered it to be the most dominating factor throughout the war and the only thing that really frightened him.

It was of further concern that, following the fall of France, the Germans gained access to the Atlantic ports of Brest, Lorient, La Rochelle, Bordeaux,

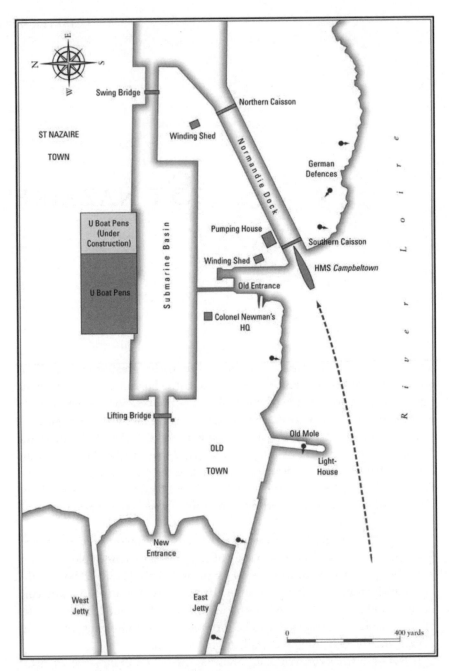

MAP 7. St Nazaire Raid

and most importantly, St Nazaire. The latter was critical because it contained a huge dry dock, the largest in the world, capable of accommodating the enemy's capital fighting ships, in particular their most powerful, the *Tirpitz*. With its eight 15-inch guns and a speed of some 30 knots, the *Tirpitz* could out-gun and out-speed the largest of the Royal Navy's battleships. But if this dry dock and other harbour facilities at St Nazaire could be destroyed, it would help considerably to reduce the dangers from such formidable enemy surface raiders on our vulnerable sea routes in the Atlantic. It was, therefore, decided in early 1942 that an operation should be mounted with this aim – Operation *Chariot* was born.

Here it should be mentioned that there are several excellent books devoted entirely to this single operation and they are listed in the 'Select Bibliography'. Also, in 2007 the BBC produced a first-class television documentary, narrated by Jeremy Clarkson, on the raid. With this in mind it is emphasised that these sources record the full story from the planning to the final outcome of the operation in great detail, and the following account here is, in effect, a summary of No 2 Commando's part in the raid.

Initially, a major air raid by the RAF was considered but subsequently ruled out because it was decided that the bombers could not be spared for such an operation. Furthermore, at this stage of the war the RAF considered that their Wellingtons and Whitleys were not technically capable of carrying out a precision night attack on such a specific target as the dry dock; finally, there was fear that any such night air raid on the docks area of this port would inevitably inflict unwarranted and undesirable casualties on the French population.

Other possibilities were considered but eventually it was decided to employ the commandos to raid the port and carry out the demolition tasks. The planning and execution of the ambitious operation was delegated to Combined Operations, whose chief, Lord Louis Mountbatten, was keen to take it on, and No 2 Commando, commanded by Lieutenant Colonel A. C. Newman, was duly selected for the task.

The final plan was based on the Royal Navy delivering the commandos from their base in Falmouth, Cornwall, across 380 miles of sea to St Nazaire, which is located six miles up the Loire estuary – in a mixed flotilla of mainly RN motor launches (MLs), but headed by an old US destroyer, renamed HMS *Campbeltown*, which had been transferred to the Royal Navy by the Americans in exchange for rights to use bases in Bermuda. Approximately a hundred commandos were to travel aboard the destroyer, with the rest of No 2 distributed aboard the sixteen MLs.

The commandos were to land at three different places in the docks area:
(1) on the dock caisson gate itself, from the decks of HMS *Campbeltown*
(2) on the old entrance quayside
(3) on the 'Old Mole'

The commandos aboard the motor launches would use the landing places at (2) and (3). From these three main landing points assault groups would attack and kill the enemy manning the dock defences, whilst specially trained demolition parties would destroy or damage buildings, installations, and equipment, including the important pump and winding houses of the dry dock.

To destroy the main seaward caisson gate of the dry dock it was planned that HMS *Campbeltown* would sail straight into it and thus ram it – its forward holds were to be packed with some four and a quarter tons of explosives, which would be detonated by timed fuses set during the final approach to St Nazaire.

On completion of these tasks the Commandos would withdraw to the quayside of the Old Mole and re-embark in the MLs and accompanying motor gun boat (MGB) and motor torpedo boat (MTB) for the return journey back to England.

After much discussion and haggling, Bomber Command of the RAF agreed to mount a 'diversionary' raid in the area, but as James Dorrian explains in his comprehensive book, *Storming St Nazaire*, it was ineffective and the subsequent action of the aircraft only alerted the German defences in the area without providing any useful support to the seaborne raiding force.

So much for the outline plan, now for some details of the special training undertaken for this daring, but hazardous, operation. After receiving his initial briefing Colonel Newman was introduced to his opposite number in charge of the naval side of the operation, Commander R. E. D. Ryder, RN, who, because of those initials and for no other reason, was nicknamed 'Red' Ryder. Right from the onset Newman and Ryder established a warm and harmonious working relationship – a very important factor in this type of joint operation.

With less than a month to prepare for the operation there was no time to lose. For Newman there were three distinctly different training priorities: firstly, street fighting and close-quarter attacks at night; secondly, the tasks of demolishing special dockside installations and equipment; and thirdly, liaison with the Royal Navy, familiarisation and training with the craft and the ship to be used on the operation. There were no particular problems concerning the first and third of these priorities, they were consistent with normal commando training, but the second one did pose problems – the main one being that the number of demolition experts required for the numerous and specialised targets exceeded those normally trained and available in any one Commando. So it was decided to bring in demolition experts, officers, and other ranks from other Commandos, namely Nos 1, 3, 4, 5, 9, and 12. I well remember Second Lieutenant Pennington, RE, from No 4, for he was an ex-Varsity rugby 'blue', being detached together with several of our other men, who were mostly all sappers. With security foremost in mind, they were told – and it also appeared in our unit orders – that they were being detached for a 'docks demolition course'. (In the event not all of them went on the raid. Pennington went, as did Sapper Coulson, but sadly neither returned; both were killed on board their motor launch as they approached the quay.)

Initially eighty of these demolition commandos gathered at the small port of Burntisland on the Firth of Forth, under the command of Captain W. Pritchard, RE, and he was assisted by another RE officer, Captain R. Montgomery. Neither were Commando officers, but they were chosen because they had pre-war working experience in docks and also had a sound working knowledge of dockyard demolition techniques. Indeed, Pritchard, who had won a Military Cross for blowing up a vital bridge during the Dunkirk evacuation, had lately made a staff study of the feasibility of destroying enemy dockyards by raiding forces. Equally important, he was familiar with the layout and structure of the King George dry dock in Southampton, which was almost as large and very similar in many ways to the one in St Nazaire.

In the short stay in Burntisland the commandos were shown how to destroy anything and everything that contributed to the smooth and efficient running of a port; with this basic knowledge of a small port, it was time to move on to the larger ones of Cardiff and Southampton. The eighty-strong party was split into two groups for this continuation training; after a few hectic days of training at Cardiff and Southampton the groups changed over so that they got experiences of both ports. Towards the final stages of this training Pritchard and Montgomery were finally told of the plan for the operation and they were able to decide the type and size of charges necessary for the selected targets and also allot teams to the specific targets then get them to rehearse for the 'real thing'.

For example, at the King George dry dock in Southampton Lieutenant Stuart Chant, from No 5 Commando, and his men got first-hand experience of what was involved in the destruction of a pump house and practised for such a task, descending the dark metal stairways within time targets and placing dummy charges against the vulnerable impeller pumps located deep underground.

Lieutenant Gerard Brett from No 12 Commando and Lieutenant R. Burtenshaw from No 5 Commando, with their teams, each consisting of an officer and four demolitionists, tackled the hollow interiors of the caissons to place their charges against its steel sides. Lieutenants Corrin Purdon from No 12 Commando and C. J. Smalley from No 5 Commando concentrated their teams on demolishing winding houses. Similarly, other teams at both ports practised and rehearsed for tasks that covered a wide range of dockside installations, from bridges to cranes. Those in the demolition teams were so heavily laden, some with loads of up to 90 lb, that they would be easy targets so for this reason small protection teams were planned to accompany them, although these protection teams initially did their training separately and only joined up with the demolition groups in the final stages when the whole Commando was concentrated at Falmouth.

While the demolition teams were away for their special training the rest of No 2, who were to provide the assault groups to attack the enemy dock defences, as well as the protection parties for the demolition teams, trained and prepared under the Commando second-in-command, Major Bill Copland. Their priorities were concentrating on night movement, street fighting, section attacks on enemy gun emplacements, and firing practice with their troop weapons. This they did initially around their base in Ayr, then subsequently in the Falmouth area, culminating with a night exercise – a mock raid – on Plymouth docks.

To provide those troops earmarked to make the long sea journey in the MLs with some experience of such a sea crossing aboard these small craft, Newman arranged a return trip to the Isles of Scilly. Unfortunately, it was anything but a pleasant experience: the weather was foul and the sea conditions vile, with the result being that practically all who went were extremely seasick.

On 23 March the demolition teams joined up with the rest of the Commando aboard the *Princess Josephine Charlotte* moored in Falmouth, which was used as the Commando base. For security reasons the troops were now confined to the ship except when they disembarked for training.

An important feature of the overall plan was the decision to alter the silhouette of HMS *Campbeltown* to resemble a German warship. The required transformation included the removal of two of her four stacks then cutting the tops of the other two at an angle to make them appear similar to those of the German destroyers. To protect the crew and the commandos on board as she was running the anticipated gauntlet of enemy fire when sailing up the Loire to the dry dock, extra armour-plate panels were welded to the bridge and decking.

There were also, of course, structural alterations in the forward holds to accommodate the depth charges and explosives to turn the ship into a floating bomb. All these alterations were carried out in the Devonport docks, under the supervision of Lieutenant Commander Beattie, RN, who had been appointed captain of the destroyer.

Commander Ryder also had to assemble and prepare a flotilla of MLs – they also had to have an important modification because the long sea journey, there and back, meant that extra fuel had to be carried, so tanks, each holding some 500 gallons, had to be installed on the decks of every ML.

In the final stages of the preparation every one was thoroughly briefed on the operation with the aid of aerial photographs and an excellent model of the docks: all the designated targets were clearly depicted so that every single commando knew where and what his task was – and also, in less detail, those of his comrades. All going on the raid were left in no doubt of the hazards and difficulties that faced them. They were spelt out quite clearly – some eighty defence posts, including anti-aircraft guns, machine gun emplacements, and searchlights. It was estimated that the enemy, including those manning the ships and submarines in the docks plus the garrison troops in the port and adjacent area, was in the order of five thousand men altogether.

One of the briefing officers reckoned that attacking St Nazaire would stir up a 'hornets' nest' and conceded that while, with surprise and luck, they might get in and do the job, their chances of getting out were slim. 'There's certainly a VC in it,' he said. He underestimated: there were five, more than for any other single operation in the war.

The time and date fixed for the actual attack on St Nazaire was in the early hours of 28 March. However, because of the long sea journey and the slow speed of the MLs, the flotilla of raiding craft and their escorts had to leave Falmouth during the afternoon of 26 March. So earlier that day, in the morning, Colonel Newman, held his final briefing to the whole Commando, although even at this late stage he had not received the final order 'to go'.

Commenting in his diary Captain Hodgson, who commanded one of the assault parties, had this to say about Newman's final pep talk: 'A rousing speech by Charles Newman which put up morale 100% – he really is a fine chap and all of us realise how much he has done to make the job a success. If anyone has been patient, helpful and charming the whole time, it was he.'[1]

At the end of his final briefing, in which he had emphasized that it was going to be an extremely hazardous operation, Newman made a unique offer, which had been previously proffered by Lord Mountbatten: namely, that any man who considered he had family responsibilities or any other reason for not going could stand down. They were completely free to do so and nobody would think any the worse for so doing. Not a single man asked to stand down. This was to be the sort of job they had trained for and waited so long for. Now here it was and they were ready and eager to get on with it.

With most of their bulky stores, ammunition, and equipment and rations for the long sea journey already packed and stowed on either HMS *Campbeltown* or the MLs the previous day, they left their host ship, *Princess Josephine Charlotte*, early in the afternoon of the 26th to embark. Later that afternoon, escorted by two 'Hunt'-class destroyers, HMS *Tynedale* and HMS *Atherstone*, plus a motor gun boat and a motor torpedo boat, the raiding force set sail from Falmouth.

The weather and sea conditions were favourable and during that first night they made good unhindered progress. By early next morning they had rounded the Brittany peninsula and were well out in the Bay of Biscay, giving the impression that they were heading for Gibraltar. It was planned that when the vessels finally turned towards the French coast to head for St Nazaire, they would do so having already passed the mouth of the Loire. They sailed in a procession-like formation with HMS *Campbeltown* at the head and the MLs following in two columns, port and starboard. All were under the 'watchful eyes' of the two Hunt-class destroyers.

There were a couple of incidents during the day, one involving a German E-boat and the other a fleet of French fishing boats, but these problems were dealt with by the two escort destroyers without affecting the progress of the rest of the force.

As the day wore on the sky became overcast and clouds came down and so gave some cover to the raiders. Just after 8 p.m. Ryder's little fleet had reached the point where it was to alter course and head north-east for St Nazaire. In the naval plan, arrangements had been made for the Royal Navy submarine, *Sturgeon*, to be waiting just off the mouth of the estuary to act as a navigational beacon from which the force could get a pin-point chart position and plot their course for the tricky approach up the Loire to the port of St Nazaire. At 10 p.m. the submarine's light was spotted dead ahead. Operation *Chariot* was on time and on course. At this point the two destroyers left the force, their immediate task duly completed.

Sergeant Robert Barron, who was in one of the motor launches and recorded his experience in *Forgotten Voices*, related:

> I was with Captain Hodgson's assault party in Motor Launch 341. We were third in line on the port side column, but we broke down some time before our rendezvous with the submarine *Sturgeon* so we had to transfer to Motor Launch 446. We fell behind but the captain put on full speed and we tore through the night with sparks coming from the funnel and we caught up with the convoy at the entrance to the river Loire. From then on the

atmosphere was tense. It wasn't too dark as we sailed up the river. One could see the outlines of the shore. Everyone was ready for action![2]

Just before midnight the RAF began its diversionary raid on the port, but with little success – because of the overcast sky and low cloud the bombers could not press home their attacks for fear of causing French civilian casualties. All they could do was to circle around in the area in the hope that the enemy's attention would be drawn skywards. It was a vain hope – due to the unusual nature of the aerial activity the local German commander, Kapitan zur See Mecke suspected 'some devilry afoot' and ordered all his units to maintain a 'continued and increased alert' and in particular to pay special attention to the sea approaches.

Meanwhile the raiders were making steady progress over the sand banks and mud flats which bedevilled their line of approach. The *Campbeltown*, still flying the Nazi flag as part of the deception plan, twice touched bottom but her momentum carried her forward.

However, their luck could not hold much longer. At about 1.20 a.m. a piercing beam of light suddenly swept the waters behind the fleet, but then, just as suddenly, it went out. The German commander, Mecke, however, signalled to all his units the ultimate order: 'Beware landing!' Whereupon all the searchlights on both banks of the river started to sweep the water, quickly locking on to the *Campbeltown* and her accompanying fleet of small ships. In spite of the inspired use of deception messages (using German codes that had been obtained from the Vaagso raid) from the signallers on the destroyer, enemy guns of all types opened fire. Surprise had been lost. The deception Nazi flag on the *Campbeltown* was taken down and replaced by the White Ensign.

Captain Bob Montgomery, in charge of the demolition teams aboard the *Campbeltown*, in his interview for the Imperial War Museum archives, recorded the following account of what followed:

The shooting started rather slowly, but pretty soon all hell broke loose. There was banging and crashing and lights and tracer. The bridge was hit and the coxswain was killed, so another naval rating took over the wheel, but then he too fell away. I seemed to be the next in line, so I grabbed the wheel but I wasn't certain what to do with it, but luckily at that moment someone else took it away from me. The searchlights came in handy because they showed us that we were fast approaching the lighthouse on the Old Mole so we were able to change course. If we hadn't seen that, we might well have rammed the Mole rather than the gate [of the dry dock]. Soon we did hit the gate with an almighty crunch which threw me back against the bridge.[3]

The time was 1.34 a.m. The *Campbeltown* and her deadly cargo of four tons of explosives with the delay-action fuses already set by Lieutenant Tibbits, RN, had successfully reached her target – just four minutes late.

The enemy gunfire, however, had inflicted casualties not only on the crew, but also on the commandos waiting on deck ready to disembark to tackle the various enemy defence positions. Nevertheless, it did not affect their resolve to get on with these tasks, which they had rehearsed to perfection.

Major Bill Copland, directing all the commandos on the *Campbeltown*, was a wonderful example of leadership and cool determination during the extraordinary period of enemy bombardment just prior to the ramming of the dock gate. With total disregard for his own safety, he was organising and dispatching the assault teams of Captain Roy, Lieutenant Roderick, and the others over the port and starboard sides of the ship. Survivors subsequently recalled how they were greatly inspired by Copland's apparent immunity from enemy fire!

Bob Montgomery continues: 'The assault teams immediately began clambering down the front end. It was quite a game climbing down the (bamboo) ladders as there was a fire blazing in the fo'c'stle. Corporal Calloway's trousers caught fire as he climbed and he had to take them off and carried out the whole operation in his underpants.'[4]

Montgomery followed Lieutenant Chant, who had been wounded in one of his hands, and his party to the pump house, but there they found the door locked. Fortunately Montgomery had a small limpet mine and he used it to blow the lock and Chant and his men dashed into the pump house. Montgomery and Sergeant Jameson decided to board one of two tankers in the dry dock, but they were thwarted by a machine gunner on board, so they went back to meet up with Lieutenant Chant who reported that he had successfully laid his charges in the pump house. After the explosions Montgomery went inside to check on the results and found them most satisfactory – not only had the motors that pumped the shaft been destroyed, but the explosions had also caused structural damage. Furthermore Chant's men had smashed up the switchboards and cut the transformer pipes. They had done all that they had set out to do.

Minutes later there was a loud explosion from the area of the winding house, so that was assumed to be a write-off. At the caisson gate of the dry dock Montgomery met up with Lieutenant Brett's party and learned of their problems, including that Brett had been wounded and Lieutenant Burtenshaw had been killed. The team had not been able to get into the caisson because the Germans had covered the hatches and built a road on top. Eventually they managed to detonate underwater charges on the side of the caisson and heard the satisfying noise of water entering the dock from either end of the caisson – the charges had done their jobs.

Satisfied that they had achieved all their various tasks Montgomery and the demolition teams set off to find and to report to Colonel Newman, who by now had landed and established his headquarters in the area of the Old Entrance. En route they came to the bridge that was one of the targets for the assault team from the *Campbeltown* led by Captain Donald Roy, who had landed wearing his kilt as befitted his nickname of 'the Laird'. Roy's only other officer in his group had been very badly wounded during the shelling of the ship. In spite of this and other casualties he and the other assault group, led by Lieutenant John Roderick, had successfully dealt with various enemy positions covering the pump house and the caisson, thus providing the protection that had enabled the demolition teams to carry out their missions as already outlined.

Eventually Montgomery and his men and the others found and reported to Colonel Newman. As their operations had successfully gone according to plan, they all assumed they would soon be re-embarking to sail back home. But these commandos, who had been on the *Campbeltown*, soon realised as they looked out across the river that re-embarkation was most unlikely because so many of the small launches were alight. They had been so involved in their own tasks that they had no idea of how their comrades aboard the motor launches had fared and were unaware of their fate – that was a different story.

The MLs, after moving upstream in double column astern of *Campbeltown*, were to land their troops on the pre-selected landing points, namely those in the starboard column on the Old Entrance and those in the port column on the Old Mole. However, it was at this stage of the raid that the weaknesses and disadvantages of the motor launches, – which had up to this part of the operation done all that was required of them – began to become terribly and tragically apparent. Being constructed of wood, with practically no metal protective plating, they were extremely vulnerable to all types of enemy fire, even smallarms fire at short range. Captain Micky Burn, who was in one of the MLs, was later very scathing about their vulnerability, but had to concede that they were the only ones available for the raid.

So once the enemy spotted them, guns of all types, with the aid of the searchlights, were able to pour accurate fire on the vulnerable craft. It soon became doubtful whether they would even be able to close to land and put the troops ashore, much less remain afloat long enough to be able to return and re-embark them.

In Ken Ford's admirable book *St Nazaire 1942: The Great Commando Raid* there is an excellent and detailed account of the fate of each of the motor launches and the commandos aboard. The following is a summary of that account, dealing first with those planned to land on the Old Entrance quayside.[5]

The leading launch, ML 162, containing the assault group of Captain 'Micky' Burn, got hit by a large shell, even before the *Campbeltown* had rammed the dock, creating a large hole in the engine room that crippled her immediately. As a result she swung athwart the port column and struck the high wall of the quayside. Other shells struck the ship and started a fire. The situation was dire, both the naval crew and the commandos suffered heavy casualties and the order to abandon ship was given. The wounded were put into rafts as the craft began to drift downstream, but Captain Burn, who had not been wounded, was determined to press on. He made his own way ashore, determined to fulfil his mission, even though he was only armed with his Colt 45 and hand grenades; he found the flak towers, his objective, but they were deserted.

The next two craft (MLs 262 and 267) were confused and misled by the action of ML 162 – as a result both overshot their landing marks and continued upstream, but subsequently turned back and managed to land their commandos. Lieutenant Woodcock and his demolition team – preceded by their protection group, led by Lieutenant Morgan – managed to scramble ashore from ML 262 at the northern quay, but they came under intense fire. Morgan saw what he thought was the recall flare and so both parties retraced their steps to re-embark. As it happened, their ML was just pulling away, but the skipper saw Morgan and Woodcock's commandos running back down the jetty towards his launch so he pulled in and was able to pick them up.

Lieutenant Beart's ML (267) with Regimental Sergeant Major Moss's party aboard – Colonel Newman's reserve – came in to land at the steps of the Old Entrance. Some did manage to scramble up the steps and ashore, but the launch came under such intense fire that, besides killing or wounding both crew members and commandos, fires started aboard and within a few minutes the launch was ablaze and drifting helplessly towards the middle of the river. The order was given to abandon ship and those who were able tried to slip on to rafts or swim; sadly Moss with most of his comrades and crew members were killed by machine-gun fire whilst in the water.

In the meanwhile the fourth craft in the column (ML 268) was heading for the right landing place, but was subjected to sustained and accurate fire from close range. As a result the launch became a blazing inferno when the extra fuel tank on the deck was hit. Seconds later she blew up, spreading the burning fuel on to the surface of the water. Although the skipper and some of his crew did survive, all but two of the eighteen commandos aboard perished.

The fifth boat (ML 156) was repeatedly hit well before reaching the dock area, yet in spite of this the skipper, Lieutenant Fenton, kept on course for his proper landing place; obliged to take late evasive action, however, he missed it. Although badly wounded, Fenton brought his launch around in a wide circle and tried again for the Old Entrance landing point, but then he collapsed and Sub Lieutenant Machin took over. Within seconds he too fell victim to the enemy fire, as did the ship's steering gear and port engine. By now, not only had these two naval officers been wounded, but also Captain Hooper and some of his assault group – with the craft in such a poor way and with heavy casualties to both the crew and the commandos the decision was made to withdraw downstream.

The last launch (ML 177) of this column had better luck. Lieutenant Rodier brought his craft towards the Old Entrance where devastation – blazing craft, pools of fire, and shouting men – marked the way in. Rodier succeeded in landing his party of commandos, led by Sergeant Major Haines, at the steps of the Old Entrance. This assault group of some fourteen men dashed up the steps and past the sheds to their planned rendezvous with Captain Hooper from ML 156. Together these two groups were to tackle the enemy guns located between the Old Entrance and the Old Mole, but of course Hooper's party had not got ashore. In the event Haines found that the expected enemy gun positions were non-existent so he and his group were able to join Colonel Newman where he was more than welcome as Newman's planned reserve had been wiped out in ML 267. Haines also had the very handy two-inch mortar, which he set up and used to good effect on the enemy situated on the roof of the U-boat shelters opposite.

Concurrent with all these actions, the port column of motor launches was also making its incursion up the river to the docks, aiming for the Old Mole jetty. Leading the column was ML 447 with Captain Birney and his assault team on board – their targets were the pillboxes on the quay. This craft suffered the same fate as its counterpart leading the starboard column. It came under heavy enemy fire, which knocked out its main weapon, the Oerlikon, also killing crew members and commandos. However, the skipper persevered and after going astern made a second attempt, but to no avail. The craft took a direct hit from a large-calibre shell that penetrated the engine house and set the craft ablaze. Orders to abandon the ship were given and in so doing many were washed away and drowned, although there were a few survivors who were later picked up by Lieutenant Boyd's MTB after he had fired his torpedoes into the outer lock gate of the submarine basin.

Coming up close behind ML 447 was Lieutenant Collier in ML 457; his approach was more successful and the landing parties were delivered right to the landing steps of the Old Mole. Off rushed the three teams; in the lead was the assault team of Lieutenant 'Tiger' Watson, who was followed by Captain Pritchard with his demolition party, who in turn was followed by another demolition party led by Lieutenant Walton. In spite of coming under enemy fire all three teams made steady progress towards their main target, which was the destruction of the bridge separating the old town from the remainder of St Nazaire to deny the Germans access to counter-attack. On their way Watson's and Walton's teams got pinned down; by taking a different route Pritchard got to the bridge but it was covered by an enemy pillbox – as his team were only armed with their personal weapons they were unable to mount an attack on it. Pritchard decided to find alternative targets, but unfortunately they met stiff enemy opposition and Captain Pritchard was killed. Meanwhile Watson, although wounded, managed to extricate his team and they were able to join up with Colonel Newman at his headquarters.

Next in the column was Lieutenant Wallis's ML 307, with a demolition team but no protection party. As this craft neared the quay German defenders on the high wall above the ML were not only able to rake it with their light machine guns, but also drop grenades into it. It was an impossible situation – the demolition team of eight suffered casualties so it was decided to abandon the landing. Wallis withdrew his craft to the other side of the river and engaged enemy guns and searchlights located there with his main armament.

Next in was ML 443, but the skipper, Lieutenant Horlock, was dazzled by searchlights and overshot the Old Mole; he headed out and circled back to try again, but the chaos on the river and the strength of the enemy fire forced him to withdraw. The following ML 306 also came under heavy fire; suffering heavy casualties. The skipper, Lieutenant Henderson, had no option but to withdraw too.

The last ML of this column was none other than the one carrying Captain Hodgson and his men who had been transferred to this craft when their original ML broke down earlier. They too overshot the Old Mole and came under heavy enemy fire, destroying both their main guns and killing Captain Hodgson and wounding his two sergeants. Lieutenant Falconer, then in charge of the ML, decided that any further attempt to land was not feasible and he also withdrew.

Therefore, of the six MLs due to land at the Old Mole only ML 457 had succeeded – so that just twenty Commandos out of the planned seventy got ashore in this part of the operation. They did what they could and the survivors then joined up at Colonel Newman's headquarters

By now it was apparent to Newman that the planned re-embarkation of his men was out of the question, so he held a hasty conference with those survivors from the *Campbeltown* and the other two landing points, to consider their next move. There were two options – fight or surrender.

Major Bill Copland was at hand and when Newman asked him the question, 'Shall we call it a day', received the answer he expected from his second-in-command: 'Certainly not, Colonel. We'll fight our way out.' And off they went, after being split into groups of about twenty. They aimed to make their own separate ways out of the docks and in to open country beyond – hopefully to Spain and on to Britain, via Gibraltar. It was customary in the briefings for the cross-Channel raids to always include details on 'escape and evasion'; it was also a subject that featured in commando training. In this case the odds were heavily stacked against success – nevertheless, five of Newman's men did make it all the way from St Nazaire back to England, via Gibraltar, thanks to the very generous and risky help given to them by individual French families.

By daylight the raid was well and truly over, although the explosives aboard the *Campbeltown* were still dormant. Nevertheless, the devastation that the commandos had wrought in the port was evident and impressive. There were many fires still burning, started by the commandos' incendiaries, dockside buildings and equipment had been destroyed, and ships sunk in the harbour, whilst bodies – commandos and Germans – littered the dock-side streets and alleyways. Throughout the early hours of the morning nervous Germans scoured berths, buildings, and sheds in the docks searching for the raiders, whilst other Germans in the town and beyond were looking for those who had taken to flight, until one by one the commandos – and sailors – were forced to surrender and become prisoners.

Meanwhile out at sea those MLs that had survived, along with the MTB and MGB, continued on course to rendezvous with two destroyers sent out to escort them back to England; all but one did manage to limp back to Falmouth. ML 306, skippered by Lieutenant Henderson, was the missing one and was unfortunate enough to run into five German ships, which circled around the ML. Expecting this isolated craft to surrender, the Germans opened up with just small-arms fire. However, the naval gunners on their Oerlikon and the commandos with two Brens and a twin Lewis gun, manned by Sergeant Tom Durrant, on Henderson's orders, returned fire. One of the enemy ships tried to ram the ML; they did no damage but they did rake the ML with more short-range small-arms fire, inflicting casualties, but once again the crew and commandos returned this enemy fire. It was then that an enemy destroyer opened up with its heavier four-inch gun, hitting the bridge of the ML and killing

Henderson and wounding others, including Durrant. The German destroyer *Jaguar* then closed on the ML and again called for it to surrender, but the wounded Sergeant Durrant on his twin Lewis replied with fire that raked the deck of the German ship. Again the German skipper called in broken English for the surrender and once again he received the same answer from Durrant – another burst of fire that swept across the bridge of Kapitan Paul's destroyer. The Germans then concentrated their small-arms fire on this lone commando Lewis gunner – he was repeatedly hit, shot through both arms, legs, stomach, chest, and head. He collapsed and died immediately from these horrific wounds.

The only surviving commando officer, Lieutenant Swayne, although wounded himself at this stage, hailed the Germans and offered to surrender. This was accepted and the wounded naval crew and commandos were taken aboard the *Jaguar* and were well treated. Indeed Kapitan Paul commended Swayne and the commando survivors on their gallant fight. Later Paul actually suggested to Colonel Newman, in his POW camp at Rennes, that Durrant should be recommended for a 'high award' and so it was that a commando army sergeant, Tom Durrant, was awarded the Victoria Cross for his part in a naval action at the suggestion of a German officer, undoubtedly a unique circumstance.[6]

Meanwhile in the dry dock area swarms of German officials and curious sightseers had been boarding the *Campbeltown* from early morning onwards, unaware of its hidden lethal cargo. They naturally assumed that the raiders had planned to destroy the dry dock merely by ramming the gates. Mid-morning at 10.35 a.m. they found out differently. The four and a quarter tons of depth charges exploded, sending a great shudder through the town. The ancient destroyer was rent in two, the caisson collapsed and sea water rushed into the dock. On board, hundreds of 'sightseeing' Germans and French collaborators were blown to oblivion. To the captive British sailors and soldiers the explosion brought compensating elation – their efforts and sufferings had finally been rewarded.

The object of Operation *Chariot* been achieved. The dry dock and its installations had been rendered completely useless and remained so for the rest of the war. The Germans were denied its use by *Tirpitz* and other German battleships.

But this success came at a cost – of the 611 men who entered the Loire in the early hours of 28 March, 169 were killed, the majority victims of the river battles, 105 of them were naval losses, whilst 64 were commandos.

The raid, quite rightly, led to a high number of awards for gallantry, headed by five Victoria Crosses: two to commandos, Lieutenant Colonel Charles Newman and Sergeant Durrant, and the other three to Commander Ryder,

Lieutenant Commander Beattie, and Able Seaman Savage of the Royal Navy.

However, perhaps the most enduring and permanently visible award will be the battle honour of ST NAZAIRE emblazoned on the Commando flag in Westminster Abbey, for it is there on display permanently for all to see, honouring every commando who went on the 'greatest raid of all'.

CHAPTER 5

DIEPPE

ARGUABLY NO SINGLE LAND BATTLE in the Second World War has provoked more controversy than the Dieppe raid of 19 August 1942.

In the course of just a few hours on a glorious summer day the casualties suffered by the British, Canadian, and other Allied forces involved were horrendous. Some ten thousand men – navy, army and air force – took part in the five-hour raid on the German-occupied French port of Dieppe. Of the almost 5,000 Canadians who embarked for the operation, only 2,121 returned to England and many of these were wounded; 907 lost their lives and 1,946 were marched off as prisoners. The naval losses were also severe with 550 casualties, plus thirty-three landing craft lost and the destroyer, HMS *Berkeley*, torpedoed after she had been severely damaged by enemy bombers. Allied losses in the air were equally heavy: 108 planes were shot down – more than any other day of the war – with 60 pilots lost, as the Luftwaffe committed 956 aircraft to attack the Allied shipping and beachhead, losing just 48 of them.

For more than sixty years historians have sought answers to many questions concerning this controversial and costly operation, but this is neither the place nor the time to discuss these contentious issues. The main object here is to record the part played by the Army Commandos in the operation, codename '*Jubilee*', which was undoubtedly the largest amphibious raid in modern history

— for make no mistake, the operation was planned from the outset to be no more than a 'reconnaissance raid in force'.

Without going into details it is necessary to briefly outline the background to the raid. The Allied situation in 1942 was grim: the Germans had penetrated into Russia, the British Eighth Army in North Africa had been forced back to the frontier of Egypt, and in the Far East the Japanese advances in Burma had yet to be contained. However, at the same time the Americans and the Russians were insisting on some positive action by the British in western Europe, advocating a landing and limited occupation, with the call, 'A second front now'.

The British Chiefs of Staff rightly maintained that the time was not yet ripe for even a limited incursion into western Europe, but in the event agreed to mount a major raid on Dieppe, arguing that this type of operation would provoke German fears of an attack on the mainland of north-west Europe and compel them to strengthen their Channel defences with men and materials at the expense of other operational areas — which it did — and so help to relieve pressure on the Russians.

Accordingly plans were made, under the codename 'Rutter', for a large-scale raid that was to be carried out on 4 July, with the Canadians providing the main landing force. However, the operation was cancelled on 2 July for two reasons: firstly, the onset of unfavourable weather conditions; secondly, an air attack by German fighters on some of the assembled shipping. Nevertheless, because of continued political pressure the plan was revived, duly modified, and reappeared as Operation *Jubilee* under the direction of Admiral Lord Louis Mountbatten, Chief of Combined Operations.

One of the major alterations to the old plan was that whereas in 'Rutter' two battalions of the Parachute Regiment were to attack and destroy two coastal batteries dominating the main landing beaches at Dieppe, in the revised plan these tasks were allocated to Nos 3 and 4 Commandos instead.

The plan called for landings at five different points on a coastal front of approximately ten miles with simultaneous attacks on the batteries at dawn by No 3 on the eastern flank at Berneval and the other by No 4 at Varengeville on the western flank.

Then half an hour later the Canadians would start the main attack on the town of Dieppe itself supported by attacks at Pourville in the east and Puys to the west of the port. The Royal Marine Commando was to follow up the Canadians and land in the port area to carry out its allotted tasks there.

Towards the end of July the commanding officers of No 3 (Lieutenant Colonel Durnford-Slater) and No 4 (Lieutenant Colonel Lord Lovat) were briefed by Brigadier Laycock for their roles in the raid and the two Commandos

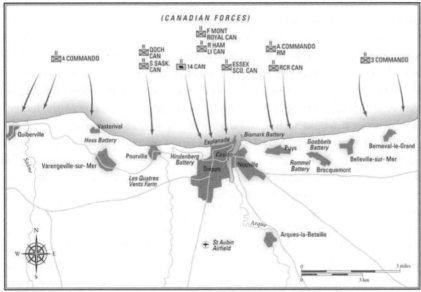

MAP 8. Dieppe Raid: Operation *Jubilee*

immediately started their training and preparations on the south coast of England: No 3 in Sussex and we, in No 4, in Dorset, although for the first part of our special training we were based on board the LSI HMS *Prince Albert*, on which we would ultimately sail across the Channel for the raid.

No 3 was to land in two groups on two beaches, 'Yellow I' and 'Yellow 2', near the village of Berneval and, in a co-ordinated action, attack the battery (codename '*Goebbels*') of 5.9-inch guns. Colonel Durnford-Slater with the main body of No 3 was to land on Yellow I and Major Peter Young (now second-in-command of the Commando), with Nos 3 and 4 Troops plus a section of three-inch mortars, land on Yellow 2.

No 4 Commando was also to land on two beaches, 'Orange I' below the cliffs at Vasterival, and 'Orange 2' on the beach at Quiberville. Lord Lovat had based his plan – to destroy the battery, codename '*Hess*', of six 5.9-inch guns – on a simple 'fire and movement' plan, which involved splitting his Commando into two groups.

Group I was under the command of Major Mills-Roberts and consisted of C Troop, a fighting patrol from A Troop, and the three-inch mortars. They were to land on the beach 'Orange I', climb the cliff by one or the other of the two gullies, make a direct approach with all speed to a small wood about a thousand yards inland which was just in front of *Hess* battery, and engage it with accurate small-arms and mortar fire, thus carrying out its role as the 'fire' element of the Commando plan, which became known as Operation 'Cauldron'.

Meanwhile, Group 2, under the command of Lord Lovat, consisting of B and F Troops, plus the rest of A Troop, would land on 'Orange 2'. After dealing with the beach defences and detaching the A Troop section to act as a protective force between the two groups, it would then quickly advance along the eastern side of the small river Saane to a pre-selected position at the rear of the battery from whence it would assault and destroy the guns and its garrison.

In No 4 Commando we started our operational training on 2 August. Under the supervision of Lord Lovat and Major Mills-Roberts, both advocates of the military truism 'train hard, fight easy', the training was thorough and rigorous. We carried out field firing exercises, based on the operation plan, firing all the troop weapons – rifles, Brens, anti-tank rifles, Tommy guns, two-inch and three-inch mortars – on the ranges at Lulworth; the demolition teams prepared and fired token explosive charges and Bangalore torpedoes; the signallers tested and counter-tested their sets. We carried out landing exercises on the coast near Lulworth in daylight and at night and finally rehearsed our withdrawal plan. Nothing was left to chance.

Lord Lovat in his book *March Past* had this to say about the training:

> If Waterloo was won on the playing fields of Eton it is truer to say Operation *Cauldron* owed its success to Lulworth Cove. Here we trained tirelessly in eight rehearsals, working day and night from HMS *Prince Albert*'s landing craft. The boat crews were good and trained with a will as No 4 Commando wound up to concert pitch. Every soldier would meet the events of the day like a trained athlete, off his mark to the crack of the starting pistol. The men were splendid and I was well pleased.[1]

Towards the end of this spell of intense training and preparations five US Rangers and three Free French commandos joined us. The Rangers (who had been trained at Achnacarry) were to be the first American soldiers to see action in north-west Europe, whilst the French comrades were to act as interpreters and also collect intelligence information from the local inhabitants.

On 18 August we left our temporary base at Weymouth to join HMS *Prince Albert* in Southampton docks and once on board completed our eve-of-battle preparations. At about seven o'clock in the evening we were paraded on deck for a pep talk by Lord Louis Mountbatten, who, with a twinkle in his eye, said: 'As you shouldn't know but have no doubt guessed by now, there's a party on tonight.' He went on to tell us that it was to be the biggest raid yet, and we, in

No 4, had a very important part to play. We were to destroy a battery of coastal guns overlooking the beaches of Dieppe and we had to destroy these guns at all costs. He was full of confidence and reassurance, especially when he outlined the amount of air support we would have. He wished us good luck, we gave him a cheer, and off he went, leaving us to have a meal, complete our preparations and try to get some 'shut eye'.

In spite of the pressures as troop sergeant major, I did manage to steal away from the troop deck and go up on to the open deck. There, in the last rays of a setting sun on a perfect and peaceful summer evening, I was able to gaze onshore in the direction of Shirley, a district in my home town of Southampton, where my widowed mother lived just a couple of miles away, but was unaware of my nearby presence – or the significance of that presence. I stood there for a few minutes with my inner thoughts, then went down to rejoin the troop on the mess deck.

Later we set sail and, as we cleared the Isle of Wight, we met up with other ships and craft of the naval force; meanwhile No 3 had set sail from Newhaven. The majority of that Commando was in a convoy consisting of twenty Eurekas – unarmed landing craft, each carrying some eighteen fully equipped soldiers. The Eurekas were escorted by a steam gun boat, a motor launch and a larger landing craft carrying No 4 Troop of No 3.

All went well on the channel crossing. We had transferred from our parent ship into the landing craft with no problems and both Commandos were on their final run-in to the French coast. Then it all went wrong for No 3.

At about 3.47 a.m., when they were still about an hour's run from the coast, a star shell went up – illuminating their whole group. They were subjected to heavy fire from a whole range of naval guns and machine guns. A stream of shells, tracer, and bullets poured into their craft – they had run into an armed German convoy.

Major Young, who saw plenty of action during the war, reckoned it was by far the most unpleasant moment of his life. He recalled five enemy craft converging on them and he couldn't see them surviving for more than a few minutes: 'It was certainly very frightening – far more so than any land battle I ever saw before or since.'[2]

We in No 4 Commando had some indication of this action being fought way off to our port bow, but had no idea of the consequences of the enemy fire. In any event we could not do anything to assist, even if we had been able, because we had to carry on with our own mission. Needless to add, this unexpected attack by the German armed convoy crippled and scattered No 3 Commando's flotilla of Eurekas and even sank some of them, thus putting a premature end to the original plan — any subsequent action by the survivors, if they could get ashore, would have to be improvised. Surprisingly, several of the Eurekas did make it to their landing beaches. The first was that of Major Young: thanks to some brilliant navigation and determination by the naval officer in charge, Lieutenant Buckee, RNVR, they landed on their planned beach.

Prior to disembarking, Young and Buckee agreed that if the landing craft did not come under too much enemy fire Buckee would wait for them offshore, but if the fire became too heavy he would withdraw and the commandos would take a chance and make their own way to Dieppe and re-embark with the main Canadian force. Little did they know at the time how disastrous that would have been.

Young and his men touched down just as it was getting light at about 5.50 a.m. They crossed the narrow beach and made for the gully up which they had planned to climb, but found it choked with barbed wire. To his horror Young then discovered that the Bangalore torpedo, earmarked to deal with any barbed wire problem, had been left in the landing craft.

Exasperated, but undeterred, Young decided to carry on and after about twenty-five minutes of sheer determined efforts, during which they found that their toggle ropes came in very handy, they reached the top of the gully. During their climb the *Goebbels* battery had opened fire on the main naval force, which was just visible. With only his small force available Young decided that, although the original planned assault was obviously out of the question, they could — and should — snipe and harass the battery from short range and hopefully limit its ability to effectively engage the incoming ships and craft.

Splitting his small party into three groups they set off for the village, where they cut the telephone lines connecting the village to Dieppe, then, as they were doubling back up the main road, they came under fire from a machine gun about sixty yards ahead. In a spirited response in which all the weapons were involved — including the two-inch mortar that was deployed behind the church — the German machine gun was silenced and to the amazement of all they had no casualties. After this encounter they reformed behind the church and planned to put the Bren and a couple of snipers on the top of the church tower and engage the enemy gun position. When they went inside, however, they found there were no steps to climb up the tower, so had to abandon that idea.

Young decided to advance through the orchards behind the houses of the village towards the battery position, but again they came under enemy fire; although they suffered no casualties their advance was slow. As a result Young decided to avoid the village approach and continue his advance through a cornfield that led up to the battery position. Once in this cornfield, which offered some cover, they were able to get within two hundred yards of the battery and take up positions in an extended line with spaces between each man. In this unusual formation they started to fire at the crews of the enemy guns. Young did not claim that they caused many casualties but their fire undoubtedly harassed the gun crews, so much so that eventually the Germans turned one of their guns on to the commandos in the cornfield. Young recalls: 'Fortunately we were too close to be damaged, for the guns, not being designed to fire at point blank range, could not depress sufficiently to hit us. It was an unusual experience and for a moment I wondered what was happening.'[3]

Apparently one of Young's men indignantly said to him, 'Sir, we are being mortared' as the first shell whistled overhead, but he soon realised otherwise when he saw the smoke above the culprit gun a few seconds later. They were able to carry on with their harassing fire with a satisfying degree of impunity.

The net result of Young's men's action was impressive considering their numbers and the fact that they had only small arms. They did not destroy the battery nor stop it from firing altogether but their offensive action reduced the Germans' rate of fire considerably, thus preventing further damage and casualties to our naval force. For over three hours Young and his men were engaged in their harassing action and only when their ammunition was almost exhausted did he give the order to withdraw to the beach and re-embark.

Even on their way back to the gully and Yellow 2 they came under further enemy fire, but in a series of 'leap-frogging' bounds they managed to reach the beach where Buckee was waiting for them, having been called to come inshore by prearranged Verey light signals. The re-embarkation had its moments of excitement too. Young, together with fellow officer Ruxton and the Bren gunner Abbott, were the last to embark and had to wade out to the landing craft where they caught hold of a lifeline and were dragged out to sea some way before being hauled aboard.

Once out at sea Young and his men transferred to a motor launch for the run back to Newhaven where they disembarked at about 11 a.m. All eighteen of Young's party returned to England with only one slightly wounded.

'I was lucky enough to see plenty of action during the war,' said Peter Young later, 'but I think the best operation of all was the Dieppe raid – I took eighteen men ashore, did the job and brought eighteen men back. You can't do better than that.'

For his leadership and achievements on the raid Young was later awarded the DSO to add to the MC he received for his part in the Vaagso raid.

Whilst Young and his men were involved in their private war against *Goebbels* battery, five more Eurekas carrying men of No 3 – who had managed to survive the German onslaught on their flotilla – headed for their beach, Yellow 1, which was about two thousand yards east of Yellow 2, where Young and his men had landed, and about fourteen hundred yards from the battery. They neared the beach at about 5.30 a.m., by which time it was daylight and the alerted Germans opened fire on their landing craft as they closed on to the beach, killing two naval crewmen. Despite this the commandos managed to land without too much difficulty as the tide was well in and the beach had no mines nor wire obstacles. They were able to make their way to a gully, where, under the shelter of the cliff face, they were immune from enemy fire and out of harm's way whilst the leading troops tackled the barbed wire in the gully to force a path.

They all duly managed to climb up the gully without any further problems and Captain Geoffrey Osmond, a pre-war bank manager and Territorial officer, of No 3, took command and decided to make a limited attack, based on the original plan, on *Goebbels* battery. The group numbered about one hundred, including six US Rangers.

Unfortunately, but obviously, by this time all surprise had been lost and the enemy was fully alerted. Indeed, a strong detachment of German reinforcements had already arrived from the Dieppe area to engage the commandos and drive them into the sea. Initially, however, Osmond had some success clearing the coastal hamlet of Le Petit Berneval, wiping out a machine-gun post in the process. But then as they headed for the battery their fortunes took a turn for the worse. They met stiff opposition and repeated flank attacks. With commando casualties mounting, it was decided to abandon the attack, withdraw to the beach and re-embark. It was now about 7 a.m.

Verey light signals were fired for the landing craft to return to the beach, which they did, but then came under heavy mortar and machine-gun fire. Nevertheless, they waited for some considerable time for the commandos to return, but none came. Finally, Lieutenant Stevens, with three of his craft now out of action, decided to withdraw. Little did he know that at the time the commandos attempting to get back to the beach were still heavily engaged, but nearing the cliff top. Pinned down, the only desperate option for the commandos was to make individual mad dashes across open ground to the gully. A number of the men were killed in their efforts, including Lieutenant Loustalot of the US Rangers; he thus became the first American soldier to be killed in action in Europe during the Second World War.

Remarkably some of the commandos did make it to the beach unscathed, but to their bitter disappointment only burning or out-of-action craft awaited them and the enemy was still able to fire at them from the cliff top – it was an impossible situation. Captain Osmond, who had been wounded, decided that he had no option but to surrender and so No 3 Commando's part in the raid came to a sad but worthy end.

No one sums up their action better than Robin Neillands in his book *The Dieppe Raid* when he wrote:

No 3 Commando did very well at Dieppe, displaying a resilience and aggression typical of the very best Commando soldiers. The outstanding element in their conduct was a dogged refusal to accept defeat and a determination to press on with the task. When their convoy was disrupted and their force much reduced, they still had officers and men willing and eager to get on with the job and carry the war to the enemy. One can only wonder at what this fine unit would have achieved had it got ashore intact.[4]

No 3 Commando paid a heavy price in casualties – a total of 140 killed, wounded, and made prisoner, the majority of these being those who landed on Yellow 2 beach.

Now we look at Lord Lovat's No 4 Commando, which was to land on the west flank of the raid to destroy *Hess* battery.

Our approach to the coast, in complete contrast to that of our comrades of No 3, was uneventful and everything went according to plan. We had no enemy interference nor navigational problems, the latter largely being due to the fact that the lighthouse at Porte D'Ailly, sited between the Commando's two landing beaches, kept flashing for five minutes every quarter of an hour. We could not have had a better guiding light.

As a result we in Group I (the fire group) landed on the right beach at the right time, just before daylight, dry-shod and unopposed. We quickly cleared the beach and moved up to the left-hand gully, but found it impossible to climb because it was full of barbed wire. Attention was switched to the other gully, which proved to be a better proposition although it still needed two Bangalores to clear a passage. We had an added bonus inasmuch as the sounds of the detonations were muffled by some RAF aircraft that were overhead at the time and so was not heard by the men of the enemy battery.

We quickly scrambled up the gully and a beachhead was established on the cliff top by one section of C Troop whilst the rest of the group led by Major Mills-Roberts pressed on towards the battery; this advance up a narrow unmade road went well. En route we made enquiries at a couple of the houses to get information about the Germans in the area – the French commandos attached to our troop for this purpose were very helpful in this role.

All was going well and according to the plan, which was that we would all be in position to bring co-ordinated and concentrated fire on the battery position by 6.15 a.m. – fifteen minutes before Lovat's main assault was due to go in.

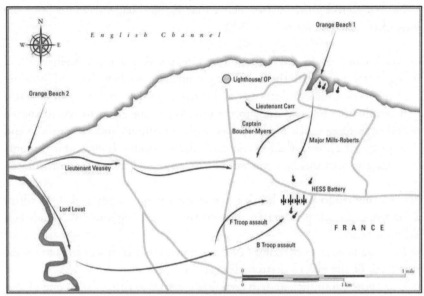

MAP 9. Dieppe: Operation *Cauldron*

However, at about 5.45 a.m., the battery suddenly opened fire, a six-gun salvo. The ground shook and shells whistled overhead. A minute or two later Mills-Roberts received a message from the intelligence officer back on Orange I beach, reporting that the main convoy was in sight and so, apparently, in range of the battery. Mills-Roberts reacted immediately – he decided to speed up the advance and engage the battery as soon as possible, ahead of the planned timetable. Within minutes – luckily meeting no opposition en route – C Troop was taking up firing positions in the wood and in an old deserted holiday home that overlooked the battery, whilst Sergeant Hugh Lindley was stealthily taking his three snipers even further forward – to within about a hundred yards from the battery. From there, Lance Corporal Mann, the troop's star sniper, would conduct his own 'private war' against the enemy. Meanwhile the battery fired another three salvoes over our heads and out to sea; fortunately, the garrison still seemed to be completely unaware of our nearby presence.

Once in position section commanders detailed their specific targets, which were now clearly visible in front of them. Fire was held until the prearranged signal was given, then all the Brens and the riflemen opened up. Out on a flank, with just his number two, Lance Bombardier McDonough started to fire at the flak tower, firing .55 armoured rounds – he scored several direct hits and put it out of action for a while (when it did open up later, it was silenced by Lord Lovat's group).

I arrived with my two-inch mortar duo at the wood a few minutes after this initial firing had started because I had not received the 'hurry-up' message. However, within a few minutes, with bombs unloaded and the weapon lined up, we were ready for action. Having no prearranged fire plan, I told the No I to aim for the centre of the battery, which was well in range. It was a fortuitous decision.

The first shot fell a little short, the second slightly to the left, but the corrected third one landed right in the centre. Luckily – and it was pure luck – we had scored a bull's eye. The result was spectacular and decisive. That third bomb had exploded among the bagged cordite charges that were stored in the open alongside one of the guns. It was a careless and fatal mistake on the part of the Germans and as result they paid the price. The guns did not fire again. They had been silenced, but not yet destroyed.

Meanwhile, Lord Lovat and his group were making good progress on their advance up from the beach towards the rear of the battery to their assault positions. They too had landed on the right beach at the right time, but their run-in had been opposed as had their landing, inflicting some casualties. However, Lieutenant Veasey and his section were able to knock out the two enemy machine guns involved.

As expected, the barbed wire on the beach presented problems, but men of B Troop, wearing leather jackets and carrying rabbit netting, overcame this hazard by flattening, wrenching, rolling, and lying on the wire thus enabling their following comrades – like loose forwards in a rugby ruck – to rush over the wire and through the beach.

In addition to the enemy machine-gun fire already mentioned, however, Lovat's group was also subjected to further small-arms fire and some mortar fire. Private Lilley recalls the reception they got on landing: 'The "muck" was coming down us and it seemed to be coming from the direction of the lighthouse probably on fixed lines, making the beach a lively place.'

What he also remembers most vividly of that time is the appearance and bearing of Lord Lovat, who was but a few feet away from him: 'His coolness seemed to be imperturbable, he was so calm. He was in corduroy slacks with his rifle, stripped down like a sporting rifle, he had the air of absolute confidence and looked as though he was off stalking deer on his highland estate in Scotland.'[5]

Once off the beach the commandos paused to regroup – they had suffered eight serious casualties on that beach – and then pressed on. There was no time to lose. The going was tough, the grass was long, and the ground soggy, 'It was just like running through rice pudding,' recalled one of B Troop, which was leading the advance.

Meanwhile Lieutenant Veasey's section, having dealt with the machine guns overlooking the beach, swung inland to cut the telephone wire and to move towards Group I and deal with any enemy who might be planning a counter-attack against that group and also to link up with the other section of A Troop who had landed with Major Mills-Roberts. It was a sound plan – on linking up with their comrades they did manage to sight, surprise, and destroy an enemy patrol, but again not without casualties, including the troop sergeant major, though he was one of the lucky ones who was able to get back to the re-embarkation point on Orange I beach with help.

Lord Lovat, with B and F Troops, continued to make good progress, meeting no opposition, to the area he had pre-selected for his whole force to pause whilst the two assault troops separated to move to their different forming-up positions (FUPs) for the final attack on the battery. Captain Pat Porteous, moving alongside F Troop with his small section as the link-reserve element between the two troops, recorded what happened just after the split up: 'We bumped into a truck of Germans who were just disembarking. We managed to kill them before they got out of the truck. We then started working our way through this very dense bit of country – all little cottages and hedges and so on.'[6]

This success was short lived. As F Troop was moving through this area of cottages they were taken by surprise and came under fire at short range. 'Ossie' Hughes, who was carrying a Bangalore torpedo for use on the barbed wire at the actual site of the battery, recalls: 'Captain Pettiward and Lieutenant McDonald were both killed outright and Troop Sergeant Major Stockdale, who had taken over, was hit by a stick grenade which landed on his foot, badly wounding him, but he kept firing from the hip.'[7]

Fortunately Captain Porteous and his little reserve section was near at hand – ready for such an eventuality – but they too came under fire. Two of them were badly wounded and Porteous got shot at very close range, the bullet passing through his hand and into his lower arm. Undaunted, he closed with his assailant, succeeded in disarming him, and killed him, thereby saving the life of one of his NCOs on whom the German had turned. In spite of his wounds, he rushed over to rally the main body of F Troop – now without an officer or their sergeant major – and lead them on to their FUP.

It was at this stage that Jim Pascale, the medical orderly with F Troop, unselfishly decided to stay and treat his badly wounded comrades who could not move, knowing it almost certainly meant that he would be captured and made a prisoner of war (POW), which is what happened. His brother, Ted, the other medical orderly with Lovat's group collected the walking wounded and took them back to Orange I beach for the re-embarkation. Tragically, on D-Day in 1944, Ted (still with No 4) was killed on the beaches and his brother Jim only learnt of the death of his brother when he was released from POW camp in 1945.

Lovat's two assault troops (B and F) duly arrived in their FUPs on time and as they fixed bayonets and prepared for their assault, a prearranged RAF strike came down to strafe the battery; Mills-Roberts's group intensified its covering fire. Right on time at 6 30 a.m. up went Lovat's Verey light signal and everyone knew what this meant. The covering fire ceased and the assault went in. It was a dramatic moment.

B Troop, led by the wounded Captain Webb, made for the battery buildings to seek out those garrison troops not in the gun emplacements and also to gather any useful intelligence information from the office. F Troop and the demolition teams, still led by the wounded Pat Porteous, made straight for the guns. In fact Porteous was one of the first to reach them and in the fighting there he was wounded again, this time in the thigh, yet he still kept going, urging his men to get to the last (sixth) gun. Then, shot once more, he passed out.

Those commandos responsible for the demolition of the guns had brought 'tailor-made' charges, specially prepared at the conclusion of the training, to deal with the guns. Sergeant Bill Portman explained: 'All we had to do was to open the breech, make sure there was a shell in it to take the blast of the explosive charge and that would do a very good job.'[8]

It did – all six guns were destroyed; the mopping up of the garrison quickly followed and then there was a brief period of reorganising before Lovat gave the order to withdraw in the manner that had been so thoroughly rehearsed back on the coast of Dorset. During the reorganising period Lovat had called for the medical officer to bring his orderlies up to the battery to help with the evacuation of the seriously wounded and to attend to the other wounded. A couple of doors were removed to use as make-shift stretchers; Pat Porteous was put on one of these to be evacuated down to the beach and two of the German prisoners were 'enlisted' to carry his stretcher.

Lovat's mission was successfully completed: *Hess* battery had been silenced and destroyed – it was to be the only success of that disastrous day.

The withdrawal went according to plan. We, in C Troop, stayed in position until all of Lovat's party had passed through then we left the wood, leaving one of our dead comrades there who had been the victim of enemy mortar fire. Then we too made our way down to the beach, via the gully, in a series of 'leap-frogging' bounds, to re-embark on our landing craft, which were waiting for us.

By 8.45 a.m. the re-embarkation was completed; as we set off we came under some enemy fire, but it was ineffective mainly due to a smoke screen that had been put down, both on the beach as we left and from smoke canisters thrown overboard as we set sail. The sea was calm and the sun shone, but overhead there was plenty of aerial activity. To the east, onshore, smoke and the sound of explosions and gunfire provided plenty of evidence of bitter fighting, although at this stage none of us knew how disastrous the landings on the sea front of Dieppe and the flanking beaches at Pourville and Puys would turn out to be.

A few miles offshore some of our more seriously wounded were transferred from our landing craft to a destroyer for a speedier return to Newhaven and hospital treatment. We also managed to pick up, out of the water, a RAF pilot who had baled out of his badly damaged fighter. The rest of the journey back in our landing crafts was quite pleasant and we finally docked at Newhaven at about 5.30 p.m. We were all pleased with the results of our mission and it was not until weeks later that the full story of the raid was made public, such was the necessity to censor news in wartime.

Some months after the raid several members of both Nos 3 and 4 Commandos were honoured with awards, including that of the DSO to Lord Lovat, but the undoubted highlight was that of the Victoria Cross to Captain Pat Porteous.

Considering the success of their operation the casualties sustained by No 4 compared with the other units were minimal — a total of forty-five all ranks, of whom seventeen were killed. The latter are all remembered by name on the memorial tablet installed on the wall of the old town hall in 'Place du 4 Commando' (No 4 Commando Square) in the inland hamlet of Sainte Marguerite, near the site of *Hess* battery. Further to the east, at Berneval, on the cliff top overlooking the 'Yellow' beaches, stands a monument commemorating the part played by those of No 3 Commando who got ashore.

In the town of Dieppe itself an interesting museum is dedicated to all those who took part in this controversial raid and each year commemorative services are held on the main landing beaches at Puys, Dieppe, and Sainte Marguerite on 19 August. These are preceded by a vigil at sunset on the evening of the 18th in the military cemetery at Dieppe and is always a moving and poignant occasion. In these ways the people of Dieppe remember and honour all those who took part in the fateful raid. In England the actions of the two Army Commandos are remembered on the Commando flag with the battle honour of DIEPPE.

Finally, mention must be made of a special War Office training pamphlet, published in 1943, devoted entirely to the 'Destruction of a German Battery by No 4 Commando during the Dieppe Raid'.[9]

CHAPTER 6

NORTH AFRICA 1942–1943

(Steamroller Farm, Sedjenane, and Djebel Choucha)

FOLLOWING THE ACTIONS OF Nos 3 and 4 Commandos in the Dieppe raid the next battles in the saga of the Commando battle honours were those fought by Nos 1 and 6 Commandos in Algeria and Tunisia from November 1942 to April 1943 and for which they were awarded the above three specific honours for their part in the Tunisia campaign, although mention must also be made of the part played by the Special Boat Section in the preparations and planning prior to the invasion of Algeria, codenamed '*Torch*', as well as the actions of the two Commandos in the landings there, and further actions in Tunisia that are implicit in the battle honour of NORTH AFRICA.

The background to Operation *Torch* once again reveals the differences in their appraisals of the direction and strategy of the war that prevailed at times between the British and US political leaders and military Chiefs of Staff. As already mentioned in the context of the Dieppe raid, the Americans were keen to invade north-west Europe in 1942–43 whereas the British, quite rightly, appreciated that the Allies were not ready for such a demanding operation. The losses on the Dieppe raid clearly revealed the problems and difficulties of mounting and sustaining even a limited incursion into occupied Europe.

Nevertheless, the Americans persisted in advocating a more aggressive policy towards Hitler's fortress in Europe, ostensibly to demonstrate to the American people that the USA was equally committed to the liberation of Europe as to defeating the Japanese in the Pacific. However, after a lot of wrangling at the highest level – and mainly due to Roosevelt's personal insistence – the Americans eventually decided to mount the invasion of French North Africa with British support; the hitherto untried American general, Dwight (Ike) Eisenhower was appointed as overall commander. The intriguing story behind this decision to invade the Vichy French territories is told in John Keegan's *The Second World War*. It makes interesting and enlightening reading.[1]

The overall plan was for three separate landings on the North Africa coastline: at Casablanca in Morocco on the western flank, Oran in the centre, and Algiers on the eastern flank in Algeria. The first two of these three landings were to be carried out by wholly American forces, whilst the attack and seizure of the third was the objective of a mixed American–British force and included the two Commandos, Nos 1 and 6. All the invasion forces except those destined for Casablanca were to mount their operations and sail direct from the United Kingdom; the troops for Casablanca were to sail across the Atlantic direct from the United States.

One of the interesting features of the preparations for the invasion involved the commandos of the Special Boat Section – they were still in existence and operating following the formal disbandment of the rest of the Middle East Commandos, and were therefore already in the Middle East.

A major problem facing the Allies in their planning was gauging the extent to which the Vichy French troops might oppose the landings. So to find the answer a daring plan was formed to land the deputy commander of the Allied Force, General Mark Clark, and some of his senior officers at a secret rendezvous some sixty miles west of Algiers to confer with the French commander of the Algiers' district, General Mast. The meeting was arranged through US diplomats already resident in Algeria. It was the typical kind of 'cloak and dagger' operation in which the SBS excelled.

My old friend, the late Captain Jimmy Foot, who took part in the mission, gave me a first-hand account, which, incidentally, I included in the tribute I was asked to give at his memorial service some years ago. The following is the gist of that account.

Prior to the operation the SBS canoeists were concentrated in Gibraltar where they were briefed for the operation. They were to ferry a formidable team of American high-ranking officers, a total of six including Mark Clark, in their canoes from their parent Royal Navy submarine HMS *Seralph*. On landing, they were to escort them to an isolated 'house with a red roof' a short distance inland where they were to meet General Mast and representatives of the US diplomatic staff – the object being to try and persuade General Mast and the rest of the Vichy French forces not to oppose the landings. The Americans were keen to emphasise the fact that the whole operation was under American control – so as to avoid any further resentment still felt by the French in Algiers towards the British following the destruction of the French Fleet by the Royal Navy at Oran in July 1940.

Once ashore, of course, the commandos were responsible for the security and safe return to the waiting submarine of those six high-ranking US officers. It was no mean task.

The landings went according to plan, thanks mainly to prearranged signals from a member of the American–French party on shore, although there were a couple of minor hiccups trying to get into the canoes from the submarine – always a tricky manoeuvre, especially if there is any sea swell. Once ashore General Clark immediately had a brief conference with a member of the shore party and as a result decided that they would not be able to conclude their discussions that night. It would take longer and the submarine would therefore have to be informed to pick them up during the next night. This was done by radio and then it was on to the meeting house where the canoes were concealed. Jimmy recalled that it was 'all hands on deck' with everyone involved in the carrying of canoes and kit up to the house. On arrival at the house food and drinks were offered and after a few hours' rest the generals and their staffs got down to serious discussions. All went well and as a result it was decided that they would leave as soon as it got dark at about 8 p.m.

Just prior to that time, as the commandos started to get their canoes out of the shed where they had been hidden, they got word from the French caretaker that the local police were on their way to the house. There was a frantic rush to rehide the canoes and it was also decided that the general and his party, including the commandos, would hide in the wine cellar, 'which was empty' mused Jimmy. There they hid whilst the French general and the American diplomats above 'gave a fine performance as honest citizens with nothing to conceal, certainly not a cargo of contraband generals in the wine cellar'. Fortunately all went well and the satisfied police went off, although the landing party was told that they had just three hours to get away because the police might return to carry out a thorough search.

There was no time to waste. Unfortunately they had problems launching their canoes due to some nasty surf, but after several attempts they all made it to the waiting submarine and they set off for a prearranged rendezvous with a Catalina seaplane from Gibraltar, which was to land near the sub and pick up the general and his staff to fly them to 'Gib'. All went according to plan with

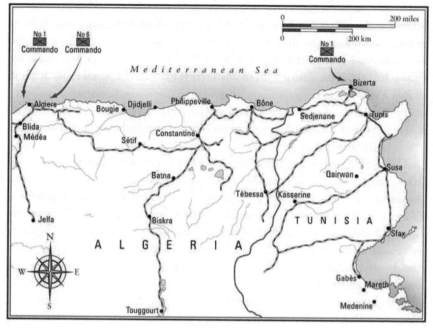

MAP 10. North Africa

the SBS ferrying their high-ranking charges from the submarine to the waiting seaplane, and then from Gibraltar General Clark returned to England satisfied with the outcome of the operation

Years later Jimmy showed me a photograph of a marble plaque that had been installed on the rendezvous 'house with the red roof' bearing details of the exploit and also the names of American, British, and French participants of this unique clandestine operation. Sadly the house and the plaque became victims of the fighting between the French and the Algerians between 1956 and 1962.

However, this was not the end of the SBS's involvement with the preparations for Operation *Torch*, for a few days later Jimmy and his comrades were sent on a mission to pick up General Giraud from Lavandou on the French Riviera. General Giraud was a French hero who had refused to accept the authority of the Vichy French government and had been imprisoned, but he had managed to escape and was 'sitting uneasily in Lyons'. Somehow the Americans had managed to get a secret message to him offering to smuggle him out of France to North Africa – it was thought that, once *Torch* had been launched, the respected general might be able to persuade the Vichy French forces to give in and join the Allies and Free French in their fight against the Nazis and Mussolini's Fascists in the struggle to liberate Europe.

Jimmy was in the small SBS party selected for this pick-up job and again they sailed from 'Gib' in the HMS submarine *Seralph* and eventually picked up General Giraud from a small local fishing boat at a prearranged offshore pick-up point in the early hours of 5 November, before the actual invasion. The whole SBS operation was fraught with incidents and problems and the account in Gruff Courtney's (he was the brother of Roger Courtney who had joined the SBS) book, *SBS in World War Two*, reads like a chapter from a James Bond novel, except the SBS version was real life.

Meanwhile, back in Britain Nos 1 and 6 Commandos in early October had been alerted for Operation *Torch* and the commanding officers, Lieutenant Colonel Tom Trevor (No 1) and Lieutenant Colonel I. F. McAlpine (No 6), had been briefed that they would be operating with an American combat team. The commandos duly left their base in Scotland for Belfast in Northern Ireland to join the US troops aboard American ships. All of No 6 Commando were in one American ship, the *Aewatea*, but No 1 Commando was split between two other American ships, the *Otranto* and the *Leedstown*. They left Belfast on 13 October and the next few days were spent settling down and preparing for a joint exercise, which was to be held at Inveraray on Loch Fyne. During this period the commandos got to know their American allies, some of whom were the US Rangers that had been trained at Achnacarry, and there were a few who had been with Nos 3 and 4 Commandos at Dieppe. The commandos were also issued with some American Garand automatic rifles and US helmets in an effort to make them look more like US soldiers because it was felt that the Vichy French forces might surrender more readily to US troops rather than to the British, for the reasons already mentioned. On board, the commandos were able to enjoy American army food which, after their austere wartime rations in civilian billets, they found rather rich; they did not complain!

Following the joint exercises at Inveraray the convoy for North Africa began to assemble off the Isle of Arran; it eventually set sail on 26 October. During the voyage via Gibraltar the commandos in their respective boats, with the aid of aerial photos and models, were able to prepare the details for their respective missions. One of the best first-hand accounts of how the commandos of No 1 Commando fared on Operation *Torch* is contained in a book by one of its wartime members, 'Tag' Barnes, who later won a Military Medal with his Commando. He also provides a vivid picture of the ensuing campaign in Tunisia as experienced by another rank. Indeed his writing prowess came to the fore after the war when he became a very successful angling writer, contributing hundreds of articles plus two authoritative books on the subject, as well as one on birds. He also made a series of fishing programmes for Yorkshire Television, so it was no wonder that the background of his accounts of his Commando's action in North Africa is often flavoured with observations on the wildlife and descriptions of the landscape and terrain.

The outline plan for the Commandos was to carry out three separate landings with three separate objectives, hence the reason for splitting the two Commandos to sail on three ships from the outset. The task for one half of No I, under the command of the colonel, Tom Trevor, was to capture the fort and battery at Cap Sidi Ferruch some ten miles west of Algiers. No 6 Commando's task was to capture another fort, Duperre, on the west side of the Bay of Algiers whilst the task of the other half of No I, under the command of the second-in-command Major Ken Trevor, a cousin of Tom Trevor, was to capture the other fort (d'Estree) and battery (Lazaret) dominating the bay from the east side. All three tasks were typical of the invasion-supporting role the Commandos were increasingly given, namely to destroy coastal batteries covering proposed landing beaches, as had so successfully been carried out by No 4 at Dieppe and No 5 in Madagascar.

The Commandos in this operation had mixed fortunes. Colonel Trevor's group had complete success with no casualties – the Vichy French forces manning their objectives at Cap Sidi Ferruch surrendered without a single shot being fired. But it was a different story at the other two objectives.

The attack by No 6 Commando on Fort Duperre went badly from the start – during the lowering of the landing craft from the transport ship, some of the craft were lost and although landing craft from other transport ships were sent to the *Aewatea* to pick up the balance of No 6, there was a lot of confusion for some time. As a result the landings were behind schedule – even worse, all surprise was lost. The enemy was not only ready but the commandos were met by withering artillery and small-arms fire. Furthermore, owing to poor navigation some of the commandos were landed on the wrong beach – one of these parties, under the second-in-command, Major A. S. Ronald, was landed in the most heavily defended area of the port and all were killed or captured. Those who had survived on the main landing beach mustered and managed to make their way to the fort, and eventually, after calling for an air strike forced the garrison to surrender.

The third landing under Major Ken Trevor was successful and it is very well chronicled, not only by 'Tag' Barnes but also by Henry Brown, who served in No I from its founding days to its disbandment (and subsequently for forty years he was the illustrious full-time secretary of the Commando Association). He wrote a very detailed account of their action at Algiers for Charles Messenger for inclusion in his book *The Commandos, 1940–1946*.[2]

Major Trevor's party got to within three hundred yards of the fort and the battery – 'It was a picture book fort complete with a draw bridge and, although dry, a moat' – before they were fired upon and had to take cover. They did manage to get their mortar in position and engage the enemy before a spirited attack was made on the fort by one of the troops; lacking heavier fire support, however, it was repulsed with the loss of one killed and seven wounded. So the commandos called for supporting fire from one of the destroyers, which came inshore to engage the fort. Still the enemy resisted, so an air strike was then called for; following the strike the commandos attacked with success and the garrison surrendered, although according to Brown the troops in the fort and those manning the battery would have given in many hours earlier had it not been for the stubborn Vichy French commandant. By now it was late afternoon and with their objectives achieved the men of No 1 Commando moved to a small nearby village where they 'brewed up', had something to eat, organised a rota of sentries, and settled down for the night.

Their comrades of No 6 were not so lucky, for after their action at Fort Duperre they had little respite before they were called for a further operation two hundred miles to the east of Algiers at Bone near the frontier of Tunisia. First, the background to this move.

It so happened that at the time of the Allied landings Admiral Darlan, who was Marshal Pétain's commander-in-chief of all the Vichy French armed forces, including those in North Africa, happened to be in Algiers on a private visit. This meant that the American's chosen man, General Giraud, who was with the invaders, because of Darlan's presence, now lacked the authority to establish local control – so they started negotiations with Darlan instead. The admiral was a realist and was quickly persuaded by the evidence of the Allied strength to change sides; an armistice was declared late that evening on 8 November. Thus at a stroke the Allies were able to subsequently take possession of all of coastal Morocco and Algeria. It was a most encouraging start.

The way was now ready for Eisenhower's Allied Army to advance and occupy Tunisia, with the aim of denying the retreating German Afrika Corps escape routes, but Hitler was furious at this turn of events, particularly with Admiral Darlan for agreeing to an armistice. He immediately ordered the occupation of all of France and forced Pétain's Vichy French government to formally abrogate the recent North African armistice. Furthermore he demanded free access to all the ports and airfields of Tunisia, which were still held by the Vichy French forces and immediately took steps to send fresh troops by sea and air transport from France to Tunisia to bolster and reinforce Rommel's retreating troops, who were being driven back towards Tunisia by Montgomery's Eighth Army, following their victory at El Alamein.

No 6 Commando was in the vanguard of the Allied thrust towards Tunisia, having boarded two destroyers soon after the armistice had been signed at Algiers. Its mission was to secure a vital airfield near Bone. Landing at the port of Bone the men duly marched on to the airfield on 11 November – at about the same time as the first 'sticks' of paratroops from the 3rd Battalion of the Parachute Regiment were dropping unopposed from Dakota aircraft of the US Air Force. Although the Commandos and their 'red beret' comrades were unopposed on the ground it was not long before they were being attacked by German Stukas, although these Luftwaffe raids were mostly confined to dawn and dusk. With typical resourcefulness they had managed to obtain some Oerlikon guns from damaged ships in the Bone harbour and used them to deter the enemy bombers. On 18 November No 6 were joined on the airfield by their comrades from No 1, who took over and relieved the paratroopers.

'Tag' Barnes relates the events that led up to the reunion of the two Commandos and how No 1 had travelled from Algiers aboard a train for the two-hundred-mile journey to Bone – a journey made in open cattle trucks that took two days and two nights. They never knew when, where, or for how long the train, which was driven by local Arabs, was going to stop so planning for the preparation of food, hot drinks, and attending to the call of nature presented problems, especially the latter when the stop was only a couple of minutes. Barnes recalls: 'There were some incredible sights to be seen when the train moved off; with several men rushing after the slow moving train trying at the same time to pull up their trousers.' On the subject of hot drinks he added: 'To help to wash down our cold rations, a dash would be made to brew tea with hot water from the engine's boilers.'[3]

During the journey they also got to realise how cold the nights were in the mountains of North Africa, and 'it came as a complete surprise to see snow falling on the morning of the second day', but 'As we descended towards the plain and Bone, once again a more pleasant climate could be felt.'[4]

No 1 Commando then joined Colonel McAlpine's No 6 Commando on the Bone airfield and after relieving the Parachute Battalion the men started to prepare their own defensive positions on the perimeter of the airfield.

At this stage there was a fear that, following the success of their airborne invasion of Crete, the Germans might consider a limited airborne operation to capture the Bone airfield. So with this mind and not knowing how long they might be kept in this defensive role, Tag Barnes tells of how his mate and he decided to turn their two-man slit trench from 'temporary digs' into an 'elaborate den' by using some wooden spars and other materials at hand, before finally completing their work with camouflage covering, adding that they 'both felt very proud of it as we crawled in through the low entrance'.[5]

In the event, although there were some false alarms and they 'stood to' regularly at dawn and dusk the only enemy attacks on the commandos on the airfield came from Luftwaffe bombers. Meanwhile, however, the Germans began to pour troops, armour, and artillery into the ports and airfields of Tunisia.

On 21 November both Commandos were ordered to cross the Algerian frontier and move into Tunisia to a place called Tabarka about sixty miles to the east. No 6 Commando was to travel by train whilst for some unexplained reason No 1 Commando went by sea in a tank-landing craft. No 6 Commando, travelling in open cattle trucks, had a horrendous experience. It was accompanied by a solitary Spitfire to provide defence against enemy air attacks, but unfortunately the 'Spit' had to return to Bone airfield every so often to refuel and it was during one of these absences that two German FW 190s flew low over the train and straffed the open trucks with cannon and machine-gun fire. The results were devastating: eleven commandos were killed and no fewer than thirty-three wounded.

Furthermore, the Arab drivers fled, but a lance corporal from No 6 was found who fortunately had some knowledge of driving a steam engine; he volunteered to get the train going and succeeded in driving it into the small port of Calle, where the commandos stayed for a couple of days. During that time they helped to unload stores at the port and a detachment was also dispatched, in 'requisitioned' local buses – as the commandos obviously had no transport of their own – to investigate a report of a German tank harbour in a nearby valley.

Apparently the tank harbour was located but there were no enemies in the area. The positions chosen for the tanks appeared so obvious that Captain Murray Scott reckoned they were decoys and so took no further action, although later he returned to the 'tank harbour' area at night and did confirm that the suspected tanks were in fact dummies, albeit very realistic ones. Whilst the commandos were at the 'harbour' they came under light enemy fire; one section went on the attack and Private Lomax of No 3 Troop was reported to have wiped out a machine-gun post single-handed. Other patrols also went into action and an estimated twenty-eight Germans were accounted for without loss. During the whole time of this little night operation the weather was terrible, it rained hard and the cold was intense – there seems no doubt, however, that these awful weather conditions favoured the commandos and once again proved the value of the exacting training that they had undertaken in the last year or so back in Scotland and elsewhere under similar conditions.

Meanwhile No 1 Commando had arrived at Tabarka after a miserable sea journey in a crowded and uncomfortable tank-landing craft, in which the men were accompanied by a 'detachment' of donkeys who were seasick! From the port No 1 Commando carried out an amphibious operation, '*Bizerta*', the object of which was to support the First Army advance to Bizerta by turning the enemy's right flank and cutting their lines of communication. No 1 Commando was supported by a strong detachment of American troops who were integrated into the Commando. The whole force embarked on a mixture of landing craft and duly landed in the early hours of 1 December. Once again the commando force was split into two detachments under the respective commands of Colonel Tom Trevor and Major Ken Trevor. Unfortunately the raiders had a very wet landing, wading ashore with the water up to their armpits, but on the positive side they landed unopposed and subsequently were able to make good progress towards their respective objectives, namely two important road junctions. One was on the main Tabarka–Bizerta road, which they held for twenty-four hours before being driven off; the other road junction they successfully held for three days. During this period they were able to harass the enemy by choosing the time and place to shoot up enemy transport.

However, with only the basic hard rations – two tins of stew, half a tin of bully beef, three bars of chocolate, two packets of hard biscuits, plus tea and milk powder per man – they were unable to stay longer. Furthermore, the fighting had inflicted losses and they were not light. Commando casualties totalled sixty all ranks and their American comrades seventy-four all ranks.

It was time to withdraw through the Allied lines back to their base in the old prison outside Sedjenane, but it took them two days before they finally took up residence once more in the old jail. In spite of the losses, this operation clearly demonstrated that the sea could no longer provide a safe protection to the flank of any enemy line and that a small force of raiders landing in the rear of the enemy lines could have a great, even a decisive, influence on a main battle. Sadly, however, this was to be the last amphibious commando operation of the Tunisian campaign. Hereafter the commandos were misused as normal infantry and came under the command of the various infantry brigades of the 78 Infantry Division.

Sedjenane where both the Commandos were then located, is, of course, one of the Commando battle honours. Firstly, it is worth highlighting the signifi-cance of this town because the immediate area became of considerable strategic importance during the Tunisian campaign. The Allied rush across the frontier, heading for Tunis, was halted by strong German forces holding the hills just east of the town –the wrecked Bren carriers and other military equipment of the leading infantry battalion of the British First Army littered the battle area for some time, becoming a grim symbol of the ensuing stalemate for all of the First Army over the following months.

The town of Sedjenane itself was an important railway town on the main line to Tunis and was on the main road as well. Just north of the town was a mountainous range and three formidable hills, several hundred feet high, dominated the pass through this rugged range. They were christened by the Allies as 'Green Hill', 'Bald Hill', and 'Sugarloaf Hill', names that were attributed to their natural features. Green Hill on the north side of the main road was smooth and rounded with green vegetation, Bald Hill was a rocky and gaunt hill typical of most in the area, and Sugarloaf Hill was so named because of its shape. The last two hills were on the south side of the pass; all three were barriers to Allied advances along the axis of the road in the north towards the ultimate Allied goal of Tunis.

Whilst No I Commando was engaged on Operation *Bizerta* No 6 Commando had moved up to the Sedjenane area and, placed under the command of 36 Infantry Brigade, ordered to attack and capture Green Hill. Two infantry battalions of the brigade had previously attempted to capture the hill without success and had suffered considerable losses. No 6's plan of attack was based on surprise and involved four troops: one troop was to engage the enemy with fire from the front, whilst the main body of three troops, under the command of Captain Bill Coade, delivered the main assault from the flank and rear.

The frontal party under Captain Mayne stealthily managed, under the cover of darkness, to get within small-arms range of the enemy position and at 'H hour' opened up with their Brens, mortars, and rifles – but this brought a quick response of heavy fire from the Germans. Meanwhile Captain Coade's party, moving to his start line on the top of the hill, came under withering fire from the enemy, who wisely had all-round defence and were obviously aware of the possibilities of attacks from their exposed flank and rear.

Captain Coade was forced to withdraw down the hill and then contacted brigade headquarters seeking both artillery and air support, without which he could not make a second attempt. His request was granted and in the afternoon a co-ordinated plan of artillery and air support was directed on the enemy position; this seemed to be accurate and as a result hopes were high and the rain-soaked commandos made their attack. However, it was to no avail – the enemy had well-prepared positions and had not only survived the artillery barrage and air strike, but forcibly hit back at the commandos, inflicting many casualties; there was nothing for it but to retire. One historian later wrote: 'Green Hill, said the press, was Green Hell for the commandos and for once they were right.'[6]

Green Hill never fell to direct attack in spite of several more attempts by much larger units than the four commando troops who had tried so bravely and suffered heavy losses – a total of eighty officers and other ranks were killed, wounded, and missing as a result of their attack on Green Hill at Sedjenane on 30 November.

Soon afterwards Colonel McAlpine suffered a heart attack and Major 'Jock' McLeod took over command. No 6 Commando, now down to a total of just 250 men all ranks, spent the next few weeks carrying out front-line duties and patrols operating from their Commando base, which was in a railway tunnel. On 5 January the Commando provided a party in support of yet another attack by 36 Infantry Brigade on Green Hill – this time the Commando's role was to provide flank protection to the main assault and although the main attack failed the commandos acquitted themselves well. They held their ground against stiff enemy opposition for over forty-eight hours and inflicted heavy losses on the enemy, although once again they suffered casualties, this time some thirty-five in all. In spite of these losses, morale in the Commando was high and they made the best of things over the Christmas period.

Early in the New Year No 6 Commando's new commanding officer, Lieutenant Colonel Mills-Roberts, the ex-second-in-command of No 4, arrived from England to take over. In his book, *Clash By Night*, he provides an amusing account of his journey out to Africa and how, in his determination to get out to his new command as quickly as possible, cut through red tape and managed to scrounge a series of 'opportunity' flights to Algiers to finally arrive at his new headquarters established in the railway tunnel just outside Sedjenane. His description of this unusual commando base is worth repeating here. He arrived in the dark and was met at the entrance of the tunnel by the adjutant, who introduced himself as 'Knox, the Adjutant, sir' – by the light of a hurricane lamp' and then:

> We went into the mouth of the tunnel behind an old tarpaulin and walked along the railway line to our Headquarters which lay a short way inside. The refuge spaces which are built into the walls of the railway tunnel are for workmen when a train goes by. They have always intrigued me and tonight I was going to sleep in one . . . All along the tunnel these refuge bays had been turned into living quarters with bunks and screens of old canvas and hessian.

It is surprising how comfortable any normal person – and the British soldier in particular – can make himself when the need arises.[7]

After a quiet night, when he had slept in his duffle coat and a blanket, he awoke at dawn and visited his new command as they 'stood to'; in the light of the early morning sun he then viewed the surrounding countryside with its series of low undulating hills covered in 'the inevitable and abounding thorn scrub' with some tracks, odd trees, and the occasional mud hut. But more to the point, he noted 'those notorious three hills Green Hill, Bald Hill and Sugarloaf Hill on which the Germans were dug in'.

However, it was not long before No 6 was on the move again, this time to a location called 'Hunts Gap' where they carried out a series of long-range patrols, rather than holding ground 'in the line'. Indeed this type of operation became the norm for the employment of both Commandos.

Mills-Roberts provides plenty of stories about the patrolling activities of his Commando and clearly spells out the differences, purposes, and nature of the two types of patrols – namely reconnaissance (sometimes referred to as 'observation patrols') and fighting. Whereas the former is sent out solely to get information – without being intrusive or stirring up the enemy – the larger fighting patrol is sent out to achieve a definite object by force.

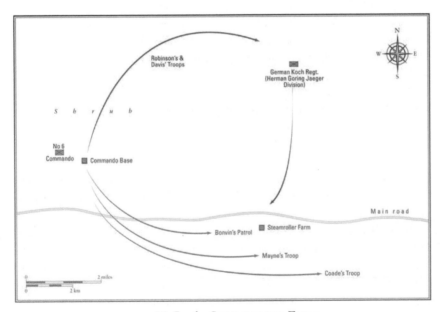

MAP 11. Battle: STEAMROLLER FARM

Tag Barnes who took part in these patrols recalls his experiences from the soldier's point of view: 'Observation patrols were launched by sections or sub-sections and led by either an officer, a sergeant or perhaps a corporal or sometimes a mixture of all three. Most of these patrols were without incident but nevertheless the strain of living *behind* the enemy lines, for sometimes a week at a time, began to play havoc with the nerves.'[8]

The final word on the subject of patrolling in North Africa during this period – which included Christmastide – must surely be attributed to Leslie Greenslade of No I Commando, who recorded his experiences in verse:

> We were spread out to work in the mountains,
>   And our Xmas was spent amongst mud,
> But our NAAFI supplied us with beer and fags,
>   But they couldn't supply us the pud.
>
> The rumour of going home had faded,
>   As they moved us from front to front,
> And the rains were falling so heavy,
>   For patrolling we thought we'd punt.
>
> We now come to a mountainous sector,
>   Where patrols have come a routine,
> All round a strong point called Green Hill,
>   Which is more of a nightmare than a dream.
>
> We got swopped from sector to sector,
>   From Green Hill to Beja and back,
> The mountains we got used to,
>   We could tell you offhand every track.[9]

Greenslade's verses might not qualify for a prize in a poetry competition, but they do paint a clear picture of how one commando soldier remembered his war in Tunisia that winter.

In mid-January No 6 Commando was now down to a total of about 250 men all ranks and organised into just four troops instead of the normal six. Mills-Roberts, with the approval of the divisional commander, decided to dominate his area of responsibility of about seventy-five square miles by vigorous patrolling from an established Commando strongpoint on the Goubellat Plain area. This bold policy was most successful, and about a month later, towards the end of February when No 6 was moved to another locality, Mills-Roberts decided to employ these same tactics again in his new location. So it was that the Commando fought, arguably, its most successful action against one of the Germans' finest units then in Tunisia – the Herman Göring Jaeger Parachute Regiment.

Mills-Roberts provides a detailed account of this action and the following is but a brief résumé with some comments from the men who took part in this action, which became recognised as the battle honour of STEAMROLLER FARM (see Map 11, page 103).

The Commando had established their strongpoint on a spur in the scrub-covered area called 'Green Patch', which, according to the nearby brigade commander, was a 'happy hunting ground' for large German patrols – often as many as a hundred parachute troops, seeking targets on the British front. Mills-Roberts was ordered to patrol the area and keep divisional headquarters informed of any large and concentrated effort by the Germans to advance through this largely undefended gap. Furthermore if the enemy did infiltrate towards the British lines he was to hold them for as long as possible by harassing them in every possible way. It was a daunting commitment, especially with just 250 men.

By 25 February Mills-Roberts's Commando was well established on Green Patch and he recalls that he was well satisfied with the way his men had prepared and camouflaged their tents and positions – they were ready for action. At dawn on 26 February the commandos heard small-arms fire away on a flank, so a patrol was sent out to investigate, and to save time they were transported in a couple of trucks. It was getting light and the patrol had gone barely half a mile when they were fired upon. Lieutenant Bonvin quickly got his men out of their vehicles and into a ditch that ran alongside the road; from its cover, they returned the enemy fire. They had bumped into a patrol of the Herman Göring Division.

Mills-Roberts could see what was going on and reckoned that the enemy force could be one of their large patrols, probably up to a hundred men strong. He decided he must take immediate offensive action and attack the enemy in their rear and thus try to cut off their line of retreat back to their own lines. Fortunately the rest of his Commando, having 'stood to' at dawn, was ready for action – all four troops. He detailed Captain Coade's troop to stay put in the stronghold position and engage the enemy, whom they could see across the valley. This they did with some success, apparently taking the enemy by surprise – they had not expected fire from this quarter and range, although they soon started to return the commandos' fire.

He then sent Captain Mayne's troop down to the area where Bonvin's men had been ambushed to engage the enemy there and ordered the troops of captains Robinson and Davis to move along the spur, where they were positioned, and then cross the valley, which was about six hundred yards wide, to attack the enemy in their rear. This they did with initial success, but then reported that a further large German column was approaching along the same axis of advance as the initial German force. At this stage it clearly seemed to Mills-Roberts that the enemy force was not the normal large enemy patrol, but was possibly a full-scale regimental attack on the British lines – in which case No 6 Commando was facing an enemy in the order of over a thousand men!

Meanwhile Captain Mayne had not managed to get as far as Bonvin's men before he came under fire from the enemy, who were in a farm, and so they too now had a battle on their hands. All of No 6 Commando were now in action, fighting three separate actions, and Mills-Roberts was most concerned that, having committed all his men, he had no reserve, so he called for assistance from the Divisional Reconnaissance Regiment. It was a crucial stage of the battle and the fighting in all three localities was intense, as Mills-Roberts explains:

> At this time one hell of a racket was in progress. The German advance had been halted and they were temporarily pinned down. It was essential for them to get on; essential for us to delay them. Time was of the essence of the contract for both of us. It was now four and half hours since the battle had started.[10]

A little while later carriers from the Reconnaissance Regiment appeared and with their aid Captain Mayne's troop were able to counter-attack against the Germans who had originally ambushed Lieutenant's Bonvin's patrol. As a result Mayne's men managed to get some of the commando patrol back, but Bonvin had been killed and a few of the commandos had been captured. Nevertheless, Mayne later captured about twenty Germans; from these captives it was confirmed that the German troops were of the Koch Regiment in the Herman Göring Jaeger Division.

Among those commandos who were in this particular action was Frank Barton: he had been in Bonvin's patrol and recalls:

> I was captured when we engaged the Germans at Steamroller Farm – there was a steamroller in the farmyard – near Mejas-el-Bab in Tunisia. We were

getting the better of this Herman Göring Division when they brought up some Mark IV tanks. We were ordered to withdraw when Sergeant Bob Harris was killed at my side and Lieutenant Bonvin was badly wounded. I was captured while tending him.[11]

Barton was subsequently transported as a prisoner to Italy, where by a most extraordinary twist of fate he ended up at Camp 54 near Rome – there he met his brother who had been captured whilst serving with his regiment, not the commandos, at Tobruk in 1942. Barton and his brother managed to escape in September 1943 and after two and a half months walking and with aid from friendly Italians, they made it back to the British lines. They were subsequently repatriated to England, where Frank rejoined No 6 Commando, which was preparing for its part on D-Day and he served with that Commando until the end of the war.

Back to the battle around Steamroller Farm – at about midday the enemy brought up the tanks as mentioned by Barton and they also threatened Captain Coade's troop who were still in their original position in the Commando stronghold on the spur, so Mills-Roberts sent them down to the area of Steamroller Farm to join Captain Mayne's troop, which they did. Soon afterwards, however, with ammunition running out Mills-Roberts decided that this was the time to break off the engagement and start a general withdrawal back to the British lines. They had done all that had been asked of them – and more. They had halted and held up the German advance for more than six hours and severely mauled the enemy, inflicting heavy casualties. Furthermore, with the information they had sent back to the divisional commander, he was able to mount a successful counter-attack of two infantry battalions – the Coldstream Guards and the Royal Sussex Regiment – supported by tanks, and they managed to push the enemy back over the hills.

No 6 Commando's action in and around Steamroller Farm was an outstanding success and a worthy battle honour. Sadly it came at a high price, incurring the loss of about one hundred men, killed, wounded, and missing. Mills-Roberts tells of how during the next day commandos were still returning back to the British lines and some told how they had seen their comrades taken as prisoners, even though they managed to escape themselves, such as Captain Knox, the adjutant, who had seen Captain Mayne and Major Jock McLeod being led away.

In a moving couple of paragraphs Mills-Roberts describes how he and his men, after the enemy had retreated, went back to the Steamroller Farm area to collect in the dead:

Men lay in the attitudes in which they had fallen. It was a hot turgid morning when we brought them down to an olive grove for burial. When we had finally collected all the dead we could find from the area of the battle we had a full military funeral . . . One by one over thirty sad, blanketed figures were placed in their graves . . . Eventually when they all lay in their graves the Padre read the burial service. At the head of each man was a white wooden cross on which was painted his name and regiment. His Regimental badge was fastened to the cross — a commando soldier always wore the cap badge of his regiment.'[12]

As part of the recognition to the commandos for their part in the battle Colonel Mills-Roberts was awarded the DSO.

After this action Mills-Roberts was told to prepare to move to a new location for further action, but although they got ready to move to the new area they received a counter-order — they were to return to 'Blighty'. It was welcome news.

Whilst No 6 had been involved in the operations outlined above, No 1, from New Year onwards, had been similarly active on long-range patrols, under the command of 78 Infantry Division, but in a different area. However, at the beginning of February they were warned to prepare for an operation in the sector of the Allied line that stretched from the Sedjenane area towards the coast at Cap Serrat. Their mission was to be a most unusual one, which Barnes called the 'Italian Job'.

Their objective was a small village some thirty-five miles deep into 'No Mans Land', in the area held by one of Mussolini's crack units, the Bersaglieri. Apparently the Arab villagers, who were openly hostile to the Allies, were co-operating with the Axis forces and giving the Italians in the area 'shelter and sustenance'. The aim of the raid was to occupy the village, destroy some of buildings and lay an ambush for the Italians who would inevitably come to the aid of the villagers.

The operation was planned to take three days and at dusk on the evening of 8 February the commando patrol, commanded by Captain Tim Evill, set off. Barnes tells how in addition to his arms, ammunition and other stores needed for demolition, each man carried his own rations for the three days. The latter were most frugal and consisted of just highly concentrated chocolate and dried biscuits — what we normally called 'emergency rations'. It is interesting to mention that most of the riflemen were still armed with the US Garand rifles issued to them prior to embarking on Operation *Torch* — which they now greatly favoured, having successfully used them in action.

They marched through the night, making regular short stops, but the going was slow because of the nature of the ground: long stretches of wet and boggy ground alternated with rocky terrain covered with tall shrub. They arrived at a wood overlooking the village whilst it was still dark and there they rested until dawn. They started to rouse the villagers and move them under guard to places of safety, while those detailed for demolitions set about their tasks on what appeared to be official buildings. The rest of the party under Captain Evill reconnoitred ambush positions based on information gleaned from the villagers.

Following the demolitions the commandos did not have to wait long for the Italians to appear. Barnes recalled that he was with the troop leader when a lone Italian figure appeared over the skyline en route to the village. Using his Garand rifle, with its telescopic sight, he took aim and was about to fire when Captain Evill ordered him to hold his fire because just at that moment more enemy troops were appearing over the crest – obviously this lone man was just a scout. Evill waited until well over twenty Italians, moving in single file, started to come down the slope and into range before he gave the order to fire. Most of the Italians were killed, but a few escaped back over the hill to rejoin their main body. No further Italians appeared; instead, within minutes, the commandos came under quite heavy enemy mortar fire and so Captain Evill gave orders to start withdrawing using the normal tactics of leap-frogging back, section by section. There was no point in staying: the commandos had done their job and they had a long journey ahead of them to get back to their own lines.

To avoid being sighted by any enemy spotter planes Evill decided to take a longer route back that offered far more cover. This detour took much longer than anticipated, but they avoided any contact with the enemy. It was in the early hours of 11 February when Evill's troop of very weary commandos arrived back at their prison base outside Sedjenane – mission successfully accomplished with no casualties. It had been a typical little commando raid but this time it did not involve a wet landing in assault craft from the sea.

The next major action involving men from No 1 was at the end of the month, by which time two troops of the Commando, which had previously been attached to a battalion of the Durham Light Infantry, went into action again with them under the following circumstances.

On 26 February the Germans had started a major offensive, the object of which was to outflank the British positions – around Sedjenane and the high ground opposite the infamous trio of Green Hill, Bald Hill, and Sugarloaf Hill – by attacking on the hilly coastal strip of 'djebels' (hills) between the town of Sedjenane and Cap Serrat on the coast. This area was mainly held by ill-equipped French troops and the Germans were able to push through their positions towards a ridge of hills about two miles north of the actual town of Sedjenane, so it was essential to mount a counter-attack and deny the enemy this high ground.

The Durham Light Infantry and the two troops of No 1 were at the time bivouacked and resting behind the front line, having only recently been relieved from positions facing Green Hill. Indeed, No 4 Troop had only just returned from a five-day patrol, but for the men of the Durham Light Infantry (DLI) it was to be their first experience of a full-scale attack. On the afternoon of 26 February the DLI, with Nos 2 and 4 Troops of No 1 Commando, moved forward to within a short distance from the objective and prepared for their advance to seize a hill called Djebel Guerba, which was occupied by a German parachute regiment.

The commandos were to operate on the left flank of the main DLI attack, but both troops were very much under strength – in fact, No 2 Troop, with the Commando's two three-inch mortars, had only twenty-odd men. A heavy artillery-fire plan was arranged to support the attack and by midday on 27 February No 4 Troop, led by Captain Davidson, crossed their start line and moved in bounds up the steep and rocky side of the hill – a feat that reflected the special mountain training undertaken by the commandos. They reached the unoccupied part of the djebel without any casualties, but unfortunately Davidson then had to withdraw his troop because they came under 'friendly fire' from our own guns. He did, however, subsequently succeed in getting the gunfire lifted and made another attempt to reoccupy the position. In the meantime, however, men of the German parachute regiment had occupied it. Nevertheless, moving in bounds and using 'fire and movement' tactics Davidson's men succeeded in recapturing the position, with Davidson in the forefront of the final assault. During those bounds up the hill the commandos came under some enemy fire and were pinned down several times, suffering minor casualties, but the final toll was low.

For his leadership in this action and during the following days Captain Davidson was awarded the Military Cross, whilst one of his section sergeants, Sergeant Southworth, received a well-earned Military Medal for repeated acts of bravery and leadership during the attack; unfortunately he was later wounded and had to be evacuated. (He did make a full recovery and later in 1943 joined me as an instructor at the Commando Basic Training Centre at Achnacarry, though after a while he asked 'to get back to his mates in No 1 Commando', so we granted his wishes and he rejoined them in time for their subsequent campaign in Burma.)

The commandos were reinforced by a detachment from the Durham Light Infantry (DLI) and together they prepared a defensive position, while the rest of the DLI companies, who had suffered a considerable number of casualties, were withdrawn back to woods near Sedjenane.

For the next couple of days the situation in the commando location remained quiet except for some enemy gunfire and very heavy rain, which seemingly put operations by both sides on hold. On 2 March the DLI made another attack on their original objective, but it failed and suffering heavy casualties, they were forced to withdraw, as were the commandos who also came under a heavy enemy attack. Prior to this withdrawal, Private Williams, one of the troop's Bren gunners had displayed great coolness and excellent marksmanship in silencing two of the enemy's machine guns with his accurate fire and then, during the actual withdrawal, he stayed behind to give covering fire with his Bren, which enabled his sub-section to successfully withdraw to a wooded area just outside Sedjenane. Williams was later awarded a Military Medal for his heroism in this action.

In this wooded area the commandos of No 4 Troop and the survivors from the DLI were joined by men of the Lincolnshire Regiment and the commandos of No 3 Troop who had been attached to the 'Lincolns'. Together this joint force, with the support of eight Churchill tanks from the North Irish Horse, endeavoured throughout the day to prevent the enemy from getting a foothold in the important rail and road centre of Sedjenane. That night a patrol from No 3 Troop came back with the news that the battalion of the Sherwood Foresters on their flank had been overrun; indeed, soon afterwards stragglers from the Foresters started to arrive back in the DLI area. Next morning the mixed force of DLI, Lincolns, and Commandos, supported by the tanks, struggled to hold their ground – the enemy, with support not only from their artillery and fresh reinforcements of armour but also air support, finally forced the mixed force of infantrymen and commandos to withdraw and in the early afternoon of 4 March the Germans marched into the town. Meanwhile the rest of No 1 Commando, who had been holding a position in a mine area, were being heavily shelled and mortared, and appeared to be threatened on three sides, so Colonel Tom Trevor decided he had no option but to withdraw too.

With the Germans now in possession of the rail and road network the First Battle of Sedjenane was over and as the Allies withdrew, under heavy German ground and air attacks, a further defence line was being established on the hills near the town of Tamara to halt the enemy advance, prior to the Allies preparing and mounting a major counter-attack.

However, it was for their part in the battle for Sedjenane that No 1 Commando was awarded the battle honour and it is fitting to conclude with an extract from the 46 Division news summary of 5 March 1943, which sums up its part in the last day of the battle there: '2/5 Foresters, 16 DLI, 6 Lincolns and 1 Commando yesterday fought wonderfully well. They were constantly being attacked. Attempts to surround them were constantly being made.

Nevertheless they continued to counter-attack over and over again. Eventually Sedjenane was left in the hands of the enemy. Our own casualties have been heavy . . .'[13]

Tag Barnes describes how the commandos withdrew and comments that he and his mates found 'the situation difficult to grasp. Without the full facts the average soldier had to do a lot of surmising,' but adds that the withdrawal to the new defence line on the line of several dejbels was 'carried out smoothly and efficiently with few casualties'.[14]

During this withdrawal the commandos were involved in patrols and covering actions, which again were noted in the divisional daily news of 19 March, with this single sentence: 'The withdrawal was successfully covered by I Para Bn and I Commando.' Towards the end of March the Allies had blunted the German advance and on 26 March No I Commando was called upon to take part in a divisional counter-attack, its task being to mount a diversionary operation to capture and hold a hill feature called Djebel Choucha. No I Commando Operation Order No 7, dated 26 March, provides the details and plan for their operation.

For this operation No I Commando, by now much understrength, was organised into three groups, each made up of two very depleted troops; these three groups were under the command of captains Evill, Davies and Pollitt.

Unfortunately the details of this particular operation are not reported in any of the many books on the commandos of the Second World War. In fact, although the battle honour of DJEBEL CHOUCHA was awarded to No I – and only No I – there is no account of it except in the official operation order mentioned above and the unit war diary covering the period of the operation – and even the details in the latter are scanty.

Searching for further information I contacted ten veterans of No I who were thought to have taken part in this last commando battle in Tunisia – none of them knew the action by its official name and only two were actually involved in the battle. Both wrote to me with their memories, recalled after sixty-four years. Idris Jones, who was in No 5 Troop, remembers taking part in the last Commando battle of the Tunisian campaign at the end of March, and so believed it to be Djebel Choucha and below are extracts from his letter. On the whole his memories fit in with the entries in the unit war diary.

The other ex-No I veteran, Gwyn Bowen, also remembers being in the Commando's last battle when he was in Commando headquarters. He followed the rest of the Commando in the approach march – which 'went well thanks to a white taped route through a suspected mine field' – and then subsequently joined the forward troops of the Commando on the djebel itself. He had no special memories of the battle except being heavily shelled over two/three days and an interesting incident involving the reburial of one of the Goum soldiers (in the supporting native French 5th Thabor Regiment) who had apparently been buried incorrectly, according to the Muslim tradition (presumably facing Mecca).

Back to the action – the Commando left its previous position at Tabarka at 1 a.m. in the early morning of 27 March and travelled by motor transport to a mine in the area of Sidi Ahmed, where the men debussed after a journey of a couple of hours and there they spent the next day, preparing for the operation – including the making of arrangements for the resupply of ammunition and food, etc. by mules; being fed; and 'visited by some officer with red tabs', recalls Bowen.

At 10.30 p.m. that night (27 March) the Commando set off along a taped route to their start line, which it reached without any trouble, then proceeded on a compass bearing of 325 degrees to a distinctive track at a specific map reference. From there, aided by local Arab guides, they continued on to their objective, Djebel Choucha, as planned, arriving at about 7 a.m., having met no opposition. Idris Jones, having described their approach march much as above, takes up the story:

> We formed all round defence. I was down a bit over the ridge, say about 100 yards with mates each side. The sergeant came over to order 'Stand To' as dawn was near . . . everywhere was covered with mist. This soon cleared and I found myself about 200 yards from a well built German strong point . . . there were plenty of targets and we made the best of it.'

The Commando war diary reports: 'At 0730 [7.30 a.m.] Group 1 [the group Jones was in] engages enemy – casualties inflicted – one prisoner taken.'[14]

Jones recalls that in spite of this success his section withdrew from their original position back towards the main position over a small ridge. He had a nasty experience as they were crawling back under fire when he felt a thump on his back and thought he had been hit, especially when 'I felt blood running down my back, but no pain. On being assisted to remove my pack we found the water bottle riddled – that was my blood . . .'

Although no enemy attacks were made on their position they did come under heavy enemy shelling and mortar fire throughout that day. Unfortunately some of the shelling was 'friendly fire' from our own artillery. The war diary records that, at 4 p.m., 'Own troops shelled by our artillery (Capt Davies and five other ranks of Group 1 injured and 1 other rank killed).'

In spite of the shelling and mortar fire the Commando did manage to carry out some fighting patrols, so that by the end of the day they had six prisoners. During the night (28–29 March) Colonel Trevor reorganised his defences, which now included those of the French Goum infantry battalion on his right flank.

They remained on Djebel Choucha all next day (30 March) and as No 1 had an excellent position for observing the enemy's movements they were able to bring fire down on them. This was most effective and the war diary entries for that day provide plenty of evidence of this successful activity.

Although No 1 Commando was not attacked, the French Goums were and, as they were on the right flank of the commandos, reinforcements – initially from the King's Own Light Infantry and later from the Buffs – were sent to help the Goums and, most importantly, keep the Commando's main position on the djebel secure, with the added bonus of that excellent observation position for directing artillery fire onto the enemy.

No 1 Commando remained on the djebel until 2 p.m. on 1 April, when the men handed over their positions and withdrew to a rest area at Tabarka, thus bringing to an end an apparently small but important action that undoubtedly contributed to the successful start of the Allied counter-attack which ultimately culminated in the capture of Tunis and the end of the war in North Africa. The specific award of the battle honour of DJEBEL CHOUCHA to the commandos emphasises the importance of this little-known action.

In the rest area No 1 Commando received the welcome news that they were to return to Britain and after reorganising and re-equipping they moved to Algiers, where they and their comrades of No 6 Commando, towards the end of April, duly set sail for England. But not before both commanding officers, Colonels Trevor and Mills-Roberts, on 15 April, each received personal letters from the Commander-in-Chief of the Allied forces, General Dwight Eisenhower, in which he recalled that both Commandos 'had been identified with the Tunisian campaign from the very day on which the initial landings were made and since then they had been actively engaged on the most difficult mountain terrain of the entire front.' He added: 'As the time draws near for your departure from this theatre, it is a real pleasure to me to express to you and your gallant men commendations for a job well done. You have exemplified those rugged, self-reliant qualities which the entire world associates with the very name commando.'[17]

It provided a fitting official recognition of the commandos' active service in the North African campaign.

CHAPTER 7

SICILY 1943

(Landing in Sicily and Pursuit to Messina)

THE WAR IN NORTH AFRICA came to an end in May 1943 with the defeat of the Axis forces there, culminating with the surrender of 275,000 German and Italian soldiers, the largest capitulation yet imposed by the Allies upon the Axis armies of Hitler and Mussolini. It was a bitter and humiliating blow for both dictators, but particularly for Mussolini, whose aspirations for a great Italian empire had now ended in catastrophe and the loss of the greater part of his army.

Meanwhile, back in Britain the Commandos were being reorganised as a result of battle experiences and new thinking on the future roles of these special forces. In the Middle East no new Commandos were raised – those survivors of the earlier ME Commandos and Nos 8 and 11 had been absorbed in David Stirling's Special Air Service Regiment; following the capture of Stirling, whilst raiding behind the enemy lines in January 1943, this unit was split up to form two further specialist groups: the Special Raiding Squadron (SRS) under Major Paddy Mayne, ex-No 11 Commando who had been in action with them in Syria, and the Special Boat Section under Major Lord Jellicoe (son of the famous First World War naval hero, Admiral Jellicoe) who was one of the original volunteers for No 8 Commando. Major Mayne's SRS was to operate with Nos 3 and 9 Commandos in Italy.

At this time there were also some major changes to the organisation and armoury of all the Commandos. Battle experiences, particularly those in North Africa, and the projected roles for the Commandos in future operations had made it imperative for the issue of heavier infantry weapons. As a result a heavy-weapons troop was established as an inherent, albeit separate, troop in every Commando. It was commanded by a captain and consisted of a little headquarters, one mortar section of two three-inch mortars, and one medium-machine-gun (MMG) section of two Vickers machine guns.

These weapons, their crews, and ammunition were transported in a total of fourteen jeeps, but of course the latter were not available in normal landings from LCAs, so the heavy weapons and ammunition needed for immediate action and close support on landing had to be manhandled ashore – the jeeps could only arrive later in the follow-up waves of landing craft. This meant, of course, that the members of the heavy-weapons troop endured plenty of tough and exacting training to prepare them for their operational role in an initial landing. Another development with the introduction of this new troop was the distribution of spare ammunition, particularly mortar bombs, to men in the rifle troops – this was not very popular with the riflemen!

Another alteration to the structure at this time was a reduction in the number of the rifle troops from six to five, although they became slightly larger, increased from a total of fifty to sixty-two all ranks.

A major development of the war, following the Casablanca Conference in January 1943, was the decision to invade Sicily, under the codename 'Husky', for which four Commandos were to be involved, namely Nos 2, 3, 40 (RM), and 41 (RM). It was also decided that these four Commandos were to be under the command of Brigadier Laycock, who after his 'escapades' in the Middle East had returned to Britain and been placed in command of all the Commandos and specialist groups, including the Special Boat Section, the Commando Basic Training Centre (Achnacarry), and the Small Scale Raiding Force. Following Laycock's departure for the *Husky* operation, Lord Lovat, then commanding No 4 Commando, was promoted to brigadier and took over command of the 'Special Service Brigade' as this grouping of UK commandos was then known.

The responsibility for the planning of Operation *Husky* was delegated to General Eisenhower as supreme allied commander of the invasion force, which consisted of General Montgomery's Eighth Army, General ('Blood and Guts') Patton's US Seventh Army and the 1st Canadian Division. Critical of Eisenhower's original invasion plan, Montgomery was mainly responsible for the revised version, which was, briefly, based on seizing the south-east corner of

MAP 12. Actions in Sicily

the island with simultaneous landings on the south-coast beaches by Patton's army and Monty's Eighth Army, plus the Canadian division, on the south-east tip (see Map 12, page 117).

Having secured the beaches the plan was for Monty's forces to advance via the coastal road through the ports of Syracuse and Augusta to Catania and on to the major port of Messina. Meanwhile Patton's army was to advance inland, also aiming for Messina. The aim being to capture this vital port and so deny the Axis forces its use for supplies from the mainland, without which they would not be able to hold out for long. Messina would then provide the 'launch pad' for the invasion of Mussolini's Italy and so become the first major step in the liberation of Europe – with, in Churchill's words, the invasion of 'the underbelly of Europe'.

Montgomery's and Patton's armies were already in North Africa but the Canadians were in Britain and arrangements had to be made for them to join the invasion fleet direct, just prior to the landings on Sicily.

For the Commandos' involvement in Operation *Husky*, the Canadians had asked for the support of the two RM Commandos to assist them in their landings, whilst No 3 Commando – already in the Mediterranean, but stationed on Gibraltar – was to support the landings of General Dempsey's 13 Corps of the Eighth Army. The Canadians were to land on the left flank of the Eighth Army on beaches on the south coast west of Cape Passero and the task of the Royal Marine Commandos was to knock out the enemy defences covering these landing beaches. No 3 Commando had a similar task: to destroy coastal and beach defences dominating the landing beaches of Dempsey's corps

However, before continuing with the Sicily story it is interesting to recall the background to No 3 Commando's presence in Gibraltar. They had been sent out to 'The Rock' in February 1943 to take over from No 9 Commando, who had arrived there in the early stages of Operation *Torch*. The role of No 9 was to launch raids on various objectives on the coast of Spain should Hitler decide to occupy that country. To that end Lieutenant Colonel R. Tod had drawn up a list of potential targets and his Commando had trained for such an eventuality. On being relieved by No 3 Colonel Tod had passed on this role and all details to his successor, Lieutenant Colonel Durnford-Slater. Although No 3 also prepared and trained for this type of operation, they were ordered to move to Egypt in April and No 2 Commando, under the command of Lieutenant Colonel Jack Churchill was sent out from Britain to take over from them.

No 3's move to Egypt was quite an experience – having reached Algiers by sea they travelled on that infamous cattle-truck train, as had Nos 1 and 6 Commandos en route to Tunisia some seven months earlier. Sad to say conditions had not improved, in fact they had worsened. This time the journey through to Tunisia took three days and on the last night the 'train broke in half'.

Apparently, following one of the night's 'comfort stops' – there were still no toilets on board – the couplings connecting the rear half of the train to the front half somehow came adrift and on restarting the journey the front half trundled off leaving the rear half behind. When the mishap was discovered there was quite a scene – involving the adjutant, Captain Head, and the Vichy French train guard – which the colonel had to sort out. The outcome resolved, the engine was uncoupled and went back to retrieve the missing rear trucks; later that night Durnford-Slater's Commando was 'reunited'. On arrival in Egypt Durnford-Slater was briefed by General Dempsey who had taken over the final stages of the planning for Operation *Husky* whilst Monty 'finished off the war in Tunisia'. No 3 was to operate on the left flank of 50 Infantry Division and land ahead of the main force to destroy a coastal battery at Avola, about three miles inland, as well as the enemy pillboxes covering the main beaches. Having been briefed and expressed his appreciation of the plan, Durnford-Slater told the general that, provided they were landed on the right beach at the right time, No 3 could put the battery out of action in ninety minutes! General Dempsey was impressed and told Durnford-Slater to carry on with his final training and that he would come and see him in a week's time, which he subsequently did.

No 3 Commando moved down to the Port Tewfik area by the Bay of Suez where the vessels were assembled for the invasion. There the men carried out some twelve rehearsals; to add realism to this training, they even constructed a dummy battery. Once again, as at Vaagso and Dieppe, Durnford-Slater planned to split his Commando into two forces: he was to lead Group I for the main assault on the battery, whilst Major Peter Young, in charge of the second group, tackled the pillboxes and other beach defences.

On 5 July 1943 Durnford-Slater and Group I embarked on the *Prince Albert*, a well-run and excellent landing ship, as we had found out when it took us (No 4) to Dieppe in August 1942. As it only had sufficient landing craft for half of the Commando, however, Major Young's group had to embark on the transport ship *Dunera*. Although the two groups were to land on different beaches and tackle different targets they were to join up afterwards at a rendezvous at nearby Cassibile.

Among those in Group I was an ex-No 4 Commando officer, who had been with us at Lofoten and also at Dieppe, namely Lieutenant S. Veasey. He had arrived in Egypt with some reinforcements for No 3 just a few days before they sailed for Sicily following an eventful journey through the Mediterranean – on their way from Algiers to Alexandria the transport ship on which they were embarked was torpedoed. Happily Veasey and most of his men were rescued by an Australian corvette and so continued on their journey to Egypt to join No 3.

This single incident well illustrates the inherent problems of sending troops from Britain to theatres overseas and the dangers they faced even before going into battle. In the context of the invasion fleet for Sicily there were two British convoys and they had to be co-ordinated to arrive off the landing beaches at the same time. The first convoy, sailing from Britain, was carrying the Canadians and Laycock's two RM Commandos; the second convoy, carrying the Eighth Army and No 3 Commando, set sail from North Africa. That these two fleets were able to converge off Sicily with no mishaps and on time was no mean achievement.

The evening of 9 July saw all the ships of the landing forces in position offshore, ready for the launch of Operation *Husky*. Next morning Brigadier Laycock with the Royal Marines Commandos successfully carried out their missions in support of the Canadians' landings, but with casualties – seven killed and thirty wounded. The wounded were evacuated to the Canadian field hospital established in the beach area, whilst those killed were given a brief, but respectful, burial before the commandos pushed on inland.

As explained in the introduction, this book deals exclusively with the Army Commandos and their battle honours. Nevertheless I am conscious that hereafter the Royal Marine Commandos who, not only in Sicily, but in other subsequent campaigns in Italy, north-west Europe, and Burma, fought side-by-side with their comrades in the Army Commandos will receive scant mention.[1]

And so to No 3 Commando – as Group I approached Sicily in the fading light of the evening of 9 July, Mount Etna could be seen from the decks of *Prince Albert* and Durnford-Slater recorded that although the sea was very rough and it seemed impossible that they could achieve a surprise attack his men were in high spirits, singing and laughing – their morale was high.

Later, however, after the transfer to their landing craft and approaching the beach, Durnford-Slater and the flotilla commander, Lieutenant Holt, RN, both had the 'gut feeling' that they were not heading in the right direction. To make sure they hailed a nearby destroyer and asked for a compass bearing to Scoglio. Their hunch turned out to be justified and with the correct bearing they set off for the right beach, only to be greeted by some machine-gun fire from one of the pillboxes. Luckily it was inaccurate and after a prompt response from the Lewis guns mounted on the bows of the landing craft the enemy gun was quickly silenced.

They touched down on time at 2 a.m.; apart from some sporadic, inaccurate and ineffective gunfire, they were able, with the aid of a couple of Bangalore torpedoes, to get through the barbed-wire obstacles and on to their FUP, where they assembled without any casualties. So far, so good.

They started on the approach to the Avola battery without further opposition, but Durnford-Slater, determined to fulfil his assurance to Demsey that they would destroy the battery in ninety minutes, i.e by 3.30 a.m., was not satisfied that the leading troop was pushing on fast enough so he decided to take the lead in person. With his shaded torch at the ready to flash back a directing light when necessary to the following troop, he took over from the leading commando scouts and so was able to hasten the advance.

The plan for the assault on the battery was based on 'fire and movement' tactics using a three-prong attack, with Lieutenant Roy Wesley's section being the fire element – consisting of Brens, a two-inch mortar, and rifles, supplemented by the three-inch mortar detachment – whilst the 'movement' group outflanked the battery position to attack it from the rear. The fire plan was controlled by wireless communications, although true to form Durnford-Slater added a cavalier touch: when they were all set for the final assault on the Italian battery he got his batman/orderly, Charlesworth, to sound 'the advance' on his bugle.

A couple of gaps were blown through the barbed wire and in they all charged, firing their automatics from the hip, and the riflemen with bayonets fixed. There was little resistance, although there were some anxious moments when an 'over-enthusiastic' officer decided to blow up the battery's spare ammunition. The result was a very loud bang and the air was full of flying debris, but there were no casualties.

The battery had been destroyed and the time was 3.25 a.m. – Durnford-Slater had fulfilled his mission with five minutes to spare. He later wrote: 'Of all the operations in which I took part, I enjoyed this the most. It was carried to a successful conclusion without a single casualty.'[2]

After a short break, reorganisation, and a quick breakfast, Durnford-Slater's group moved off to meet up with Young's group at the prearranged rendezvous at Cassibile. As it happened they arrived there just in time to greet the leading troops of 15th Infantry Division who had landed safely and were advancing into the town headed by the regimental piper.

Major Young duly arrived though he was apparently in a foul mood, and with good reason. His group was to have landed during the night but owing to serious errors of navigation they not only landed very late – it was broad daylight – but also on the wrong beach. Fortunately they had met no opposition, but nevertheless Peter Young was not a happy man. However, Durnford-Slater had been ordered to send a party out to a nearby fortified farm where some Italians were holding out – so he sent the frustrated Major Young.

Young took No 3 Troop, under the command of Captain Lash; it included the stalwart George Herbert who had been commissioned when the Commando was in North Africa. They carried out a text-book assault on the farm, which was fortified with high walls and strong buildings, but their final engagement, including close-quarter fighting against Italians who were 'not unduly anxious to do battle', lasted barely fifteen minutes. Young recorded: 'The bag was two officers and fifty-one men of the 260th (Italian) Coastal Division, under Captain Covatto. One British officer and ten men, prisoners taken from a nearby glider, were set free. We had one casualty.'[3]

The prisoners were sent back to Cassibile; Young then continued, keeping Captain Covatto with him, to seek out another little stronghold of Italians. On reaching their position Young sent Covatto in to tell the Italians what to expect if they decided to fight – they willingly gave in. Young had another officer and sixteen more men as prisoners, which he took back with his group to rejoin the rest of No 3 at Cassibile. He was able to finish the day in a much better mood as No 3 moved to a position in the nearby foothills to provide flank protection to the main force. It was, however, a quiet night – so ended a very satisfactory and successful first twenty-four hours on the island of Sicily for No 3 Commando.

The following day, 12 July, the whole Commando re-embarked on the *Prince Albert* to be available for any further amphibious operations. As it happened they did not have to wait long, for later that same day the colonel was sent for and told to proceed to Syracuse to meet Montgomery, Dempsey, and the naval commander-in-chief, Admiral McGrigor, for a briefing and orders for a further seaborne operation.

On arrival at the quayside, Durnford-Slater was firstly congratulated on the success of the initial assault on the battery at Avola and then told by Dempsey that he had another job for No 3 that same night – it seemed a tall order at short notice.

The job was to land up the coast just short of the village of Agnone and advance some seven miles inland to seize and hold a vital road bridge near Lentini on the main road to Catania, towards which the leading troops of 50 Infantry Division were now heading; it was important to capture this bridge not only to maintain the momentum of the Allies' advance, but also to prevent the enemy from being able to send reinforcements to the fighting area or, worse, demolishing the bridge.

With only a few hours to prepare for this operation Durnford-Slater hastened back to the *Prince Albert* to plan the operation and brief his troop commanders: much of the detailed orders and preparations had to be given after they had sailed. General Dempsey had warned Durnford-Slater that it was an ambitious mission and he assured the commando colonel that he appreciated that with their limited fire power and without any artillery or armoured support, the commandos on their own could not be expected to hold the bridge should they be attacked. If 50 Infantry Division was unable to relieve them by daylight next day they were, under these circumstances, to withdraw and hide up for the day until the main force arrived.

The landing at Agnone was scheduled for 10 p.m. that night, so there was no time to lose. Planning was made difficult because, as already mentioned, the *Prince Albert* only had enough landing craft for half of the Commando and so the plan had to be based on two separate trips to the landing beach. However, apart from a narrow escape when a German E-boat fired a couple of torpedoes at the landing ship – fortunately passing under the stern – the short sea journey went well and the first group, again led by the colonel, arrived off the beach on time. They were met by some sporadic enemy machine-gun fire from a pillbox covering the beach, but retaliatory Lewis gunfire from the landing craft enabled the commandos to land. They breached the barbed-wire obstacles before making a successful attack on the pillbox, which resulted in the capture of two prisoners. Having cleared the beaches the commandos moved on towards the village of Agnone where they met opposition – there followed a series of small battles. Although the commandos were successful, they did suffer approximately twenty casualties in these village engagements, including Captain Tim Leese, OC No 1 Troop, who was shot in the eye. The mopping up of the enemy in the village was left for Captain John Pooley and his follow-up group, who were due about one and a half hours later. Meanwhile the wounded were led back to the beach area for attention from Captain 'Doc' Moore and his commando medical orderlies.

Having cleared the village, the commandos started their five-mile march to the bridge. Durnford-Slater decided to use the railway line that went almost to the bridge itself. It was a wise choice as there were no enemy posts on it at all and so their approach march was unopposed. Led by Captain Bill Lloyd and his No 4 Troop they made good progress; as they neared the bridge they needed to leave the railway line and cross the river to be in a position to attack the bridge from the north and so surprise the defenders who would not be expecting an attack from this quarter.

Bill Lloyd reckoned he had found a fordable crossing place but when he waded into the water he found, to his horror, it was head deep, so he waded back to the bank and continued his search. Fortunately he soon found a suitable alternative crossing and No 3 was able to wade across without any difficulties and continue towards the bridge.

There were four pillboxes guarding the bridge and the Italian defenders were in all of them. The plan was for the four sub-sections of Captain Lloyd's troop to take on a pillbox apiece, stealthily approaching the unsuspecting defenders and hurling grenades into the gun ports. Apparently, as they approached they could hear the Italians chatting and laughing. The outcome was quick and decisive, and by midnight the bridge was in No 3 Commando's hands. Durnford-Slater deployed his two other troops to take up defensive positions around the bridge, though the ground was too rocky to dig so they had to make use of the smaller rocks to provide some cover. Captain Lloyd's troop took over the pillboxes.

At this stage Captain Pooley arrived on the scene – he had had to fight his way through the village and his two troops had suffered casualties as well, so that the total strength of the Commando at this stage was in the order of three hundred all ranks.

It was not long before they came under mortar fire, though they did have the satisfaction of shooting up several vehicles that came down the road from the north. One of these lorries contained ammunition and unfortunately Lieutenant Cave fired his PIAT (Projector Infantry Anti-Tank) at it from point-blank range. There was a tremendous explosion and Cave was caught in the blast; he died shortly afterwards.

The enemy mortar fire increased and the Germans also sent a Tiger tank into the fray, which started to spray one of Pooley's troops with machine-gun fire. As they had poor cover they tried to move in small groups to the cover of a nearby farm building, which offered some protection – but even this building received a direct hit. Casualties were mounting and enemy infantry were now seen approaching on the far bank. It was daylight and there was no sign of the relieving troops of 50 Infantry Division. The situation was dire and, mindful of General Dempsey's directive, Durnford-Slater had no other option than to order a general withdrawal of his Commando. They had done all that had been asked of them – capturing the bridge on time and removing the demolition charges that had been placed underneath it – this alone was of great value when the leading troops of 50 Infantry Division, finding the bridge intact, were then able to maintain the momentum of their advance towards Catania.

Reluctantly Durnford-Slater had to give the order to withdraw, which his men did in the usual manner – thinning out and leap-frogging back into the hills, although some tried to make their way back to their original landing beach beyond Agnone. Peter Young, who was withdrawing with Nos 1, 3, and 6 Troops paid tribute to his men for their conduct in this difficult type of manoeuvre, which, above all, requires – indeed, demands – the highest degree of discipline to be successful. He recorded:

Then giving I Troop a bit of a start, we moved slowly in extended order, ten paces between each man, across the field. With proper intervals this is a most useful formation; it is good for control, for developing fire and avoiding casualties, particularly under shell or mortar fire. For this reason we had practised it again and again (in training previously) and the men did it extremely well, keeping their dressing by their sub-section commanders, not hurrying not bunching. One reads in old books of men under fire moving as steadily as on parade; for once in my life I was actually seeing it. It was good to see.'[4]

In spite of such tactics, however, the Commando did suffer more casualties during the withdrawal and a number of the commandos were captured as they fought their way back to Allied lines. Among these was Lieutenant Veasey, so unfortunately his service in No 3 was cut short to little more than a fortnight. Although he was subsequently taken to Italy with other members of No 3 as a POW, he managed to escape from a cattle-truck on a prisoner-train bound for Germany – his adventures as a fugitive on the run and in hiding make exciting and fascinating reading. As someone who had no knowledge of the local languages, he beat the odds to reach safety in neutral Switzerland; his story is told in his book, *Night Train to Innsbruck.*

Although No 3 Commando had succeeded in its mission there were considerable casualties. The unit had gone into Agnone numbering some 350 men but in the action they suffered just over one hundred casualties, killed, wounded, and missing. As a result the Commando was down to some 240 men all ranks and the number of fighting troops had been reduced to just four.

Nevertheless, higher command was very pleased with their achievements and General Montgomery was so pleased that he ordered that a local mason should carve a stone bearing the title 'No 3 Commando Bridge' and insert it on the parapet of the Lentini bridge. The engraved stone is still there and the bridge is still called by that name. Indeed, a friend who had just returned from taking a military history tour of Sicily recently gave me a photograph of the bridge, in which it is possible to still see one of the pillboxes that Bill Lloyd's men successfully attacked that night in July 1943. However, for Colonel Durnford-Slater and his commandos, the best tribute came from General Dempsey himself when he told Brigadier Laycock that: 'The men of No 3 Commando are the finest body of soldiers I have seen anywhere.'[5]

It is for their two actions at Avola and the Lentini bridge that No 3 Commando earned the battle honour of LANDING IN SICILY. Among the immediate awards for bravery in this action was a bar to his Distinguished

Service Order for Lieutenant Colonel Durnford-Slater, a bar to his Military Cross for Major Young, Military Crosses for captains Head, Pooley, and Moore, and Military Medals for sergeants King and Taylor and corporals Spears and Dowling.

The other battle honour awarded for the campaign in Sicily, apart from the general one of SICILY 1943, was that of PURSUIT TO MESSINA, which covered the period 2–17 August and was in recognition of an action fought during this period by No 2 Commando.

This Commando had arrived in Sicily from Gibraltar after the initial landings and the men were anxious to get into action, although for most them it was going to be their first time in action. Meanwhile, however, the commandos of No 2, like the rest of their comrades of Nos 3, 40, and 41, were bivouacking in the olive groves: relaxing, enjoying some swimming in the sea, and sampling some of the local food and wine. No 3 Commando, making the most of the respite, actually staged a concert with a show aptly named the 'Syracuse Follies'. Although the Sicily campaign was not yet over, plans were being made for the employment of the four Commandos in the forthcoming invasion of Italy. As a result of these plans the Commando Brigade was to be split into two 'mini' brigades with Nos 3 and 40 (RM) Commandos being attached to the Eighth Army and the other two Commandos, Nos 2 and 41 (RM), earmarked to operate with US 5th Army; the two groups were to operate under the command of Colonel Durnford-Slater and Brigadier Laycock respectively.

However that was a future plan – the battle for Sicily was not yet over. Unfortunately, following the capture of the Lentini bridge by No 3 and the capture of the Primosole bridge, further north, by the Parachute Regiment, the Allies failed to exploit these successes to quickly capture Catania and sweep on towards Messina. This failure resulted in a change to the original Allied invasion plan: instead of the main thrust concentrating on the coastal approaches to Messina the emphasis switched inland. This meant that there was no prospect of the Commandos being employed on amphibious operations in the immediate future, hence the 'out-of-battle' respite enjoyed by the commandos already mentioned.

Nevertheless, by 14 August the Axis forces in the coastal strip were in full retreat to the port of Messina and the Eighth Army planned an amphibious operation using 4 Armoured Brigade supported by No 2 Commando, the object being to cut off the enemy's retreat to the evacuation port. No 2 embarked at Augusta on the *Princess Beatrix*. Bob Bishop, who had joined No 2 in 1942 and continued to serve in that unit until the disbandment of the Army Commandos, aptly introduces the raid with these words: 'No 2 Commando came off the unemployment list on the night of 15 August for a landing near Scaletta. Our landing was a bit off the intended spot.'[6]

Actually the landing, made at 4.30 a.m., was about three miles from the correct landing beach; apparently the navigational error was due to the failure to recognise a prominent white house that had been selected as a 'marker' from aerial photographs, but the approach from the sea meant that the house could not be seen because it was masked by a line of trees.

Despite landing on the wrong beach the commandos were soon in action and Bishop recalls: 'We were soon engaged with the luckless tail-enders of the German rearguard who were heading at top speed for their evacuation port of Messina. The enemy vehicle drivers and their troop passengers didn't have much of a chance and the fight was over in a short time.'

Dudley Cooper was one of the those policemen who had volunteered for the Commandos in mid–1942 and later with No 2 was awarded the Military Medal. After recalling the landing on the wrong beach, he had this to say on his first taste of action:

> We moved on to the road, with the beach on one side and a wall on the other. Suddenly there was a lorry, right in the middle of our troop, and three Germans in the back firing at everyone. Someone threw a grenade into the lorry, which unfortunately was loaded with ammunition. The grenade set the ammunition ablaze and it exploded in all directions.[7]

Although all the enemy in the lorry were killed the explosion also killed two of Cooper's comrades. As the commandos moved into the village of Scaletta later that morning, they met opposition from soldiers occupying some of the houses and there was street fighting, with both sides suffering casualties; sadly No 2 lost five men, killed in the skirmishes. Bishop, after naming the five, adds: 'They were buried alongside many more of their comrades from No 3 at Catania War Cemetery.'

After clearing the village Colonel Jack Churchill was determined to get into Messina, so with some of his commandos being carried on tanks and in other vehicles of 4th Armoured Brigade, he led them, in a jeep with a US war photographer, onwards to the port. On their way they came across scores of Italians soldiers who wanted to surrender, but they could not stop and just told them to go back towards the Eighth Army lines. On arrival in Messina they found, as Bishop says, that 'the Americans had gotten there before us.' Patton's US Seventh Army had taken the port and were in charge of the situation. No

2 Commando stayed there overnight and then returned back to the Scaletta area, its mission completed.

Overall the operation was rated as rather disappointing inasmuch as the main Allied forces, having arrived too late, failed in their main objective, which was to cut off the main Axis retreat. This allowed the enemy to successfully carry out a general evacuation from Messina and it was estimated that as many as forty thousand Germans and sixty thousand Italians were safely evacuated to the Italian mainland to live and fight another day. No blame, however, can be levied at the commandos for this failure: they had carried out their mission as ordered, and in spite of being landed on the wrong beach, had shown dash and initiative, successfully carrying out their allotted tasks and so justly deserved the battle honour of PURSUIT TO MESSINA.

With the whole of the island of Sicily now (17 August 1943) in Allied hands the stage was set to carry the war on to the mainland of Europe, where once again the commandos were to be in the vanguard of the invasion and their last days on Sicily saw them preparing for the invasion of Italy – with No 3 Commando taking part in some typical commando pre-invasion reconnaissance raids on the toe of mainland Italy.

CHAPTER 8

ITALY 1943–1945 (PART I)
(Porte San Venere, Salerno, and Termoli)

AS MENTIONED IN THE LAST CHAPTER the planning for the invasion of Italy was started before the end of the Sicily campaign, with the Commando Brigade being split up for separate forthcoming operations. As a result Nos 3 and 40 (RM) Commandos plus Paddy Mayne's Special Raiding Squadron, under the command of Colonel Durnford-Slater, were earmarked to operate with the Eighth Army in Operation 'Baytown', the object of which was to invade the toe of Italy across the Straits of Messina.

Following the appointment of Durnford-Slater to take charge of this commando force, it fell to Major Peter Young to take over No 3 Commando and he recalls that it was one of the happiest days of his life. Soon after taking over he was sent for by General Dempsey and ordered to carry out some reconnaissance raids in the proposed area of the landings to get up-to-date information on the strength and dispositions of the enemy there, particularly in the Bova Marina sector.

The first raid was launched on the evening of 24 August when Young sailed from Taormina with two patrols, under lieutenants Nixon and Reynolds, but the weather and sea conditions were so bad that they had to return to port and try the following night. The second attempt proved more successful and they landed without any problems. Surprisingly they found the coastal area devoid of any enemy defences or troops, but they did bring back a captured Italian workman who was able to provide some useful information.

As a follow up Dempsey ordered Young to send more small parties over to reconnoitre further inland; they were to stay there until after the invasion had started, reporting regularly with their findings. They were told that in an emergency they would be ordered back. However, as the commando wireless sets were inadequate for this type of work, specialist signallers from the Royal Artillery, with their better, but heavier and bulkier, No 21 sets, were assigned to each of the five patrols, led by Captain Pollitt and lieutenants Wardle, Ellis, Reynolds and Cummings. They successfully landed during the night of 26–27 August and had initial success, capturing some Italians and obtaining a map of the Calabria area showing the sectors of all the coastal divisions in the toe of Italy. But unfortunately they had no means of sending this information back because none of the wireless sets were working.

Various suggestions for getting this information back to headquarters in Sicily were considered, but none were practical; furthermore, by this time the enemy had become aware of their presence in the area so they had to take evasive action, which they did for the next six days. The patrols had a mixed collection of experiences, including skirmishes with the enemy; on a couple of occasions they were also on the receiving end of Allied bombing raids.

Fortunately on several occasions they were helped by friendly local Italians who gave them food and shelter, although they did also suffer casualties. Among the casualties was Lieutenant Cummings, who was wounded in one of the skirmishes and taken prisoner; nine others were posted as missing – five of these were the RA signallers, 'not commando soldiers and therefore not used to commando tactics'. In addition, several of the commandos unfortunately came back suffering from malnutrition, some had become victims of malaria, and a few, including Major Young himself, were struck down with jaundice as well. These latter two problems had also affected the two Royal Marine Commandos during their campaign in Sicily, mostly attributable to the unhealthy conditions prevalent in the Catania area where they were committed. It was a notorious area, described by Eisenhower as 'the pest-hole malaria'. Suppressive mepacrine held the malaria at bay but further treatment was needed when the victims were out of the line.

Major Peter Young, who had been with these patrols from their second day – he had returned to Bova Marina when no messages were coming through, to find out what was happening – devotes a whole chapter in his book, *Storm from the Sea*, to this operation.

He sums up the Bova Marina operation, frankly admitting that 'as a reconnaissance the expedition could hardly have been a more complete failure', but adds that his masters at corps headquarters never held this against his men, accepting that they were victims of the unsuitable wireless equipment. They preferred to recognise that, under the circumstances of hardship, difficulties, and danger, his men had displayed the true qualities of their commando training.

Back in Sicily, the rest of No 3 Commando, now down to just two reinforced troops – and with the hospitalisation of Major Young, now under the command of Captain Arthur Komrower – was preparing for further action. Together with the Special Raiding Squadron (SRS) and No 40 (RM) Commando they were to support the landings (Operation *Baytown*) by 231 Infantry Brigade in the Calabria sector on the mainland of Italy.

In the early hours of 3 September 231 Infantry Brigade successfully landed and went on to quickly capture its main objectives of Reggio and Santa Giovanni. Meanwhile the two troops of No 3 and the Special Raiding Squadron remained afloat on their respective landing ships in reserve, ready to carry out an amphibious operation at short notice – the order for which came the following morning when Paddy Mayne's SRS were landed to outflank the enemy defences by capturing Bagnara Calabria. Although their landing was delayed some two and a half hours their operation was a great success. They accounted for forty-seven Germans killed and wounded and they took thirty-five prisoners, while their own losses were five killed and six wounded. Apparently the prisoners stated that they were taken completely by surprise and were unaware of a landing until engaged, Paddy Mayne reckoned that if his landing had not been delayed, as it was, the whole of the enemy position might have been cleared with far fewer casualties.

At this stage the Royal Marine Commando was brought into action. However, not only had it suffered battle casualties in Sicily, but it had further casualties caused by malaria. To further aggravate these problems, the unit suffered even more casualties – some seventy – during an enemy air raid while on board the *Queen Emma* awaiting further action on Operation *Baytown*. Albeit the commandos weathered the storm and on 8 September, together with No 3 Commando, they were ordered to land in the San Venere area in another outflanking amphibious operation supporting 231 Infantry Brigade. The two Commandos were to land thirty minutes ahead of the brigade and establish a secure bridgehead for the main landings.

The plan entailed securing three landing beaches, one by No 3 and the other two by No 40, then once 231 Infantry Brigade had successfully landed, the

MAP I3. Italy, Sicily and Adriatic

commandos were to push on through San Venere and take up a protective position beyond the town and hold it until relieved by the leading troops of the Infantry Brigade.

In the early hours of 8 September the commandos, who were aboard US landing ships (LSIs), arrived offshore in the transfer area for the run-in. Heavily laden with arms, ammunition, and emergency rations – along with having to cope with a heavy sea swell in the dark – the troops had difficulties transferring to the assault landing craft (LCAs). The American LCAs, unlike their British counterpart, could not be loaded with troops on the parent ship and then lowered into the sea, and so this delayed the landings for nearly an hour and a half. To make matters worse there were then also navigational problems trying to identity the correct landing places.

As a result the commandos landed only a few minutes before the main force of 231 Infantry Brigade. Fortunately there little opposition, except for some sporadic gunfire from the quayside of San Venere, which was on the left flank of the landings. This was quickly silenced by the commandos, enabling them to push on beyond the town to take up defensive positions so that the brigade could prepare for a further advance along the restrictive coastal road.

Then came the inevitable enemy counter-attack, but with the aid of an air strike and support from Royal Navy ships they were able to successfully beat off the enemy and secure the base. However, this was not all – a fighting patrol from No 40 even successfully entered the neighbouring town of Pizza, enabling the Eighth Army to continue the advance. Their mission accomplished, the commandos subsequently followed the advance to the next town of Vibo Valentia where they briefly stayed.

There is an amusing story contained in an Eighth Army intelligence report warning the troops about philandering with the local girls of Vibo Valentia. Apparently there was a folklore tradition that these ladies had, from time immemorial, concealed poison in their mouths and given poisonous kisses to any invading soldiers. The intelligence report also warned troops that the women of Vibo Valentia were of 'very powerful physique, of strong Fascist sympathies and adherents of an ancient order which ordained upon them the duty of kissing an invader and at the same time injecting poison into his mouth'.[1] Johnny White, who was with No 3 Commando, apparently did not know of this warning, neither did he note any strong looking women – but he does remember seeing 'red light area' prohibition signs in the town.

This operation concluded No 3 Commando's involvement in Operation *Baytown* and they returned to Sicily; although their involvement in the landings was minimal the commandos had helped the Eighth Army to gain twenty valuable miles in a single operation with hardly any casualties. For their part they were awarded the battle honour of LANDING AT PORTE SAN VENERE.

During this period when Nos 3 and 40 Commandos, under Colonel Durnford-Slater, were involved in the operations with the Eighth Army, the other two Commandos, Nos 2 and 41 (RM), were still in Sicily preparing for their involvement in the forthcoming Operation *Avalanche*, in which they were to be in the vanguard of the Allied landings in the Bay of Salerno.

The strategic objective of this operation for the main force, comprising an American and a British corps, was to land on the long sandy beaches of Salerno Bay, quickly establish secure beachheads and then advance inland through two vital road passes in the mountains to the Plains of Naples and push on some twenty-five miles to seize Naples itself – with the ultimate aim of continuing the advance to Rome. It was a bold and feasible plan, not only from the military perspective, but also within the context of the political situation at the time. The landing beaches were within range of air support from Sicily and the Allies' Mediterranean Fleet was fully capable of delivering and supporting the landing Force. The political situation in Italy also favoured such a bold landing attempt: following their humiliating defeat in Sicily, the Fascist Grand Council had not only forced Mussolini to resign, but he was later imprisoned. King Victor Emmanuel had been appointed as commander-in-chief of the Italian armed forces with Marshal Bagdoli as prime minister.

Although the new government had announced it would remain in the war on Hitler's side, it had secretly initiated talks with the Allies to negotiate an armistice, but these talks were making no headway and so the Allies decided to go ahead with their invasion plans.

Ironically, on 8 September, just hours before the Salerno landings, General Eisenhower made the announcement that the Italians had signed the armistice, but meanwhile Hitler had not only decided to occupy Italy but had been sending reinforcements to strengthen his forces in the peninsula.

This was the background to Operation *Avalanche*, now for some details and the tasks of the two Commandos involved in the landings. The Commandos were under the command of Brigadier Laycock, with his small headquarters staff including Lieutenant Colonel Tom Churchill (the younger brother of 'Mad Jack'), who had joined the Commandos as a staff officer in 1942, and Captain Randolph Churchill (son of Winston), who was employed as a liaison officer – and there are a host of amusing stories told of his activities in this role.

The task of No 2 Commando was to land first, climb the cliff, then assault and destroy the coastal battery of four dual-purpose 90-mm guns. After this,

No 2, in the role of brigade reserve, was to extend the original beachhead by pushing out patrols towards the main town of Salerno in the east and also make contact with the American Rangers in the west. Brigade headquarters were to land ten minutes later, followed by No 41 (RM) Commando ten minutes after that. No 41 was to move inland to clear the village of Vietri (see Map 14, page 136) and then push up the main road for about a mile and a half and establish defensive positions on the hills of the Molina Pass and prevent any enemy action that might delay the advance of the Allied Fifth Army. There the marines were to hold on to their position until relieved by the advance troops of 46 Infantry Division, who were expected within a matter of hours – twenty-four hours at the most. To help them in this role the two medium machine-gun teams of No 2 were attached to the marines as well as the 4.2 mortars from the US Rangers, whilst No 41's mortars were attached to No 2; these attachments had been effected in the planning period back in Sicily.

During the planning stages of Operation *Avalanche*, Laycock, with his bitter experience of the limitations of the inherent fire power and administrative set-up of the Commandos, had managed to get attached to his force some six-pounder anti-tank guns to supplement the transfer of heavy infantry support weapons within his two Commandos already mentioned. In the week before the operation the commandos carried out useful training exercises to rehearse their role in the operation in the Fifth Army area near the port of Palermo in Sicily, where they were also able to enjoy American army rations, and from whence they ultimately sailed for Salerno on 8 September – No 2 aboard the landing ship *Prince Albert* and No 41 aboard two LCIs. They had an uneventful passage, almost to their launch area, at which point there were two incidents of note.

First, some details about the LCIs because they were quite different from the normal LCA assault craft. To begin with, they were much larger and could carry one hundred fully equipped troops compared with thirty-five in the LCA. They also had a much greater operational range of about seven hundred miles, compared with eighty in the LCAs. Finally, whereas the landings from the smaller craft were directly off the lowered ramp straight onto the beach, in the case of the LCIs the troops had to descend two bow gangways/steps – although more often than not, because of the risk of the LCIs getting stuck, they offloaded their troops off-beach into the water, making them wade ashore.

Now for those two incidents: the first was the radio announcement made by General Eisenhower that the Italians 'had thrown their hand in' and signed an armistice. According to Tom Churchill, when the news was received on board, it gave rise to a lot of wishful thinking: 'Some seemed to expect that this would

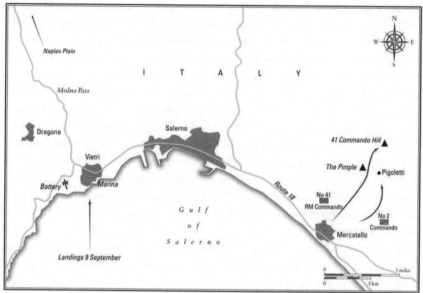

MAP 14. Nos 2 and 41 Commandos at Salerno

mean we should be met on the beaches by the local mayor with a reception committee and a brass band.'[2] But this was not to be: obviously everything depended on the reactions of the Germans in the area and whether the Italian troops had been forewarned of the armistice.

The second event was an attack by the Luftwaffe, just after dark, when the Germans dropped flares to illuminate the convoy and then bombed it. Tom Churchill reckoned there were some close shaves and it was an uncomfortable experience, but fortunately they did not suffer any casualties nor damage. It was, of course, a timely warning, after the earlier speculation of a friendly Italian reception.

In the event the Commandos' landings, to the west of the main force, were unopposed. Bob Bishop, who was in No 4 Troop of No 2 Commando, with his tongue in his cheek, recalls that their landing 'at 3.30 a.m. on 9 September was 'an absolute breeze! The ramp of the LCA went down and the troop made a comfortable landing. Not a spot of water on our boots. Needless to say the boys were not at all unhappy to find there was no "welcoming" party awaiting our arrival, indeed no signs of angry men in grey hanging around.'[3]

As No 2 headed for the landing beach a Royal Navy destroyer provided some prearranged fire on the site of the coastal battery on the cliff. Among the first ashore were the three-inch mortars under Captain Brunswick, who quickly set them up on the beach to provide further overhead fire support. The assault commandos, with Jack Churchill in front, dashed towards the cliff and on to their objective. The gunners did not put up a fight: the guns were unmanned – apparently most had fled during and after the initial naval bombardment. Churchill's men soon had a group of sullen Italian prisoners whom they brought back to the prisoners' cage hastily established near the beach. And so the first commando mission had been quickly and successfully concluded.

Whilst Churchill's men were assaulting the battery the rest of No 2 had extended and secured the beachhead ready for the arrival of No 41 on the LCIs. Landing unopposed, No 41 advanced into Vietri, and Raymond Mitchell's description of the initial stages of No 41's operation aptly sums up the situation and sets the scene for the subsequent action. The marine commandos' unopposed landing was in 'marked contrast to the reception being given to the main body of the assault some miles along the coast. Multitudinous flashes in the night sky and the rumble of many explosions told it all.'[4]

Mitchell goes on to speculate that the enemy had anticipated the likelihood of an Allied landing in the Salerno area, indeed from enemy intelligence papers collected by Colonel Churchill's men from the battery office, the enemy did have a prearranged plan to repel any such landings. However, what they had not visualised was the use of Allied special forces to land to the west of Salerno and seize the main road passes to the Plains of Naples, hence the absence in these early stages of any enemy forces in the landing area of Marina/Vietri. As a result Mitchell records that consequently 'the capture of Vietri and seizing control of the road and rail route through the La Molina Defile involved only a few disjointed encounters with the enemy.'[5] Whilst the marine commandos were advancing up the main road to occupy their defensive positions on two hills astride the road at Molina, No 2 was regrouping in and around a school house in Vietri. Unfortunately the troops were without their heavy kit, including their packs containing their rations with the magic 'char' (tea – the British Tommy's panacea for all problems, giving rise to the old adage, 'when in doubt, brew up'), and equally important in those days – their 'fags'. So some men were sent back down to the beach, where the packs were to have been offloaded from the LCAs on their second run-in. Unfortunately, the Germans, located to the north beyond Molina had started to mortar the beach and the 'pack retrievers' and some of the prisoners in the cage there became casualties, though they were able to receive treatment in Captain Lees's first-aid post, which had been established in a large house in Vietri. Regrettably, although a couple of landing craft had brought in some of the packs, the other landing craft had turned back from the beach when they came under the enemy mortar fire and, much to the chagrin of the commandos, most of their packs were now back on their parent ships. The faintheartedness of these LCA crews was the cause of much hardship and discomfort to the commandos in the days that followed: they would have run short of food and ammunition had not the maintenance parties on the main beaches been able to keep them supplied. Bob Bishop was very critical of these LCA crews: 'The faint hearted sailors shot off from the beach taking with them our reserve ammunition and the other items of our gear – including that other essential life-support item, our cigarettes! Nelson would have had that miserable lot keel-hauled!'[6]

No 41, after a successful skirmish with an enemy tank finally took up hilltop positions overlooking the Molina Pass, but from the afternoon onwards came under both enemy mortar and artillery fire; the resulting casualties were sent back to Vietri for treatment.

Earlier that morning Laycock had sent two troops of No 2, those of Captain Pat Henderson and Captain the Duke of Wellington, down to the nearby northern outskirts of Salerno to see if they could bring pressure to bear on the rear of the enemy opposing the main landings. They reported some enemy tanks in the area and actually managed to put one of them out of action with two bombs from a PIAT rocket launcher.

During the afternoon of that first day it became quite clear that all was not going well on the main beaches and the divisional commander confirmed that belief when he told Laycock that severe opposition on all the main beaches had been encountered and the relief of his commandos would subsequently be delayed. It was bad news, but hopes were raised later when a couple of armoured cars of the Reconnaissance Squadron of 138 Brigade got as far as Vietri with news that the two troops of No 2 were okay and still hanging on in the western suburbs of Salerno. With no prospects of being relieved as planned, both Commandos settled down for the night, which fortunately was a quiet one.

Early next day, 10 September, the armoured cars tried to probe beyond the Molina Pass, but without success; they reported that the enemy had moved troops up near to the Molina area and taken up positions that threatened both Commandos, No 41 in particular. From Vietri an enemy heavy-machine-gun team was spotted moving uphill to take up a firing position that overlooked the village, so Jack Churchill, from the roof of his headquarters, directed the fire of both his own three-inch mortars and those of the attached US Rangers to successfully eliminate this threat. However, as a further precaution Churchill sent two of his reserve troops to occupy the area, which became known as 'Dragone Hill', after the name of the nearby hamlet.

Throughout the morning the enemy attacked No 41's position, but the marines held on and an attempt to outflank the marines' position was thwarted by the presence of those two troops of No 2 at Dragone Hill – it had been a timely move.

Around 3 p.m., however, No 41 was subjected to very heavy artillery fire and a direct hit on their little Commando headquarters post inflicted heavy casualties, not only to men but also to the wireless equipment. Among the casualties was the CO, Colonel Lumsden, causing his second-in-command, Major Edwards to take over. Later that afternoon one of No 41's troops, which had already been heavily attacked, was rescued from further disaster by a counter-attack by another troop of No 41. Casualties among the Commandos were beginning to mount and now, – well into the second day of a holding operation that was only expected to last twenty-four hours at the most – fresh appeals were made by Laycock for at least some reinforcements if a full-scale relief was not possible. Fortunately, the next day, 11 September, was relatively quiet and the commandos had further cause to feel happier when detachments of the Lincolnshire Regiment arrived to support them on Dragone Hill with a further detachment, from the Kings Own Yorkshire Light Infantry, the followng day arriving in the Vietra area. As a result the commandos were withdrawn and moved down to a narrow strip of land towards Salerno to bivouac and get some rest; there they were also resupplied with food and ammunition.

However, their time out of the line was short-lived. It appears that the relieving infantrymen on Dragone Hill had been pulled back and No 2 Commando was ordered to return and reoccupy that area; No 41 was ordered to return to its previous position too. The relieving infantrymen had been called back to the beachhead area, where the Germans had made a heavy counter-attack supported by tanks.

By the evening of 12 September the commandos were back in their former localities and there was growing evidence, from the commando patrols sent out, that a full-scale German thrust was likely on the Dragone–Vietra positions.

On 13 September the commandos' worse fears materialised and the enemy attacked with full artillery support. On the Dragone positions, which included the village, the situation became grim: both flanks were turned, although with artillery support the commandos were able to hold on. Laycock then ordered No 41 to help out, so, together with the reserve troop of No 2 Commando (all under the command of Major Lawrie), this combined force was able to push the enemy back – by the early afternoon the situation had been restored. As usual, this success came at a price: Bob Bishop records the names of twenty of his comrades who were killed and adds that a further fifty-three were wounded in this battle at Dragone; among those killed was Major Tom Lawrie.

Bishop also recalls a most moving incident that occurred in the village during this operation:

It came during the counter-attack by the Commando. A group of four men including two walking wounded found themselves in a narrow alley which passed for the main street of the hamlet [Dragone] and saw two German paratroopers, with rifles slung across their backs, attempting to carry a wounded comrade to safety. The No 2 boys knew they were paratroopers because of their bulbous trousers and distinctive rimless helmets. The paratroopers turned and found themselves looking at our four with weapons pointing in their direction. The NCO leading our group said, 'No firing, lads!' and motioned with his arm for the Germans to keep going and get their wounded man out of there. One paratrooper raised his arm in acknowledgement and they vanished round the corner of the alley.[7]

Bishop added that it seemed to him, at that moment, that humanity had arrived to reassert itself in his world.

The battle for Dragone Hill was the last attempt by the enemy to capture the road and rail centre based on Vietri and those in high command were not slow in recognising the vital role that the commandos had played in this battle. Both the general officer commanding, General Alexander, and the corps commander, General McCreery, gave instructions to Laycock to congratulate all ranks for the magnificent part that they had played in the operation. Significantly, next day, 14 September, the commandos were relieved and American troop-carrying vehicles (TCVs) transported the two Commandos to some buildings in the northern suburbs of Salerno to be in reserve for the 46 Infantry Division. There at last they had a chance to rest, wash, and sort themselves out after the continuous commitment of the last five testing days. Some of the lads even managed to get down to the sea for a bathe, but as Colonel Tom Churchill commented: 'They had to choose their time as they were liable to coincide with a mortar concentration.' But this welcome rest and relaxation break did not last long, for within twenty-four hours, in the late afternoon of 15 September, the Commandos were on the move in the TCVs again – this time to Mercatello, about three miles east of Salerno, to a rendezvous in the 46 Infantry Division area. A threat had developed when the enemy seized three hills overlooking the division's beachhead and route inland. Laycock's commandos were to eliminate this threat with the following outline plan.

No 41 Commando was to advance up the valley and capture one of these features, which was named, appropriately, '41 Commando Hill'. The attack was to be followed one hour later by No 2 sweeping up the valley to the east of No 41's route to flush out any enemy, before taking the village of Pigoletti and moving on to the second hill feature, known as the 'Pimple'.

No 41 crossed its start line (SL) with three tanks in support, at 5.30 p.m. just as darkness was falling. Unfortunately one of the tanks soon became a casualty as it crashed through a bridge, whilst neither of the other tanks got far before getting bogged down. Fortunately, however, a well-planned and directed artillery barrage by the divisional gunners enabled No 41 to successfully storm and capture its objective, with just one killed and only two wounded.

No 2 Commando crossed its SL at 6.30 p.m. Colonel Jack Churchill had devised a plan that on the face of it seemed very unorthodox – to say the least. From his perspective he reckoned that the terrain of terraced vine-covered slopes, abounding with rocky outcrops and other obstacles, would preclude any chances of a silent surprise advance. In any case, he did not want to pass by the enemy unnoticed – he wanted to bring them to battle. He therefore decided to organise his force into a formation to carry out a sweep that would cover the whole width of the valley. Accordingly he divided his Commando into six columns, which would advance spread out to cover the frontage; he would place himself – sword in hand – in the lead between the third and fourth columns. But the key to his ultimate success was that instead of a stealthy and silent approach – and this would also, most importantly, allow him to keep control and enable the columns to maintain contact with each other as they advanced in the darkness – his men would shout out as loudly as possible the word 'Commando' every five minutes. In this novel way they swept up the valley, crashing through the undergrowth and over obstacles, yelling 'Commando' all the while.

'It must have been an awe inspiring experience for the enemy – the noise of the advance as the men trudged and climbed through the vines, the shouts of the troops and the incessant rattle of Tommy guns,' wrote Tom Churchill.[8] Indeed, several German prisoners who were later captured admitted that the noise made by the commandos as they came up the valley, shouting and crashing, was so great that it seemed to them that at least a division was advancing towards them. No wonder they felt like fish caught in a net and most surrendered without a fight. Captain Tom Hemmings and his No 4 Troop took thirty-five prisoners; other groups also collected prisoners en route up the valley. All went well for No 2 as the men steadily advanced to clear the village of Pigoletti. There Colonel Jack Churchill, assisted by one of his men, surprised and captured the crew of an 81-mm mortar in the skirmish. Altogether another forty-two prisoners gave themselves up. With the village secured they pressed on towards the Pimple, which was unoccupied, so their mission was complete and the Commandos started to retrace their steps back to the divisional front line. They found the Pimple unoccupied, so their mission was complete and the commandos started to retrace their steps back to the divisional front line. They had no problems on the return journey and arrived back at their original starting point at about midnight with the incredible 'bag' of 136 German prisoners – more than the whole division had captured in their five days of fighting at Salerno to date.

By all standards it was a unique operation and reminded the author of the Biblical story of how Gideon, with guile and the use of trumpets and pitchers, had defeated a superior force to liberate his tribe from the yoke of the Midianites in the days of the Old Testament.

Frustratingly, however, as the commandos were on their way back to the location of the original rendezvous, to rest and recover from their efforts, Churchill got the message on his wireless link that there was a change of plan and his troops were to return up the valley, clear Pigoletti once again, then move on to take and occupy the Pimple – it appeared that reports had been received at divisional headquarters that, following No 2's departure from that area, a strong force of Germans was now established there.

The moon had risen as the commandos started their return journey up the valley and they made good progress and encountered no problems until reaching the village of Pigoletti which was indeed now reoccupied. However, with some reinforcements from No 41 Commando they once more cleared the village in some fierce fighting, in which Jack Churchill played a prominent role.

Preparations followed to send a force forward and capture the Pimple, again with support from No 41. Two troops from No 2, led by Captain the Duke of Wellington, attacked the enemy position, but from the outset they were met by withering machine-gun fire and grenades. One of the first to fall was the gallant Duke: he and several of his men were killed instantly. It was a tragic and devastating blow and the commandos were forced to withdraw back to Pigoletti.

Commenting on the loss of the Duke, Tom Churchill offered this tribute: 'He had fought like a lion through all those bitter days, and proved himself a fine and resolute leader.'[9]

No 2 had lost one of their most respected and popular troop leaders and many found it difficult to accept that the descendent of such an illustrious military leader, the 'Iron Duke', should have perished in an assault on a small hill in Italy with the insignificant name of the 'Pimple'.

Following this setback the surviving commandos fell back to the village, where they held out all the next day. Their three-inch mortars, along with the 4.2 mortars of the US Rangers, who were still attached to their British comrades, pounded the enemy relentlessly with effect, keeping them at bay. There were orders for further attacks on the Pimple, but these did not materialise. One attempt involving No 41 was mounted, but the prearranged barrage planned to cover their initial move to and across their SL went horribly wrong, with our 'friendly fire' falling on the marines, inflicting many casualties and forcing them reluctantly to abort the operation. However, the two Commandos consolidated their positions on the Pigoletti Ridge and stubbornly held on until 19 September when finally the Germans pulled out from the area, leaving it in the commandos' hands. Altogether they had fought almost non-stop for eleven days.

As in North Africa the men of No 2 and 41 Commandos had been deployed in sustained defensive operations for which they were neither equipped, organised, nor trained, and as a result their casualties at Salerno were high – a total of nearly four hundred killed, wounded, and missing between the two Commandos, representing some 48 per cent of Laycock's original force that had landed unopposed in the early hours of 9 September.

Thankfully the commandos were pulled out of the line from the Pigoletti positions and taken to an orchard area near the sea that had been cleared of mines and other obstacles. Here they were able to recover, bathe, and relax, although from time to time they were subject to odd enemy shells.

On the third day the corps commander, General Sir Richard McCreery, came to personally thank them for their resolute fighting and the sacrifices made. More importantly he made a point of emphasising the effect their example had on the morale of the rest of his troops and added that it was considerable.

Two days later the surviving commandos sailed back to Sicily thus ending their involvement at Salerno. The Fifth Army subsequently secured their beachhead and were able to advance in force through Vietri and the Molina Pass on to the Plains of Naples where they linked up with the Eighth Army; on 20 September they entered the city of Naples itself.

The commandos had undoubtedly made a great contribution to this success and in so doing were worthy recipients of the battle honour of SALERNO, which ranks as one of the most glorious of the war. Many awards were made to the commandos, but none more worthy than that of the Distinguished Service Order to Lieutenant Colonel Jack Churchill, for his outstanding leadership and inspirational courage throughout the fighting, especially in the Pigoletti operation – although many of his men reckoned that he deserved the Victoria Cross.

Just before the commandos left Salerno their commander, Brigadier Laycock, was called to London for high-level discussions that eventually led to his appointment as Chief of Combined Operations in succession to Lord Louis Mountbatten, who was promoted to Supreme Commander of South-East Asia

Command (SEAC) with his headquarters in Ceylon (Sri Lanka).

At the age of thirty-six, for 'Lucky' Laycock, now Major General Laycock, this promotion was no mean achievement. Just three years earlier, as a regular army officer, he was serving as a captain in the Royal Household Cavalry. As one of the first volunteers for special service in the commandos he was promoted to lieutenant colonel to command No 8 Commando and subsequently commanded *'Layforce'* in the Middle East. He had seen at first hand a fair amount of amphibious action and was fully aware of some of the problems and lessons learnt. He was therefore going to a post of command with experience and knowledge of combined operations and ideally qualified to meet the challenges of planning and preparing for the greatest amphibious operation of all time: D-Day and the Normandy landings. He took with him on this challenging appointment the best wishes of all of us in the 'green beret fraternity'.

Back in Sicily, Nos 2 and 41 settled down for the next month to reorganise with reinforcements and train for further operations. No 41 had bivouacs in a pleasant orchard location whilst their comrades in No 2 took over a nearby old Italian barracks.

Durnford-Slater's force of No 3, No 40, and the SRS was still under the command of General Dempsey's 13 Corps, which had gone up the west coast of Italy to help the Fifth Army, as needed, in their advance to Naples. In the event they were not required and so were ordered to cross over to the east side of Italy and rejoin the Eighth Army, who were making steady progress against General Kesselring's forces.

However, intelligence sources seemed to suggest that Kesselring might pull back to a natural defensive line based on the river Biferno, which flows from the Apennines eastwards down to the Adriatic, just south of the town of Termoli – a port with a useful harbour. Appreciating this possibility Montgomery decided to forestall the Germans by making a landing with Durnford-Slater's commandos in the rear of the enemy's lines at beaches north of the river, to capture and hold the town of Termoli long enough for the leading elements of his Eighth Army to take over. This would deny the Germans the natural defence line on the Biferno, forcing them to retreat further to the north to find an alternative defensive position.

With this outline plan in mind the commandos boarded LCIs and sailed along the coast to Bari, although Durnford-Slater decided to travel by road because it was quicker and it would afford him more time for planning. In his memoirs there is an amusing and light-hearted account of his experiences on this trip.

At Bari Durnford-Slater received the latest intelligence on the enemy forces

The Bren Light Machine Gun (LMG) provided the major fire power of every Commando subsection. The No. 1 on the gun – seen here – is carrying the weapon, a spare magazine (holding 30 rounds of .303 ball ammunition) tucked into his leather jarkin, ready for immediate use. Spare magazines were normally carried in the body pouches of the No. 2 on the LMG and also by other members of the sub-section. The personal weapon of the No. 1 (.45 Colt automatic) is seen tucked into his belt, but normally carried in the holster. *(Author's collection)*

A group of the first Commando volunteers of No. 4 Commando at Weymouth in July 1940. They came from many different regiments and corps as can be seen here e.g., Lieutenant 'Monty' Banks (Royal Tank Corps) and Captain Le Butt (Black Watch). Many were survivors from Dunkirk, such as young John Skerry, seated second from left, then a private but by D-Day, after active service on raids, including Dieppe, promoted to sergeant. *(Author's Collection)*

'Living off the land' was a feature of Commando training. Here can be seen a group of F Troop, No. 4, with the haul of a night's scavenging during the period when the Commando was 'standing by' to repel any enemy invasion on the South Coast in early September 1940. The author is standing third from the left. *(Author's Collection)*

The first 'Great Commando Raid' was on Vaagso, Norway, in December 1941 carried out by No. 3 Commando with the support of two Troops from No. 2 Commando. It was a highly successful raid but saw a lot of bitter fighting – and casualties. Seen here the destruction of one of the fish oil warehouses. *(By permission of the Imperial War Museum, N459)*

Following the Commandos' experiences on the Vaagso raid in December 1941 special emphasis was placed on training and developing drills for street fighting and house clearing. At Achnacarry improvised structures were made from local materials, as seen here, for this important aspect of training. Later Commandos were also able to carry out realistic training with live ammunition and explosives in blitzed areas of London and other damaged towns and cities. *(Author's Collection)*

6 July 2001, the scene of the dedication service and unveiling of the memorial on the site of the Sauchenhausen Concentration Camp, Germany, where the seven commandos of the Glomfjord raid were shot on 22 October 1942. *(Courtesy of Mrs. D. Roderick, MBE)*

HMS *Cambeltown* rammed hard and fast on the southern caisson of the St Nazaire dry dock. This photograph was taken on the morning before the explosion that put the dock out of action for rest of the war and brought to a conclusion a highly successful commando raid, albeit a costly one in terms of casualties. In the background can be seen the enemy gun emplacements attacked by Lieutenant Roderick's group during the previous night's fighting. *(By permission of the Imperial War Museum, HU2242)*

Colonel Charles Newman VC, leader of the Commando raid on St Nazaire. After the War he was President of the Commando Association and a prime mover in applying for the Battle Honours and the Laying up of the Commando Flag in Westminster Abbey. *(Michael Burn, MC, ex No. 2 Commando)*

Colonel Charles Vaughan (*left*), commandant of the Commando Basic Training Centre at Achnacarry, with Brigadier Lord Lovat during a visit by the latter to the centre in November 1943. *(Author's Collection)*

'Madagascar Memories' … (*Top*) One of the Vichy French guns captured by No. 5 Commando in their initial assault. (*Centre*) Relaxing after the capture of Diego Suarez. (*Bottom*) Training exercise in preparation for further operations on the island. (*Courtesy of John Wall, ex No. 5 Commando*)

North Africa. One of the prison cells at Sedjenane from whence No. 1 Commando carried out many patrols including those on Green Hill and 'the Italian Job'. *(Spellmount Publishers Ltd.)*

One of the six 155mm guns of Hess Battery. This picture was taken before the Dieppe raid and obtained from German archives by Emyr Jones during his research to produce a Nominal Roll of all those in No. 4 Commando who were on the operation. *(Courtesy of Emyr Jones)*

No. 2 Commando officers at Gibraltar prior to their going on active service in Sicily, Italy and the Adriatic. Seated in front row from left to right: Lieutenant Keep, (awarded MC in Sicily), Captain Broome, (killed in action – KIA – in Salerno), Captain the Duke of Wellington, (KIA Salerno), Lieutenant Colonel Jack Churchill awarded DSO and bar (Salerno and Adriatic), Captain Bissett, Captain Hooper (survivor of St Nazaire Raid and awarded the MC in Sicily) and Lieutenant Lees. *(Photograph CVA/Mrs D Roderick MBE)*

LAKE COMACCHIO. Men of No. 9 Commando's mortar section loading their mortar, ammunition and equipment into a storm boat prior to crossing the lake. *(By permission of the Imperial War Museum)*

The Sarande operation, Albania, July 1944. A casualty of No. 2 Commando Brigade being evacuated to the base at the landing beach for treatment on board an LCI before shipment back for hospitalisation in Italy. Evacuation of casualties was always a major problem. *(Photograph by permission of the Imperial War Museum)*

Commandos of Lovat's Brigade move off from their Normandy landing beach to join up with their parachute comrades at Pegasus Bridge. One can see how heavily they are laden, with weapons, ammunition, digging tools/ammunition making loads that ranged from 80 to 100 lb (50 to 62.5 kg). *(By permission of the Imperial War Museum, B5063)*

Normandy July 1944. Left to right: Captain Charles Head, Brigadier John Durnford-Slater and Colonel Peter Young – then commanding No. 3 Commando. All three were original volunteers for Commandos in 1940 and subsequently saw action in Vaagso, Dieppe, Sicily, and Italy before the Normandy campaign. Peter Young, as Deputy Commander of No. 3 Commando Brigade, was also in Burma. *(Courtesy of Greenhill Books)*

Commandos killed in action initially had to be buried on the battle field, later they were reinterned in the military cemeteries created, world-wide, by the Commonwealth Graves Commission. This picture shows the graves of some of No. 4 Commando in their first defensive position at Hauger in Normandy. *(Roland Oliver)*

FLUSHING. Some of the German prisoners being collected by No. 4 Commando on Uncle Beach before being shipped back to Breskens during the early stages of this very successful operation on Walcheren. *(Photograph by Capt A Thorburn)*

The crossing of the Rhine. The devastation of the heavy bombing on the Wesel area can be seen here as commandos take up their initial defensive positions on the northern outskirts of the town. *(By permission of the Imperial War Museum)*

A special bodyguard from Nos. 4 and 6 Commandos was organised to protect Field Marshal Montgomery during the Allies' dramatic break-out from Falaise in the Normandy campaign and the subsequent pursuit of the enemy to liberate Brussels. At the end of this tour of duty Montgomery had this photograph taken and presented each one of his 'commando bodyguard' with a signed copy. *(Alex Morris – 4 Commando)*

FLUSHING. Commandos of No. 2 Troop, No. 4 Commando, take over a captured German position in the area of 'Troon' – see map on page 214. *(Photograph Joe Spicer)*

The leading elements of No. 3 Commando Brigade wading ashore at Myebon from a landing craft on 12 January 1945. The follow-up commandos had to wade through an ebb tide with water up to their armpits. *(By permission of the Imperial War Museum)*

Tag Barnes, MM, author of *Commando Diary*, in which he describes his service in No. 1 Commando in both the North Africa and Burma campaigns. He provides a rare insight into the experiences of a commando soldier 'in action and out of action'. *(Spellmount Publishers Ltd.)*

Lieutenant George Knowland won his VC on Hill 170 in Burma. See Chapter 13.

Corporal Tom Hunter, No. 43 (RM) Commando won his VC at Comacchio. See Chapter 9.

Lieutenant Colonel Geoffrey, KEYES, VC, No. 11 Commando, lost his life leading the raid on Rommel's Headquarters in North Africa. See Chapter 3.

Lance Corporal Eric Harden, RAMC, won his VC in action with No. 45 (RM) Commando. See Chapter 12.

Henry Brown OBE, MBE served in No. 1 Commando throughout its wartime existence. After the war he served as secretary of the Commando Association for forty years, and was honoured to be appointed as its final president prior to disbandment in 2005. Seen here in front of the Commando Flag and holding the Commando Roll of Honour, which is permanently on view in the nave of Westminster Abbey. *(Commando Association)*

Officers Mess (Instructors and Staff) of the famous Commando Basic Training Centre at Achnacarry in the Western Highlands late 1943. Seated in front row from left to right; Captain K. Allen (later No. 2 Commando), Captain J. Symondson, Medical Officer, Captain G. Kaye, Captain J. Joy, Adjutant, Major A. Komrower, DSO, (who had commanded No. 3 Commando at Termoli), Lieutenant Colonel Charles Vaughan, OBE Commandant, Major D. Cotton-Minchen, Chief Instructor, (later reported missing on operations in Albania), Captain J. Carlos, Quartermaster, Captain F. Benwell, Captain J. Dunning (author) and Captain L. Sharples, ex No. 4 Commando. *(Author's Collection)*

Forty Years On. Veterans of No. 4 Commando reunited at St Marguerite, the site of Hess battery (Dieppe), in 1982. Left to right: Jim Pascale, James Dunning, head of John Skerry, Eric Cross MBE, Bill Boucher-Myers DSO, Robert Dawson DSO, Captain Pat Porteous VC, George Cook, Pete Burrows, Donald Gilchrist and Maurice Chauvet. *(Author's Collection)*

Countess Mountbatten (Patron of the Commando Association from 1981 to 2005) with Lord Lovat and his D-Day piper, Bill Millin, at the unveiling of the D-Day plaque at Warsash, Hampshire, where most of Lovat's Brigade set sail for the Normandy beaches on the evening of 5 June 1944. *(Author's collection)*

in the Termoli area. It was reckoned that the garrison in the town and immediate area consisted of about five hundred paratroopers of the 4th German Parachute Brigade, who were, coincidentally, the opponents that No 3 Commando faced in the epic battle at 'Commando Bridge' in Sicily. So Durnford-Slater reckoned it was not going to be an easy affair, but nevertheless felt confident of carrying out his assignment. After consulting the operational planning staff he decided on the following simple plan.

No 3 Commando (still commanded by Arthur Komrower, though now as a major), because it was the numerically weakest unit, would land first and establish the beachhead to ensure the safe landing of the other two units. No 40 (RM) Commando, numerically the strongest unit having received reinforcements, was given the lion's share of the operation. Commanded by Lieutenant Colonel 'Pop' Manners, the Commando's tasks were to take the town and send out troops to hold the area, covering the important crossroads to the west, whilst the Special Raiding Squadron was to pass through No 3's bridgehead, skirt the western suburbs of the town, and secure the important road junction area south of Termoli.

The whole operation was a gamble but all seemed confident that it could come off; it was estimated that at the time of the commandos' planned landings the leading troops of the Eighth Army would be about twenty miles from Termoli, and both Monty and Dempsey had assured Durnford-Slater that they would make every effort to relieve the commandos quickly. So with these assurances preparations went ahead – the first stage being the move of embarked commandos from Bari to the port of Manfredonia to complete their preparations for the operation, codenamed 'Devon'.

The commando convoy of LCIs plus six LCAs left Manfredonia during the evening of 1 October and set sail unescorted on the 120-mile journey to Termoli. The journey proved uneventful and the force arrived at the launch area on time. The transfer of brigade headquarters and No 3 Commando from their LCIs to the LCAs went well and, thanks to some excellent navigation by the navy, their unopposed landings touched down at 2 a.m. on 2 October – spot on time. Once ashore No 3 Commando quickly established an extended bridgehead and Durnford-Slater set up his headquarters on the forward edge of the bridgehead near the railway line. All was going well, but then problems developed.

The LCIs carrying the No 40 Commando and the SRS got stuck on an uncharted sandbank and many men from both units had very wet landings. Fortunately Durnford-Slater was able to get the LCAs to help out, so that in spite of this little setback both units got ashore on time to pass through No 3's bridgehead and press on towards their objectives.

Although their landing had been unopposed the men of No 40 were soon in action as they entered the outer streets of Termoli itself, but nevertheless by 6 a.m. they had succeeded in overcoming all opposition in the town and were not only securely established there, but had pushed their forward troops to the crossroads in the western suburbs and successfully shot up and destroyed several enemy vehicles that were using the main road.

The SRS had also fought its way around the town to its allotted area in the south and taken up positions centred on the local cemetery and the railway line covering the main Termoli to Vieste road; it was not long before they too were engaging and destroying enemy vehicles on this main road. Throughout the early hours of that morning German supply lorries were using the roads, seemingly unaware of the commandos' incursion. At one stage No 40 had ambushed some twelve lorries – 'greeting each vehicle with long bursts of Bren fire until it ran off the road and overturned, often in flames'.

During the next few hours calm settled on the town, which was now firmly in the hands of No 40, supported by a troop of No 3; they had between them a total of some seventy prisoners, including some who had been captured on a train by Durnford-Slater's headquarters personnel in the following circumstances. In the early stages of the advance to the town after leaving the bridgehead they moved along the railway line towards the town station. As they approached they unexpectedly heard a steam engine apparently just pulling out and coming slowly towards them. Major Brian Franks, the senior staff officer, jumped into the engine cab, pistol in hand, and ordered the driver to stop, which he did. Meanwhile the rest of headquarters staff boarded the train to find sleeping German soldiers, whom they woke up and made prisoners. Apparently the Germans took quite a bit of awakening and could scarcely believe what was happening, believing they were safe and sound twenty-odd miles behind their front line!

As the morning wore on the Germans began to appreciate what had happened and launched some local counter-attacks, but these were repelled. By midday elements from 78 Infantry Division began to appear and started to relieve some of the commandos. Among these relieving forces was the Divisional Reconnaissance Regiment, commanded by Colonel Chevasse, who had fought alongside Colonel Mills-Roberts's No 6 Commando in Tunisia – he was a welcome ally. As a result of these reinforcements Durnford-Slater was able to gradually pull in his men to the town itself for a rest and reorganisation. Among these relieving forces were infantry from the Argyle and Sutherland Highlanders, the Royal West Kent Regiment, and The Buffs and they were able to take over and even strengthen (with their heavier fire power of anti-tank guns and medium machine gun) the original defensive perimeter around the town and also cover those important junctions astride the main coastal roads.

The situation began to worsen, however, following strong enemy counter-attacks in the early afternoon and the commandos had to return to the perimeter and start to dig in. The enemy attacks included heavy shelling on the town itself, inflicting damage and casualties, particularly to civilian property and the local inhabitants. To add to the gloom of the situation the weather deteriorated and there was heavy rainfall, adding to the discomfort of the troops in their slit trenches and other make-shift defences. This heavy rainfall also caused a temporary bridge that had been erected by the divisional engineers across the river to be swept away, disrupting the build-up of reinforcements from the Eighth Army. There was some compensation inasmuch as the awful weather did curtail the enemy's attacks: they stopped altogether towards the evening and the night itself was relatively peaceful.

Soon after dawn on 5 October twelve enemy planes bombed the town and made low-level strafing attacks on some of the perimeter defensive positions. Then came the inevitable enemy probing patrols, followed by the main counter-attacks supported by Mark IV tanks. The action went on all that day with the enemy bringing up more tanks; Colonel Chevasse, having more powerful wireless sets and being on the divisional network, was able to call for artillery and air support, but the enemy pressure continued. No 3 Commando was relocated near a farm in an olive grove and was in the thick of the fighting; fortunately it had the support of the heavy machine guns of one of the relieving battalions. In spite of this help and support, however, by nightfall the enemy were so close that Komrower reckoned that he could hear them talking. There is also the lovely story that the Germans had lit a fire in the courtyard of the farm and kept it stoked up throughout the night, and 'this was too great a temptation for Troop Sergeant Major King, MM, of headquarters, who was very partial to tea. He crept up to the fire and succeeded in remaining unnoticed on the other side of it while he boiled a mess-tin of water.'[10]

There is no doubt that at this stage – the night of 5–6 October – the situation in Termoli was grim; Durnford-Slater later admitted that he had felt for the first time in all his battles that defeat was possible, yet at the same time he contended that his comrades of No 3 had their finest hour at Termoli.

During the night limited withdrawals were made from the perimeter into the town itself, the Eighth Army was now well on its way to Termoli, and the engineers, struggling in the adverse weather conditions, had also replaced the bridge that had been swept away. As a result of all these factors the late morning saw the full artillery of 13 Corps and the Allied Air Force bringing down 'a terrific finale to the battle. Every gun we had, every mortar, tank, aeroplane and man combined to devastate the Germans'.[11] By midday the enemy was in full retreat and the battle for Termoli was over. The bold venture had paid off: that unopposed landing by the commandos in the early hours of 3 October and the subsequent bitter fighting had brought success, but at a cost. Durnford-Slater's force of 2 Commandos and the Special Raiding Squadron in their tenacious fighting had lost a total of three officers and twenty-nine other ranks killed, seven officers and seventy-eight other ranks wounded and a further twenty-two all ranks missing. Considering the size of the force these were relatively heavy losses, especially following on those already suffered in Sicily and the toe of Italy. However, Operation *Devon* had been a great success for the commandos – they had surprised the Germans and seized the town, subsequently fought hard to hold it, and with the timely assistance of those units from the Eighth Army achieved a notable victory. The special service troops had won for Monty's army not only a valuable harbour, but had also denied Kesselring the possibility of a vital natural defensive line on the Biferno. Their achievements were recognised by General Montgomery, who, later on that final day personally congratulated Durnford-Slater's men and told them to get back to Bari and 'enjoy themselves' – a somewhat unexpected choice of words from the normally austere general. Needless to say, in due course they were able to carry out Monty's instructions.

So ended Operation *Devon* and with its conclusion came, ultimately, full recognition of the commandos' involvement with the battle honour of TERMOLI; among the awards for bravery and leadership was that of the DSO to Major Arthur Komrower of No 3 Commando.

CHAPTER 9

ITALY 1943–1945 (PART II)

(Anzio, Monte Ornito, Valli di Comacchio, and Argenta Gap)

BEFORE CONTINUING THE ACCOUNTS of the other Commando battle honours in Italy, it is relevant to mention the important changes in the structure and organisation of the Commandos that were initiated in early 1943.

By then the prestige and reputation of the commandos were well established, both in the hearts and imagination of the general public and in the esteem of the armed forces. Their green beret was a coveted symbol of an elite fighting force. Indeed, when recruiting teams for No 2 Commando, following their losses at Salerno, went around Italy, Sicily, and North Africa seeking volunteer reinforcements they were inundated with applications – so many that Tom Churchill (now promoted to brigadier, following Laycock's elevation to Chief of Combined Operations) recorded that they had enough volunteers to fill three Commandos, not just one. So they could be selective before subsequently training them at Bari, where three of my comrade instructors at Achnacarry were sent to help out in the training.

Over the three years since the formation of the Commandos in the summer of 1940, against the backdrop of the fear of a Nazi invasion, the proposed role and purpose of the Commandos had changed from that of 'tip-and-run' raids to the full-scale raids of Lofoten, Vaagso, and St Nazaire. This had been followed by specific supporting actions in major amphibious operations such as the destruction of coastal batteries as at Dieppe, Madagascar, and Algiers, and then 'behind-the-enemy-lines' landings to turn their flanks and assist the main army's advance on coastal roads in Tunisia, Sicily, and Italy – plus, of course, taking their place to bolster the defence of infantry formations 'in the line' in Crete and Tunisia.

As a result of all these developments, the original concept of small raids was mainly delegated to specialised smaller units such as SSRF (No 62 Commando) although ad hoc raiding parties were formed within the standard Commandos for small raids, especially at the end of 1943 and during the months of 1944 in the run up to D-Day.

Accordingly the whole structure of the Commandos was reorganised as a Special Service Group (SS Group) under the overall command of Major General R. G. Sturges, CB, DSO, RM. His deputy, on his return from Italy after Termoli, was none other than Brigadier Durnford-Slater, DSO.

The SS Group was planned to have four brigades, each of four Commandos and, although no extra Army Commandos were raised, six more Royal Marine Commandos were eventually created. Disliking the use of the words 'special service' in the context of battalions and brigades for its connotation with Hitler's 'SS', I will continue to refer to them as 'Commando Brigades' – as indeed they were officially designated from late 1944 onwards.

There were two other innovations as a result of the reorganisation worthy of mention. The first was the formation of the Commando Snow and Mountain Warfare Camp in the Cairngorms in Scotland, the purpose of which is evident from its title, and the other newcomer was the Holding Operational Commando (HOC), based in Wrexham. The latter was where volunteer trainees were mustered and prepared for their basic Commando training at Achnacarry and it was here also that those who passed the training returned, wearing the coveted green beret, to await postings as reinforcements to operational Commandos.

Now to return to those Commandos still in Italy. The serious losses suffered by No 3 in its battles in Sicily and Italy made it necessary to return to Britain to reform and prepare for D-Day as part of No 1 Commando Brigade. No 2 Commando was made up to strength with volunteers from the field forces in the theatre, as already mentioned, whilst No 40 (RM) Commando was made up to strength with marines from the RM Division. No 41 (RM) Commando returned to Britain and was replaced by No 43 (RM) Commando, which had recently been raised. Two troops from No 10 (Inter-Allied) Commando, namely the Belgian and Polish troops, also joined Churchill's brigade, as did, finally, Colonel Ronnie Tod's No 9 Commando, which had recently arrived from Britain.

No 10 Commando was very different from the other Army Commandos inasmuch as it was composed of volunteers from countries that were under Nazi occupation and were serving in the 'liberation' forces established in Britain. These volunteers included French, Dutch, Norwegian, Belgian, and Polish soldiers, plus some, surprisingly, from Nazi Germany itself – the latter were mostly Jews who had managed to escape from both Nazi Germany and Austria, and they formed the mysterious 'X Troop'. For obvious security reasons very little was either published or known about the exploits of these troops until their respective countries were liberated. Certainly the existence of X Troop was kept secret until well after the end of hostilities. It was not until the launch of an appeal for the Commando Benevolent Fund, held under the patronage of the Right Honourable Lord Mayor of London in the Mansion House in October 1946 (which I had the honour of attending, having been involved in the training of some of these commandos, including a section of X Troop) that Admiral Lord Mountbatten in his toast of 'The Commandos' disclosed for the first time details of the hitherto secret X Troop, which was subsequently widely reported in the newspapers next day.

Brigadier Tom Churchill was anxious that the two troops from No 10 should obtain some battle experience as soon as possible because they had not been in action before, so he approached General Dempsey to enquire if they could operate on his corps front to get their 'baptism of fire'. Dempsey replied that there would be a role for them carrying out fighting and reconnaissance patrols in the rugged mountain areas overlooking the river Sangro on the enemy's front; this was agreed and the Polish and Belgian commandos moved up to that sector of the front. Based in two remote mountain villages and in atrocious and bitter winter conditions, from 13 December 1943 until 9 January 1944 they carried out a series of patrol activities, including some over the actual Christmastide period.

On 21 December, the Polish troop had a night-long battle when the Germans mounted an attack on one of the villages where they had established their base – the commandos not only beat off the attack but inflicted heavy casualties. One contemporary report written on 23 December ends: 'Towards 1000 hours Lieutenant Dauppe takes the daily patrol of three men down to the Sangro, not seeing any enemy activity. He returns towards 1400 hours with half a butchered pig and three sheep which will serve as the Troop Christmas dinner.'[1] And so it did – in spite of having to patrol on Christmas Day itself, the Poles did have a really good Christmas dinner (the menu did, of course, include pork and lamb dishes) at 2030 hours; they even toasted their absent CO, Colonel Lister – who had led No 4 on the Lofoten raid way back in 1941, before being appointed as the founding commanding officer of No 10 – with these words: 'the commander who formed us and who is unhappily not here to harvest with us the fruits of his excellent work in directing our training.'[2]

No 9 Commando, although one of the original Commandos, had not taken part in any major raid or operations to date either, except for a disappointing raid on an enemy gun emplacement on the occupied French coast in November 1941. They had been standing by in Gibraltar in support of Operation *Torch*, prior to arriving in Italy. On arrival there they had taken part in a reconnaissance raid on two small islands in the Adriatic, but found no enemy on either island.

So their first taste of action was to come when they too arrived on the west coast of Italy and were ordered to take part in an operation, code name '*Partridge*', in support of the Fifth Army on the Gustav line (the most rearward of three German defensive lines on the Italian peninsula). No 9 Commando's task in this operation was to outflank the enemy on the north banks of the Garigliano river. Although their subsequent action in this operation on the night of 29–30 December is not listed as a battle honour it was a major action for No 9 and is well documented in Messenger's book and several others. Once again, although the commandos enjoyed success it came at a price: they lost nine killed and twenty one wounded, although they killed some twenty Germans and took twenty-eight prisoners. One of the interesting asides of this action was the use by No 9 of the bagpipes. Being raised originally from units in Scotland the Commando was naturally proud of this heritage – to the extent that in their head-dress, even before the advent of the green beret, they wore a black heckle in their 'bonnets'. Every troop also had its own piper and in Operation *Partridge* they used their bagpipes for communicating between the troops.

Following these actions on the west coast of Italy Churchill's Commandos' next major operations, for which they were awarded battle honours, were at Anzio and Monte Ornito. It should be noted that after Christmas 1943 No 2 Commando was detached from the brigade and sent on a separate mission in the Adriatic – their exploits there are fully told in the next chapter.

Briefly the object of the operations at Anzio, codenamed '*Shingle*', was to outflank the enemy's Gustav line and force them to withdraw from their stronghold positions based on Monte Cassino, where they had stubbornly resisted sustained Allied land and air attacks and bombardments for months – during the course of which the Allies had suffered many casualties.

The initial landings of Operation *Shingle*, mounted during the night of 20–21 January, were most successful and effected with few casualties. Unfortunately these successes were not followed up and exploited, for reasons too detailed to discuss here; suffice it to quote Brigadier Tom Churchill's opinion on this issue:

'Anzio was mounted with too few divisions in the first place and for this Winston Churchill and Field Marshal Alexander [who had been promoted to Field Marshal following General Eisenhower's departure to England to prepare for the invasion in his role as Supreme Allied Commander] are primarily to blame. Churchill because he insisted on the operation when there were not enough troops, landing ships and craft available and Alexander because he let Churchill have his way.'[3]

As a result Anzio became a beleaguered beachhead and the battle there raged for months until the enemy on the Gustav line were finally defeated and the way to Rome was opened. However, although the commandos took part in those initial landings they were withdrawn after a short stay and took part in a separate, but related, operation at Monte Ornito, before returning to Anzio.

Captain Lucas, who commanded the heavy-weapons troop of No 9 Commando provides an excellent account of the build-up to Operation *Shingle* and their part in those initial landings, in Robin Neillands's *The Raiders*.

According to Lucas it was some time in early January that the troop leaders of No 9 Commando became aware that they were to take part in a major amphibious operation, followed by a dash (in which the commandos would be conveyed in jeeps) to a major city, parts of which they would have to hold until a larger force arrived to relieve them. They started to train and prepare for such an operation. He went on to say that they all speculated that the 'major city' was to be Rome and adds: 'Theirs not to reason why; but I believe most of us were not sorry to learn that such a harebrain scheme – even for the Commandos – had been abandoned.'[4]

Lucas then continues to provide a full description of their landing and subsequent action in Operation *Shingle*. Nos 9 and 43 (RM) Commandos embarked on HMS *Derbyshire* on 21 January and landed shortly before dawn the following morning; they were virtually unopposed and passed through the beachhead and perimeter that had been established by the Scots Guards. The Commandos' objective was a hill feature about seven miles inland on the main road to Rome, about five miles north of Anzio itself. Once established on the hill, with all-round defence, they were to stay until relieved by the main force, who were to extend their bridgehead to include the hill. Once relieved they were to return back to their base at Bacoli.

Having landed, the commandos made good progress and passed through the Guards' beachhead, although thereafter they did have the odd 88-mm shell fired in their direction, though with no effect. It is interesting to note that for this operation, and expecting the worst, the commandos were fully prepared with plenty of ammunition and emergency rations: it is recorded that the weight of each man's load was nigh on ninety pounds. Furthermore, in the absence of jeeps to lift the heavy weapons Lucas's men had steel-framed canvas hand-carts to convey their Vickers medium machine guns, three-inch mortars, and the ammunition for these weapons – they certainly were taking no chances.

Fortunately the going to the objective was good and they were able to follow decent tracks without any difficulties. Lucas and his batman, Healey, had an extraordinary experience soon after leaving the perimeter, when they stopped for a short rest, a chat, and a fag. Healey apparently said to his troop leader, 'No more from that 80-mm', and before Lucas had time to answer, thirteen German gunners suddenly and unexpectedly climbed out of a gun emplacement they had just passed, threw down their weapons, and surrendered. About the same time two follow-up troops of No 9 arrived and the prisoners were taken back to the Scots Guards, while the commandos continued on their way to their objective.

Nos 9 and 43 (RM) Commandos had planned to attack the hill simultaneously from the north-east and the west. Lucas's mortars put down a covering barrage on the hill and the co-ordinated assault went in. The marine commandos had several brushes with the enemy between the railway and the hill, taking six prisoners, but apart from that there was no opposition. Once on the hill the commandos started to dig in and prepared to defend it from any quarter; they also sent out some patrols to make sure there were not more enemy in the area. They stayed on the hill for the next twenty-four hours, during which time they were able to watch the build-up of troops and vehicles, with tanks, artillery and all the supporting services of an army in the field. Lucas aptly comments: 'We never seen anything like it, as this was No 9 Commando's first major invasion.'[5]

On being relieved the commandos were taken back to Bacoli: so ended 'Anzio One – a walk in the sun', as it was known in No 9. The other comment of note was about all that ammunition carried and not fired – the Commando history recorded: 'The Commando never carried more ammunition and fired less', but there were to be bitter and prolonged battles ahead, which would earn Anzio its awesome reputation for fierce fighting – and heavy losses.

Back at Bacoli it was not long before they were called out, but not to Anzio. Brigadier Churchill was ordered to take Nos 9 and 43 (RM) Commandos up to the Garigliano sector to join up with No 40 (RM) Commando, which was already in the area –the three Commandos were to come under the command of 56 Infantry Division and take part in a major counter-attack. However, there was a delay in arranging the necessary transport to convey Nos 9 and 43 (RM) Commandos the sixty-five miles north; as a result they did not arrive in their new sector until 31 January, by which time the corps commander had amended his original plan and decided to use the Commandos to extend his footholds in the hills west of the river by seizing three dominant peaks that made up the Monte Ornito range: Tugo at 2,000 ft, Ornito (2,400 ft), and Faito (3,000 ft). For this operation they were to come under the command of 46 Infantry Division. The terrain in this area was most hostile: rocky, uneven and in some places covered with scree slopes, but worst of all there was little or no cover. It was going to be a formidable mission.

On arrival at the river Garigliano the commandos from Bacoli crossed over on a pontoon bridge and then marched to their assembly area, where they joined up with No 43 (RM) Commando and the Belgian troop. The operation had been planned for that night, but as the commandos had had little or no sleep, and no time to prepare, it was decided to postpone it for twenty-four hours. During that time the commando officers were able to move forward and view the ground they were going to fight over. One of the problems of mounting this operation was the problem of carrying the necessary amounts of reserve ammunition (especially for the three-inch mortars), water, food, and blankets – for it was bitterly cold and even in the shelter of stone sangars one needed something warming to endure the cold and be ready to fight. So to help solve this problem the commandos were to be aided by teams of local Italian muleteers who were to deliver these reserve supplies to the area of the planned forward Commando Brigade headquarters, thus reducing the battle loads of the troops on their approach march to the objectives.

The outline plan was quite simple: the two Commandos, Nos 9 and 40 (RM) Commandos, plus the Belgian troop, would advance in a column led by No 43 – who were to seize Ornito and a subsidiary feature, Point 711 – making an approach march of about two miles from the start line. Meanwhile, No 9 Commando, which was following up, was to bypass Ornito to the east and move to an area to the north of Monte Faito and assault it from that direction, the distance to its objective being about three miles. The Belgian troop was to follow up as the force reserve while a company of an infantry battalion already in the area would provide flank protection for the initial part of the commandos' approach march.

The leading troops of No 43 set off at 6.30 p.m. on 2 February and under bright moonlight made steady progress even though the going was tough and arduous. They encountered some mortar and machine-gun fire from isolated enemy outposts en route; nevertheless they successfully secured Monte Ornito and Point 711 shortly before first light, though not without casualties. Prominent in this action was Captain John Blake, RM, who was later awarded the Military Cross for his outstanding leadership and magnificent example in leading the three assault troops. Over thirty prisoners were captured by the marine commandos in the action.

Meanwhile No 9 was making its way around Monte Ornito, but as the men continued on to get to the north of Ornito they came under machine-gun fire from enemy positions, some sited in derelict stone huts; however, No 4 Troop, supported by Nos 1 and 2 Troops, dealt with this threat, capturing several prisoners in the process. Eventually – it was now daylight – the Commando got to the rocky promontory to the east of the valley, from which, led by Nos 5 and 6 Troops, they planned to mount their final assault on Monte Faito. Captain Leslie Callf of No 5 Troop, takes up the story:

> As 5 and 6 Troops moved up, an extremely heavy stonk covered the whole of the promontory and seemed to continue for ages . . . 5 and 6 Troop kept moving, the remainder of the Commando were trying to scratch some cover in the rocky ground . . . But I preferred to keep moving as fast as possible. This was the most vivid picture of the war, which remains very clearly in my mind. The shells and mortar bombs were exploding on the rocks which covered every foot of the ground. The sight of the almost horizonal flashes with tearing pieces of rock and shrapnel, and the cries of the wounded was horrifying.'[6]

Captain Lucas, still commanding the heavy-weapons troop, was in the area of the forward brigade headquarters and had a clear view of his comrades crossing the valley towards Monte Faito; he recalled the continuous gunfire – hundreds of shells and mortar bombs, some which he reckoned came from multiple-barrel mortars as well as from the enemy's 88-mm guns – and added: 'Clearly No 9 had not achieved surprise!'

This heavy bombardment caused many casualties, but still the survivors kept going towards their objective, Monte Faito. Among those killed were the Commando second-in-command, Major Francis Clark, Lieutenant M. Porter, the intelligence officer, and Regimental Sergeant Major Beardmore. The latter was a most unfortunate case: having been wounded by the shellfire, he was being carried on a stretcher to the rear when they ran into a burst of enemy machine-gun fire and Beardmore was killed instantly. Incidentally, the commando stretcher bearers and medical orderlies did most courageous work that day, especially the former who had the exacting task of evacuating the wounded over the rough and steep slopes, often under gunfire, down the valley for further treatment.

By the time the survivors of the leading troops of No 9 reached the lower slopes of Faito, Colonel Todd, who had also been wounded, along with several of his officers, decided that to try and advance up the mountain would be suicidal – he had no other choice than to order his Commando to withdraw to Monte Ornito and join up with No 43. It was a wise decision as later interrogation of the German prisoners revealed that the enemy had withdrawn to Monte Faito and were most likely to put in a counter-attack.

Later in the morning Brigadier Churchill came forward and ratified Todd's decision that it was not possible to attack Faito without further reinforcements, and ordered a programme of active patrolling in the meanwhile. He also ordered the colonel to withdraw for medical treatment and so command of No 9 passed to the adjutant, Captain M. R. H. Allen. At about 4 p.m. the expected enemy counter-attack on Ornito was launched, centred mainly on the ground occupied by No 43, but they were able to beat it off.

Later the Belgian troop, as yet not engaged directly, was ordered to seize a small tactical feature in the valley between Ornito and Faito; they found the area unoccupied. As darkness fell, the commandos received news that they were to be relieved by the Hampshire Regiment (my old regiment, with whom I subsequently served after the war). This went well and the commandos withdrew back down the valley to a rest area in a ruined village, where they spent two nights before returning to their billets back in the Naples area.

Although they had not achieved their ultimate objective of Faito, they had extended the Allies' line beyond the river Garigliano and the capture of Ornito was a major success, as it was to be a vital tactical feature for the next three months, during which time 46 Infantry Division, with all its divisional resources plus air support, made several attempts to capture Faito, but failed. It was not until May that the mountain was eventually evacuated by the Germans when General Juin's Free French forces advanced through the Auruncian mountains to outflank them as part of Field Marshal Alexander's push to Rome.

Recognition of the commandos' achievement came in a letter from General McCreery to Brigadier Churchill, in which he said;

> ... The fact that the Bosch has reacted so strongly shows that the objectives you captured were of real importance. I want to congratulate your Brigade on the good work during 2–3 February by both Commandos. The country was extremely difficult, and the courage, enterprise and endurance shown by the many parties, after the officer casualties had made control difficult, were in the best traditions of the Commandos. . .[7]

Such then was the story behind the battle honour of MONTE ORNITO, but one must add that in addition to this emblazoned honour on the Commando flag in Westminster Abbey there is also a simple stone memorial cairn to No 9 Commando on Monte Ornito – erected to the memory of the thirty-five officers and men of that Commando who lost their lives in this action. Altogether No 9 lost a quarter of its strength in killed and wounded at Ornito, including 50 per cent of its officers, fortunately a lot of the wounded, including Colonel Tod, were able to rejoin the Commando at their base soon after treatment and care at the nearby field hospital in Naples. They all started training again for their next operation, although they were still much under strength.

The call came on 29 February (1944 was a Leap Year) when Nos 9 and 40 found themselves on their way back to the Anzio beachhead, where the Allies were bogged down under strong German pressure. On arrival back at Anzio on 2 March, in the absence of Brigadier Churchill, the two Commandos came under the direct command of two brigades of 56 Infantry Division – namely 167 Infantry Brigade and 169 Infantry Brigade respectively. Both Commandos were immediately employed on a programme of offensive patrols, which No 40 continued to carry out for the whole period that they were with 169 Infantry Brigade without being involved in a major action.

It was a different story for No 9, however: it continued its patrolling activities with 167 Infantry Brigade until 10 March, by which time they had sent out eleven fighting patrols, killing or capturing sixty-two of the enemy, but losing nineteen men killed or wounded themselves. Colonel Tod then received a warning order that his Commando was to take part in a major operation involving 5 Infantry Division, which had just arrived at Anzio. The original plan for this major operation involved two divisions but was scaled down to a local attack by No 9, whose task was to clear three wadis – only about half a mile from the perimeter of the beachhead – which the Germans had been using as a forming-up point for their counter-attacks. The wadis formed a 'U', with a small hill (*Beechers*) in the centre and some further high ground below the base of the 'U'.

Colonel Tod was given a week to plan and prepare; he decided to divide the operation into three phases. The first phase (codenamed 'Haydon'), to be mounted in darkness, was to tackle the left-hand arm of the 'U'; the second phase ('Charles'), to be carried out at first light, was to attack and clear the enemy off the base of the 'U'; and finally, in phase three ('Laycock'), to clear the enemy off the right-hand arm.

On the successful conclusion of these three phases the Commando was to consolidate in the wadi, establishing an all-round defensive position. There they were to have the support of a regiment of field artillery 'on call'.

Colonel Tod decided to split his depleted Commando into three groups, which he labelled 'squadrons' for this operation. Each squadron consisting of two troops. Some idea of how depleted No 9 was at this time can be gauged from Captain Callf's account of the operation in *The Raiders*, when he recorded that his troop, No 5, consisted of 'one officer [himself] and twenty eight men instead of the full compliment of three officers and fifty-seven men'.

At 2 a.m. on 19 March B and C Squadrons crossed their SL; although they were fired on by machine guns, these were quickly silenced and they occupied '*Haydon*', the left arm of the 'U', with no further problems.

As A Squadron, the one that included No 5 Troop, crossed their start line at first light, they came under enemy artillery fire; as they then passed through their comrades' position on *Haydon*, they came under machine-gun fire from well-dug-in positions on *Charles*, which they attacked under cover of their own No 77 smoke grenades and a final well-spirited charge. Callf recalls:

> I think we must have looked a fearsome sight as we came through the smoke on to them. Many of them were killed and others put their hands up. We suffered three killed and nine injured. I'm not sure of the German casualties, but the official report gave twenty-five killed and twenty-three POWs, which was approximately the strength of No 5 Troop on that day.[8]

The enemy soon reacted to the commandos' successes with an initial bombardment of their positions, followed by counter-attacks that forced Tod to bring all his men back to the *Haydon* position, although the continued enemy shelling made even this limited action difficult. Originally the plan was for the commandos to be resupplied during the day, but this had to be cancelled. This meant that the wounded, who were to be carried back for treatment by the porters bringing up the supplies, were stranded – as a result, Tod decided to use his own men to evacuate the wounded, though of course, with two men to a stretcher, this decision further reduced his force on *Haydon*. Happily, the enemy respected the evacuation of some twelve stretcher cases under the aegis of the Red Cross flag.

During the late afternoon the shelling intensified; as darkness fell a strong enemy attack developed from the direction of *Beechers* onto No 3 Troop's position, supported by two weaker attacks on the flanks of the Commando's position. The latter were beaten off, but the major attack was pushed home with so much determination that at one stage some of the enemy managed to get in-between No 3 Troop and Tod's headquarter's position. However, the attack was repulsed by a force under Major Mike Allen – not only were they able to beat off the enemy attack, but with the help of the other troop in the squadron they also recaptured their original positions, with 'pipes playing and all weapons firing'.

Without immediate reinforcements and resupplies the Commando could not hope to hold on to their positions on *Haydon* – it was impossible, especially as the enemy was obviously determined to regain control of the wadi feature in order to continue their operations against the Anzio beachhead. Indeed orders had come from brigade headquarters to Colonel Tod, just before that last counter-attack, to withdraw, so immediately after the retreat of the enemy Tod issued instructions for a controlled withdrawal back to their original start line. The riflemen were the first to leave and they had to help the walking wounded, as well as carry some of the more badly wounded on improvised stretchers made up from their rifles, greatcoats, and groundsheets. As they withdrew, they were covered by the Bren gunners – in this way the Commando 'thinned out' in an orderly and co-ordinated manner. Support was also forthcoming from the brigade gunners who laid down a barrage to prevent the enemy from following up on the commandos as they withdrew.

In this action, known simply as Operation 'X', No 9 lost a total of nineteen killed, fifty wounded, and four missing, believed killed. On 25 March both No 9 and No 40 Commandos left Anzio and returned to Naples, although a few days later they moved across to the east side of Italy once again, this time to Molfetta.

So ended the Commandos involvement at Anzio. On the subject of Operation X, Mike Allen wrote: 'Of all the various battles, I reckon that few will dispute that the battle of the Anzio wadis was the Commando's Longest Night and Day.' He summarised the operation, pointing out the reason for it, and adding that after Haydon had been captured and held, the Commando had 'disturbed a bees' nest', which the enemy had no intention of giving up and their repeated counter-attacks and deadly accurate shelling meant that No 9 would have been annihilated unless they had been reinforced or withdrew.[9]

Their first mission at Anzio in Operation *Shingle* had been achieved with little difficulty. Their actions on their second visit to Anzio – forceful and highly successful patrolling, followed by their courageous action and sacrifice in the subsequent battle of 'Operation *X*' – completed the commandos' participation in the battle of Anzio.

The next Commando battle honour for action on the mainland of Italy was that of VALLI DI COMACCHIO (Lake Comacchio) when, at the beginning of April 1945, the whole of No 2 Commando Brigade fought together as a brigade. This action was followed by the final battle of the Italian campaign, ARGENTA GAP.

There were other actions fought by this Commando Brigade between those at Anzio and Comacchio, but as they were fought outside the mainland of Italy – namely in the Adriatic, Greece, and the Balkans – they are covered in the next chapter.

Following these latter operations the whole of No 2 Commando Brigade, now commanded by Ronnie Tod (recently promoted to brigadier, was concentrated at Ravenna in Italy and came under the command of the British Eighth Army, commanded by General McCreery, with whom the commandos had operated before when he was a corps commander. McCreery particularly wanted the commandos to take a major part in the final offensive in the spring of 1945 against Field Marshal Kesselring – whose sorely tried but remarkably stubborn soldiers had doggedly and slowly retreated, always making clever use of the terrain, which favoured defensive lines, back to northern Italy to establish positions based on the line of the river Po.

The Allied army of the US Fifth and the British Eighth, still under the overall command of Field Marshal Alexander, was ready to launch its final offensive of the campaign and the mission of No 2 Commando Brigade was to seize a spit of land running between Lake Comacchio and the Adriatic Sea and then tie down the enemy forces on Kesselring's left flank whilst the main Eighth Army attack went through the Argenta Gap to the west of the Lake Comacchio area.

Prior to their call-up for this major operation, codenamed 'Roast', the Commando Brigade had spent some time in the line, where, as usual, they had been carrying out offensive fighting and reconnaissance patrols. They underwent a thorough preparation for Operation Roast and were able to establish a good working relationship, during this training, with the various supporting arms that were to be placed under command of Brigadier Tod for the operation.

It is quite interesting to reflect at this stage on the tremendous differences between this operation and those early raids that had been based on the original concept of Commando operations – the 'butcher-and-bolt' raids. Little did we imagine in 1940 that our future operations would mean being transported in tracked amphibious vehicles and being supported by field artillery and an air attack 'cab rank' (close air support involving detailed integration with the ground forces), as was planned for Roast.

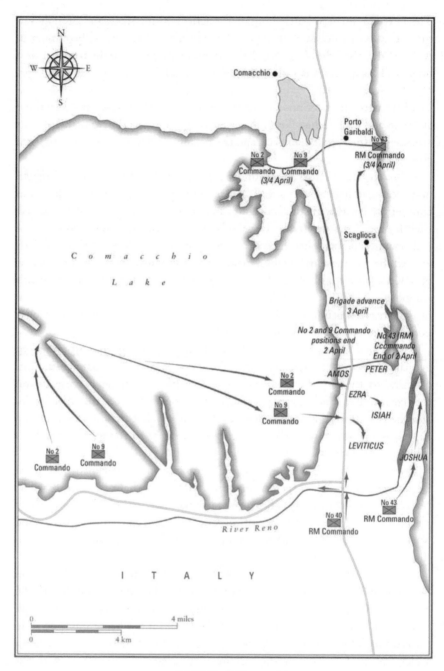

MAP 15. Valli di Comacchio

The operation was quite unique inasmuch as the commandos were to carry out co-ordinated amphibious and land actions at the same time on the coastal spit that was separated from the Adriatic sea by the river Reno and an inland lake, the latter being fed from the south by the Reno. The spit – or the 'Tongue' as it was known by the troops – was about seven miles in length and was reckoned to be held by about 1,200 troops, consisting of a mixed force of troops from the 162 (Turkoman) Infantry Division, bolstered by other units of the German army. Together they had established dugouts and strongpoints throughout the spit as well as on the north bank of the river Reno. The enemy seemed prepared to face attacks from the sea and from the south across the river, but not from the lake itself, hence the reason for planning the amphibious operation. Although mounting the attack from across the lake had the advantage of surprise, there were problems that became evident during the operation: these included the shallowness of the water, which, combined with the deep mud below the water, became a major hazard to the success of the operation, and an artificial dyke running across the approach to the eastern side of the lake.

Tod's outline plan was for No 2 and No 9 Commandos (under the command of Lieutenant Colonel F. W. Fynn and Lieutenant Colonel Dunning-White) – using a mixture of amphibian tracked vehicles, storm boats, and assault boats – to land on the inner side of the Tongue at two separate landing points for two different tasks.

No 2 was to land about three miles up from the base of the lake and capture two bridges, 'Peter' and 'Amos', which were over the Bellochio Canal, in order to cut off the enemy's line of retreat and also prevent any enemy reinforcements coming from the north. No 9's mission was to land to the south of No 2 and to clear the enemy positions in the south-west of the Tongue. Incidentally all the known enemy strongpoints had Biblical codenames.

Lieutenant Colonel L. C. Riches's No 43 (RM) Commando were to clear the enemy in the south-east of the Tongue, meanwhile Lieutenant Colonel R. W. Sankey's No 40 (RM) Commando were to mount a feint attack along the south bank of the river Reno, then one of their troops, supported by tanks, would cross over the river, further to the west, and clear the enemy on the north bank. Once the south of the Tongue had been taken, No 43 would advance on the right and No 2 on the left to the southern bank of the Valetta Canal and secure a position so that No 9 could pass through them and capture Porto Garibaldi. So much for the basic plan, now the preparations.

The four Commandos spent the week before the operation preparing and rehearsing for their various tasks: practising river crossings on the river Unito, mock attacks on strongpoints (using man-pack flamethrowers), and training on the amphibians.

Officially known as Landing Vehicles Tracked (LVTs) there were three main types of amphibians – Fantails, Kangaroos, and Weasels. Fantails were lightly armoured and designed to cross flooded areas and climb muddy banks. Kangaroos were converted Sherman tanks and used as armoured personnel carriers (APCs), whilst the Weasels were smaller tracked personnel carriers and had been very successfully used by No 4 Commando Brigade, prior to Comacchio, on Operation '*Infatuate*', as will be told in the next chapter.

All the amphibians and boats had been assembled in the launching area during the previous two days and the commandos had received a lot of help from one of the infantry battalions in the area for this task. To give all possible support to Nos 2 and 9 Commandos in their boating approach to the Tongue, a special programme of supporting fire from some 150 guns was planned, as well as an air raid on Porto Garibaldi.

Just before midnight Nos 2 and 9 set off. Dudley Cooper, who was in No 2 and won a Military Medal for his part in the action, recalls:

> We were on the Start-Line, where, according to our briefing, we would board the collapsibles (the Goatley assault boats) and be towed by the storm boats up the lake. We would then carry them over the dyke and row ashore on the east bank, after a barrage had been laid down at dawn . . . We got into the boats and the mosquitoes rose off the lake in their millions. The driver of the outboard started the engine and put it into the water. None of the engines would work. Eventually we all got in the water and found mud up to the thigh and water to the lower chest. We pushed and pulled the boats up that lake for hours. The water became deep enough to put the engine (outboard) on. We all climbed in and away we went.[10]

Cooper's experiences that night were not unique. The rest of the 2 Commandos had similar ordeals. The level of water in the lake had been previously lowered by several weeks of drought and this was the major factor for the chaos and confusion outlined above. It was the same for both Commandos: the amphibians were irrevocably bogged down, there was insufficient depth to put the outboards of the storm boats into the water, and as a result the commandos had to haul, shove, and push these unwieldy boats across nearly a mile of glutinous mud – all in the dark. The situation became so bad that at one point both colonels Fynn and Dunning-White asked the brigadier to postpone the operation. Tod, however, reckoned that, as the conditions would remain the same and as they had a well-organised fire plan of support, they must carry on. It was a bold and wise decision.

So in spite of considerable confusion in the dark, verbal orders were shouted out from boat crew to boat crew, and section to section, to carry on. Most of No 2 Commando got to the dyke and started to haul the heavy and unwieldy storm boats over a gap in the dyke, which had been located by the canoeists of the SBS, who also guided the commandos with blue lights. Beyond the dyke the water was deeper and the stormboats were able to use their outboards and tow the commandos, in their Goatley assault boats, almost to their landing places, leaving them only a short distance to paddle. In spite of all the commotion they still caught the enemy completely by surprise and pushed on towards their objectives of the *Peter* and *Amos* bridges; however, by the time they reached *Amos* the enemy had blown it. Nevertheless a formidable stronghold in the neighbourhood was silenced by an assault, which included the use of the flamethrower and several prisoners were captured.

Away to the south of No 2's landing, No 9 Commando – after their equal share of miseries in the mud and the slime – eventually made it to their landing places; supported by heavy artillery fire, which with the mist present at the time created a useful smoke screen, they made their successful attack on the stronghold of '*Isaiah*'. Those in this attack later reckoned that the coincidental smoke screen undoubtedly saved the Commando from heavy casualties.

During that period of confused activity on the lake No 40 had successfully carried out its feint attack as planned. Such was the volume of the covering artillery fire that the enemy apparently thought it heralded a major attack from that direction and consequently was unaware of the commandos' activities on the lake. No 43 had also made good progress on the Tongue: the commandos captured '*Joshua*' and subsequently crossed the river Reno. In the course of these actions they gained quite a haul of prisoners. It was by now broad daylight, with most of the above fighting having taken place after dawn.

No 2 Commando successfully captured *Peter* and subsequently started to mop up the enemy positions one by one, as did No 9. Their successes included the two major strongpoints of '*Ezra*' by No 2 and '*Leviticus*' by No 9, the latter led by their piper playing 'The Road To The Isles'; they captured nearly one hundred prisoners in the process.

Towards the evening the commandos began to consolidate in their positions; they were exhausted with all the problems and exertions of the previous night followed by a whole day's fierce fighting, so they needed to try and get some rest and have some food – emergency rations. The commandos had good reason to be satisfied with their progress to date with most of the Tongue up to the canal in their hands. Fortunately they had a fairly quiet night, with only spasmodic shelling to disturb their sleep. Next day they prepared to continue their advance to the canal itself. They were due to start at 11 a.m., but it was nearly 2 p.m. before they started to move forward – the delay was due to problems getting the supporting tanks forward. However, this delay was more than welcomed by the troops because it meant that they had a bit more rest and another brew of tea!

Initially the advance went well. No 2 Commando was in the lead, with No 43 (RM) Commando on their right. Then No 2 came under heavy artillery and mortar fire, but No 43 was able to successfully clear the hamlet of Scaglioca and pushed on towards the canal. But then they too came under heavy fire from the north bank of the canal.

> The last 600 yards in front of the canal was flat, and almost devoid of cover. When C Troop had committed themselves out in the open they came under heavy fire. Corporal Tom Hunter, in charge of the Bren group of the leading section, spotted that some houses near the south bank were occupied. He seized the Bren, charged forward on his own, and ran through the houses firing from the hip. Six Germans surrendered, and the rest retreated across a footbridge over the canal. Having eliminated this danger, he took up an exposed position on the south bank and engaged the concrete pill-boxes on the other side of the canal with accurate fire to enable the troop to get forward to the houses he had cleared. Inevitably the Spandaus focussed on him and he was killed.[11]

Corporal Hunter was later awarded a posthumous Victoria Cross and was the only royal marine to win this coveted medal in the Second World War. His citation ends with these words: 'Throughout the operation his magnificent courage, leadership and cheerfulness had been an inspiration to his comrades.'

In view of the strength of the enemy on the north bank it was obvious that a major set-piece attack with a larger force than that of the commandos would be required. With this decided the commandos were ordered to consolidate in their present positions until relieved. Accordingly, at last light on 4 April they were relieved by the 24 Guards Brigade, a much larger formation, outnumbering the commandos by about two-to-one. So ended No 2 Commando Brigade's involvement in Operation *Roast*. Although they had not completed their original mission, what they had achieved was, under any circumstances, considerable – apart from anything else, they had captured nearly a thousand prisoners. The success of their actions was reflected in the following message sent to Brigadier Ronnie Tod by General McCreery, commander of the Eighth Army:

My best congratulations to you and all ranks of your force on your most successful operation which has captured or destroyed the whole of the enemy garrison south of Porto Garibaldi. Your operation demanded very careful and detailed planning and skill in execution. All ranks have shown splendid enterprise, endurance and determination to surmount difficulties. Your success has helped the whole army plan. Well done indeed![12]

Prior to Operation *Roast* Brigadier Tod had been warned that a small operation ('*Fry*') was to be carried out by his men at about the same time as the Comacchio mission, but as it was a much smaller operation Tod had earmarked it for Major Lassen's SBS squadron along with some partisans and supporting detachments. The object of *Fry* was the seizure of four small islands on Lake Comacchio and attacks were launched during the night of 4–5 April, but all four islands were found to be unoccupied, although some Germans were caught while they were making a routine check of one of the islands. As a follow up to this raid further raids were planned to tackle a series of machine-gun posts on the narrow road connecting Porto Garibaldi and Comacchio Town. The object of these raids was to cause as many casualties to the enemy as possible and give the impression of an intended major landing. After a couple of aborted attempts on the previous nights four patrols set off on the night 8–9 April. Two of them were under the direct command of Lassen and they landed a couple of miles short of Comacchio Town and headed towards the town, but soon came under machine-gun fire. They silenced the position when Lassen, under covering fire, got near enough to lob a grenade into the enemy strongpoint. A further two machine-gun positions were also silenced under the inspiring leadership of Lassen. They pressed on, but soon came under further fire from another strongpoint; again they successfully engaged it and six of the enemy came out to surrender. Lassen went forward to gather them in, but as he did so a machine gun opened up – its fire inflicted casualties, with Lassen among those wounded; nevertheless, he and his men continued the firefight. Lassen eventually decided to withdraw and he ordered his men to do so, but he himself was near enough to the enemy strongpoint to throw a grenade, wounding more of the enemy and allowing his men to capture this last position. Sadly Lassen by now was mortally wounded, but he refused to be evacuated lest he should impede the withdrawal and endanger further lives. A few weeks after this action, Lassen's gallantry was recognised with the award of the Victoria Cross.

Lassen became the first foreigner in the Second World War to be awarded this highest of all our military honours (he was a Dane), in addition to the three

Military Crosses he had already won. Both Corporal Hunter and Major Lassen were buried with the rest of their comrades killed during Operation *Roast* in the Commonwealth War Graves Commission Cemetery at Argenta. It is fitting to add that there are memorials to both of them. The Italians erected a memorial to 'Caporale Inglese Thomas Hunter, VC, Caduto per la liberation d'Italia' just south of the Valetta Canal near the scene of his action, whilst a stone memorial to Major Lassen is located outside St Peter's Church at Praestofjord in Norway, a forest is also named after him in Israel, and his Victoria Cross is on display in the Museum of Danish Resistance in Copenhagen.

There were some further patrol activities by No 2 Commando Brigade but the actions that qualified for the battle honour of VALLI DI COMACCHIO officially ended on 8 April 1945.

No 2 Commando Brigade then had a couple of days' respite before being involved in the next phase of Field Marshal Alexander's plans for the final push in the Allies' campaign in Italy. This time, unlike the previous operation, which was focused on the spit of land (the Tongue) to the east of Lake Comacchio, the forthcoming operation (codenamed '*Impact*') was to be fought on the land between the west of the lake and the Plain of Lombardy around the town of Argenta, hence the battle title of 'Argenta Gap'.

The basic concept for this operation was to carry out a series of right-hook attacks on the enemy, of which the main opposition was to come from the German 42 Jaeger Division, reinforced by a mixture of other units and supporting arms. The terrain over which the attacks would be mounted was bedevilled with marshlands and canals, but this type of terrain favoured the right-hook tactics coming from the west side of the lake. One of these operations involved No 9 Commando, which was under the command of 56 Infantry Division, and given the task of crossing the south-west side of Lake Comacchio in amphibians then advancing to secure a major crossing over one of the canals, Fosse Marina, towards the Argenta Gap.

The commandos' daylight landing went well and was unopposed, but as they advanced towards the canal they came under fire, mostly from mortars. In spite of this they made steady progress towards their first objective, which was a group of farm buildings that dominated the bridge over the canal. As Lieutenant Peter Bolton's section was nearing the farmyard there was the unmistakable sound of a heavy armoured fighting vehicle starting its engine and then he heard a 'God-almighty bang' followed by a great blast of air. As he dropped to the ground there was another flash and bang and then, to his horror, he found himself staring into the barrel of an enormous gun. Bolton recalls:

In a flash I saw Corporal Daniels of 4 Troop moving towards it. I then heard the characteristic whirr of an engine that wouldn't fire. I immediately thought this was an enemy tank, and on the third flash-bang I saw Corporal Daniels astride the turret, tommy-gun in hand, shouting, 'Hande hoch – Raus, Raus' and out they came. It was not a tank but an SP88 gun which, as we ran in, tried to get clear and to put us off until they got it started, they fired at point blank range across the farmyard into an adjoining barn. We hustled the prisoners inside the building, found some Italians sheltering terrified in the cellar and I raced out again to see if we had secured our objective.[13]

Bolton found, in fact, that there were some more enemy in the adjoining farm building, but they were quickly dealt with and he was then happily able to give the order for the troop piper to play the tune signalling success. By now darkness had fallen and shortly afterwards Bolton was cheered to hear the 'on objective' tunes from the pipers of the other troops of No 9.

After a short rest a co-ordinated commando attack was launched to seize the bridge, but heavy enemy fire halted the commandos' advance. Following a short lull there was a loud explosion – the bridge had been blown by the Germans. By now it was almost dawn and the decision was made to consolidate and dig in. There they stayed all day while plans were made to cross the river that night, 15–16 April, using Goatley assault boats that were to be brought up by the divisional transport for the commandos.

When darkness fell the depleted No 9 made their second attempt and tried to manhandle the boats – four men to a boat – across the road and down the bank to cross the canal. But the road came under heavy fire, inflicting casualties, so it was decided to stop the carrying of boats forward – instead the possibility of wading across the canal was considered.

Lieutenant Mark Clarke went forward to reconnoitre, but he soon returned to confirm that there was only a few inches of water, but plenty of mud: 'He was literally bubbling mud and ooze,' recalled Bolton. Again the decision was made to abandon the crossing and stay put until dawn to reassess the situation.

During the day the decision was made that a full-scale assault would be needed and this task was allocated to the 24 Guards Brigade. However, the men of No 9 kept a careful watch on the enemy throughout the day – when they were relieved, they had the satisfaction of knowing that the information they were able to pass on to the Guards helped them to successfully overcome the enemy defences on the following night. No 9 Commando, already depleted from Operation *Roast*, had severe casualties from this operation on Fosse Marina. Lieutenant Bolton reckoned that, out of his section of twenty-four men, seventeen became casualties. Not all were killed or seriously wounded, but he had only seven left when they were relieved by the Guards. He added: 'Our padre, John Birbeck, was a tower of strength during the operation. His jeep with its two stretchers for our dead and seriously wounded used the open road and his presence was of great assistance.'[14]

Among the awards for this operation was, incidentally, that of the Military Medal to Daniels for his one-man assault on that self-propelled 88 gun. No 9 Commando subsequently went back to Ravenna: it had fought its last battle.

Whilst No 9 had been under the command of 56 Infantry Division and had participated in the action just described, the other Commandos had also been in action, under the command of 78 Infantry Division – they were taking part in the 'right-hook action' that opened up the Argenta Gap and allowed the British 6 Armoured Division to pass through for the final and conclusive stages of the Italian campaign.

Bill Jenkins provides an excellent account of this action, in which both the Royal Marine Commandos and No 2 took part, in his *Commando Subaltern at War*. It was a hard slog for the commandos driving the enemy from the watery flats and plains, but the choice of this hostile terrain and its conditions – in the words of General Lieutenant Graf von Schwern, who was commanding the Germans in this sector – were significant: 'The right hook came upon us as a complete surprise.'[15]

In Jenkins's account of No 43's part he modestly plays down his own part. Suffice it to record here that although he was only twenty years old at the time and a junior section leader, he single-handedly dealt with Spandau (MG 42 machine-gun) positions and was subsequently awarded the Distinguished Service Order, thus becoming the youngest and most junior officer of the Royal Marines to win this high decoration in the Second World War. He therefore joined his Army Commando counterpart, Dennis O'Flaherty, who, as a subaltern in No 3 Commando, became the youngest army officer to receive the same award, the DSO, for his gallantry in the Vaagso raid of 1941.

On 2 May the commandos and all their comrades-in-arms received the welcome news that Field Marshal Kesselring had signed the unconditional surrender of all his forces in Italy.

Next day, 3 May, General McCreery, commanding the Eighth Army, told Brigadier Tod that 'his commandos' successes, in the mud and the water flats round Argenta, had marked the decisive phase of the battle.'[16] Later this fact was acknowledged officially by the award of the battle honour the ARGENTA GAP.

CHAPTER 10

A DRIATIC AND GREECE
(Adriatic Islands, Yugoslavia, Albania, and Greece)

FOR MOST OF ITS LIFE-SPAN No 2 Commando Brigade did not fight as a brigade, for it was invariably split up and the four Commandos fought under the command of different higher formations as we have seen in Sicily and Italy. There was just that one major operation at Lake Comacchio when the Brigade fought with all four Commandos together, but even this one action was short-lived because the follow-up operation, at Argenta Gap, saw No 9 Commando detached yet again to fight under a different command to the rest of the Commandos.

A major detachment occurred in 1944 when No 2 Commando was sent to Vis, a Yugoslav island in the Adriatic (now part of Croatia), whilst their comrades in Nos 9 and 43 Commandos went back to fight at Anzio, as related in the previous chapter. The purpose of sending Jack Churchill's Commando to this island was in response to a desperate appeal made to the British and American higher command to help Tito and his Communist partisans who were faring badly on the mainland of Yugoslavia and had been forced to retreat to strongholds in the mountains. At the same time the Germans had extended their control over Yugoslavia by occupying five of the seven Dalmatian Islands in the Adriatic offshore between Split and Dubrovnik with garrisons of varying strength. It was thought, therefore, that if the Allies could conduct offensive

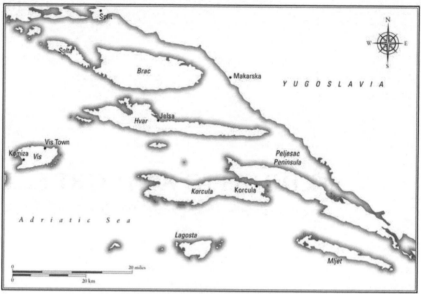

MAP 16. Dalmatian Islands

actions against the Germans on these islands, prevent further occupation, and possibly – with the cooperation and assistance of local partisans – recapture an island, it would not only keep communications with Tito open but hopefully relieve pressure on his Communist partisans on the mainland. It would be a token, but hopefully worthwhile gesture.

On 16 January the advance party of No 2 Commando under Colonel Jack Churchill landed on the island of Vis: one of the two islands not yet occupied by the Germans. (The other unoccupied island being the small one of Lagosta, whilst the five under German rule were, from north to south: Solta, Brac, Hvar, Korcula, and Mljet – a couple of which will be familiar as popular holiday resorts in the post war years.) The rest of Churchill's men soon followed, although No 2 was still under strength, with many of the replacements after the losses sustained at Salerno still completing their Commando training at Bari on the Italian mainland. Churchill's command was strengthened with various detachments, including some from the US Special Operations Group – consisting of second-generation Greek and Slav men who had a knowledge of the complex native language. There was already a large contingent of partisans on the island, who were organised in three 'brigades' under the command of Colonel Millic.

Colonel Churchill, or 'Colonel Jack' as he was soon known to all and sundry, established his headquarters in the port of Komiza, which was also the base for the Royal Navy under the resourceful command of Commander Morgan Giles, with his mixed fleet of MTBs and MGBs, plus some schooners manned by local fishermen/partisans. From the outset Churchill established a very cordial relationship with his opposite numbers Colonel Millic and Commander Morgan Giles, which continued with considerable success. Churchill had three major tasks: firstly, to co-ordinate the defence of the island with his two co-commanders; secondly, to start offensive actions with small raids; and thirdly, to build up a programme of major raids, with the possible capture of an enemy-held island. He wasted no time – within a few days he had carried out a thorough reconnaissance of the island and had liaised with both Millic and Morgan Giles to draw up a comprehensive and co-ordinated defence plan. One of the surprising finds for the commandos arriving on Vis was to learn that they were not the first British servicemen to be stationed on the island. British forces had been based on Vis during the Napoleonic Wars and had built two forts on the island – one of which was aptly named 'Fort George': still standing, it guarded the entrance to Vis harbour and it was to be garrisoned by one of No 2's troops with orders to 'hold out to the last' if attacked. The commandos occupying the fort could faintly make out the royal coat of arms engraved over the main gate and the inscription recording the building of the fort in 1811.

With his initial first task under way, Churchill immediately turned his attention to the task nearer to his heart – raiding. After all, that had been his purpose and aim when he had originally joined the commandos nearly four years earlier. He planned to start with small 'butcher-and-bolt' raids to reconnoitre and test the enemy defences and then build up a programme of bigger raids involving larger numbers of the partisans.

Living on an island with the Communist partisans was a new and unique experience for the commandos. Ted Kelly was among the first arrivals and recalls his initial reaction:

The world of the Partisans was very strange to us; it had an almost theatrical quality. The walls of the buildings were daubed with slogans and communist symbols, 'Zivio Druff Tito' (Long live Comrade Tito) took pride of place over 'Smrt Fascismo' (Death to Fascism) and 'Slobudu Nasroda' (Freedom for the People). Women soldiers carrying guns were a novelty, and the Serbo-Croat language with unpronounceable collections of consonants like 'crvna' was totally incomprehensible to us.[1]

Ted and his comrades found several other obstacles to closer understanding with their new Communist allies, not least their treatment, which they considered 'barbaric', of any captured German prisoners – for the partisans not only ill-treated them but had no hesitation in carrying out summary executions. However, although the commandos could not condone this treatment, they could understand it when they heard the stories of how the Yugoslavs had suffered under the Germans, who indiscriminately murdered and burnt villages to the ground in their reprisal attacks, in which women and children also perished.

In the mixed partisan army sex was strictly taboo and any transgressions were punishable by death. There was the case cited by Ross Hook, MC, the padre with No 43 (RM) Commando, in which he recorded: 'Some months after arriving on Vis, some men of No 2 Commando had to watch while the partisans shot three women before their eyes for the crime of pregnancy.'[2]

However, in spite of these problems, co-operation and fellowship between the commandos and the partisans gradually developed into a cordial relationship and they enjoyed many social gatherings together over a jug – or two – of local wine. Such were some of the friendships made that after the war several of the commandos revisited Vis to meet up with their old comrades-in-arms.

Just ten days after his arrival on the island and having seen to the first priority of the defence of the island, Churchill personally led his first commando raid on Hvar. It was the first of a mixture of operations undertaken by the commandos in the coming months. Bob Bishop, in his own style, summarised some of these wide-ranging activities:

> During the coming months a wide variety of activities would unfold involving conventional assaults on fixed positions with the classic bayonet charge; pirate-style boarding parties going after any German supply ship that floated; quick in-and-out raids on isolated enemy garrisons, long reconnaissance patrols; manning coast-watching positions in assorted locations, and employed as construction workers helping to build an airstrip.[3]

On the first raid Churchill, with three troops of No 2 plus men from the US Special Operations Group and some partisan guides, made a night attack on an enemy outpost near the port of Milna on Hvar. They achieved complete surprise and without loss brought back four German prisoners – who, being glad to be in British hands and not in those of the partisans, were quite forthcoming during their interrogation. Churchill got details of the Germans' strength and dispositions on the island of Hvar. The main formation providing all the garrisons on Hvar and the other islands was the German 118 Mountain Division, but most importantly the prisoners said that plans were in hand to occupy Vis.

A firm believer in the old army adage that 'attack was the best form of defence', Colonel Jack decided that although he did not have the resources, either in men or naval landing craft, for large raids at that time, he could still resort to an offensive programme of small 'butcher-and-bolt' raids. So twice in the next five days his commandos revisited Hvar successfully, using schooners manned by partisans, whom he found co-operative and capable sailors; of course, they also had first-hand knowledge of the local waters. On the second of these raids, again led by Colonel Jack, the commandos lost their first officer, Captain Jack Bare, who was mortally wounded searching the upper rooms of a German outpost; he died on the schooner during the return voyage. In spite of this setback the commandos accounted for the entire crew of the post: those not killed in the attack surrendered and were brought back to Vis.

Captain Bare was subsequently the first of the British force killed in action to be buried in the Old British Naval Cemetery at Vis. During the commandos' stay on the island a memorial plaque was erected with these words:

> AFTER MORE THAN ONE HUNDRED YEARS
> BRITISH SOLDIERS AND SAILORS
> WHO FOUGHT AND DIED FOR THEIR COUNTRY'S HONOUR
> ON THE SEAS AND ISLANDS OF DALMATIA
> HAVE AGAIN BEEN LAID TO REST
> IN THIS ISLAND CEMETERY 1944
> HERE WE LIE DEAD BECAUSE WE DID NOT CHOOSE
> TO LIVE AND SHAME THE LAND FROM WHICH WE SPRUNG
> LIFE TO BE SURE IS NOTHING MUCH TO LOSE
> BUT YOUNG MEN THINK IT IS AND WE WERE YOUNG

And Captain Jack Bare was one of those young men

Churchill followed up these raids on Hvar with a couple of small reconnaissance raids on the island of Brac in early February and from information brought back he was able to start planning for a larger raid on this island in the near future. Meanwhile, a young subaltern, Barton, with ten men, — including a signaller, so that he would be able to keep in contact with Commando headquarters — was sent to the island of Brac to harass the garrison there. Eric Buckmaster, a veteran of No 2, sent to me a copy of Barton's original typed report of the raid and the following is a summary of that report.

Having successfully landed Barton contacted the local partisan leader and from him got updated on the German garrison, which totalled nearly two hundred troops One interesting piece of information concerned the garrison commandant: he lived on his own in a house in the village Nerezisce, and he was unpopular with the local people and not often seen. He had the habit of having some of his officers each night to dine with him at seven, but they departed after the meal leaving him alone except for his personal staff of three soldiers/ batmen; the owners of the house also lived in the house. From a further reconnaissance of the layout of the house and neighbourhood carried out by one of the partisans, Barton learned that there were no sentries on the house, but there was a 6 p.m.–6 a.m. curfew enforced by German foot patrols. Barton decided to act immediately and assassinate the German commandant. Next night he set off with two partisans to approach the commandant's house from the north of the village, but they were challenged by a curfew patrol – rather than risk a gun battle he decided to quickly and quietly withdraw. However, next day he found out that the local shepherds, whose flocks grazed on the hills outside the village by day, were allowed to bring their sheep into the village during the early part of the curfew, so it was arranged by the partisans that Barton would dress up and mingle in with these shepherds to beat the curfew. The ruse worked and Barton and his two partisans successfully got to the commandant's house undetected. They found the front door locked, but when Barton knocked a woman appeared and Barton and one of the two partisans dashed in whilst the other partisan remained outside as a sentry. Initially they could not find the commandant – they were told that he had gone out to dine, but they did not believe this so decided to search the house more thoroughly. In one of the rooms that had appeared to be empty, Barton's eye was attracted by something shining near the wall, which he quickly saw to be an Iron Cross on a man's tunic, and he gave it a burst. The man fell to the floor and Barton gave him another burst.

By now there was pandemonium in the house and other partisans in the house pulled Barton away and together with the sentry outside they quickly left the house and made for the open country before any enemy reaction to their raid could be taken. They got clear away from the village before the curfew patrols and sentries appeared and all three got back safely to their hide-out and eventually to Vis. It was a most successful joint commando–partisan operation. Although Barton obviously was not able to personally check and identify the fallen German, subsequently full evidence was furnished and confirmed that the commandant had been killed and his name, rank and even the place of his burial was published.

Following Barton's daring raid there was an outburst of sabotage and even ambushes by the partisans on the island of Brac — this was just the kind of local reaction to their raids that Colonel Jack had hoped would happen. There was no doubt that the Germans became quite worried and the raids made them think that the commando force was much greater than it really was. Churchill's force was then strengthened when, towards the end of February, No 43 (RM) Commando arrived on Vis. Concurrent with their arrival was that of Brigadier Tom Churchill with his brigade headquarters, which then allowed Colonel Jack to concentrate solely on his role as commanding officer of No 2. With the arrival of the Royal Marine Commando to take over some of the commitments of the defence of Vis, Colonel Jack was now also able to commit his whole Commando on a full-scale raid on the German garrison based in the village of Grohote on Solta for which he had already been preparing.

Fortunately by this time Commander Morgan Giles had managed to add both LCIs and LCAs to his mixed fleet and Brigadier Tom Churchill was in a position to get air support from the Allied Air Forces based on the mainland of Italy for the commandos' future operations, which he duly did for his brother's raid on Solta. Thus this raid was to be the first truly combined operation of the Adriatic campaign.

Colonel Jack had already been sending reconnaissance parties to Solta for periods of up to a week at a time. There, with the assistance of the local partisans, they had gathered a wealth of intelligence information on the strength, dispositions, and habits of the German garrison. One of the leaders of these reconnaissance raids was Captain 'Ianto' Jenkins, a troop leader in No 2; using special wireless sets he had been able to send detailed and up-to-the-minute information on the enemy back to Colonel Jack's planning team back on Vis. Unfortunately, on the way back to their hide-out from their final 'recce', Jenkins's party ran into strong enemy opposition and as a result Jenkins was subsequently reported 'missing', feared killed, although the rest of the party eventually did manage to safely return to Vis.

Colonel Jack's force for the Solta raid consisted of No 2 Commando, plus the heavy-weapons troop of No 43, detachments from the US Special Operations Group, and the partisans. The basic plan was to land by night and, guided by local partisans, surround the garrison at Grohote and be in place to attack by dawn. At 6 a.m. an air strike would bomb the enemy position and before the enemy had time to recover, the commandos would immediately assault the village and destroy the garrison.

On the night of 17–18 March Churchill's force set sail in LCIs, which were towing LCAs; nearing the island they were signalled into the right landing places by Lieutenant Macminamin of No 2 who had been on the previous reconnaissance raids with Captain Jenkins and subsequently landed back on the island just prior to this raid. His role was not only to guide in the landing craft, but also to confirm that the enemy dispositions had not changed – his torch signals were therefore reassuring. The landings, shortly after midnight, were successful although it was hard going for all, but especially those carrying the heavy weapons and others detailed to carry extra ammunition, including three-inch mortar bombs. Guides led the commandos and the other detachments inland to previously selected positions outside Grohote; before dawn all were in position ready for the assault.

Stan Buckmaster – who had joined his brother, Eric, who was already in No 2, the pair of them joining the illustrious list of 'commando brothers', which included the Churchill brothers and the Pascale brothers in No 4 Commando already mentioned in the context of the Dieppe raid – provides a full and vivid description of the raid as experienced by the average commando soldier in both Messenger's and Jenkins's books.

Stan lists the items most riflemen had to carry; some had to carry six three-inch mortar bombs, which, together with their own ammunition, water, and emergency rations, etc. came to a payload of nearly one hundred pounds per man. (Way back in 1942 when we in No 4 were training for an operation we all had to carry heavy loads – those men with the exceptionally heavy loads were labelled 'pack mules'.) Stan Buckmaster provides a clear picture of the landing coast-line: 'Beyond the narrow stretch of shingle a rocky escarpment rose steeply for about one hundred feet, and across its face a boulder strewn path ran towards the top at an angle of about 45 degrees or so.' It was hard going for all, especially the pack mules, and those who had to manhandle the Commando's heavy weapons. However, they all kept going, fortunately not detected nor delayed, although they did take plenty of rests en route. Nevertheless they all got to their pre-selected positions covering the village of Grohote in good time. Thankfully those carrying the extra mortar bombs were able to drop off their loads en route at the selected mortar positions. There was one small snag, however, when a German early-morning patrol bumped into one of the commando positions and there was an exchange of fire – so complete surprise was lost. The three-inch mortars fired a few rounds into the enemy positions but had to stop because the air strike was due on the garrison in a few minutes' time.

Just before the arrival of the Kitty Hawks Colonel Jack, using a loudhailer (borrowed from the Royal Navy), called upon the garrison commander to give up and surrender, warning them that if they did not they would be bombed – this demand was made by one of the German-speaking commandos. At about this time some thirty-six Kitty Hawk light bombers had arrived over Grohote. They flew in low, just over the roof tops, then swept upwards into the sky to form a 'cab rank' ready for their strike. As no response was received nor noted from the garrison, the air attack was ordered by the ground control officer who was with Colonel Churchill.

The air attack began, first strafing the enemy positions with their 20-mm cannons, followed by low-level bombing. Whilst the aircraft were making their attack the commandos fixed bayonets and got ready to leave their positions for their assault as soon as the last aircraft had finished its run. This immediate action was, undoubtedly, the key to the success of the operation. As the last Kitty Hawk peeled off and the flight set off back to Italy the commandos rushed into the main street and began their rehearsed house-clearing action. The enemy still had their 'heads down'; there was little resistance. Among the early captives was the German commandant and he was brought to Colonel Churchill, who demanded that the Germans stop fighting, lay down their arms, and surrender — assuring them that they would be British captives and not handed over to the partisans.

Stan Buckmaster ended his full description of the raid with these words:

> Eventually we were ready to return to the beach and the prisoners were lined up, some being detailed to assist carrying the heavy equipment. Colonel Jack Churchill took his place at the head of the column and we marched away from Grohote to the tune of 'The Road to the Isles' played by the Colonel on his bagpipes. We lost two men killed and several severely wounded, but we had captured over a hundred prisoners and they had lost at least eight dead and many wounded.[4]

It had been a wholly successful combined operation and the three services had worked well together. Brigadier Tom Churchill was pleased with the outcome and in the days and weeks to follow kept up the pressure on the German-occupied islands with raids on Korkula, Brac, Hvar, and Mljet, but this raid on Solta was a significant turning point in the commandos' offensive raiding campaign.

Mention was made earlier of boarding parties on the navy's MTB sorties against the German shipping in the Dalmatian waters. Bob Bishop explains:

> Colonel Jack added a new dimension to the lives of his boys – PIRACY. Lieutenant Stilwell led the first of what was to be many boarding parties and swarmed aboard a German chartered schooner taking seventeen enemy soldiers

prisoner, after what Private Jakeman later described as only a 'third class fight'. These sojourns became very popular with the personnel of No 2.[5]

Bishop explains that the main reason for this popularity was that the commandos on board lived on naval food and rations, which were much better and more plentiful than the army rations they had on Vis. There was another bonus: on board HM ships the commandos were entitled to the navy's daily tot of rum, not infrequently they were also able to get duty-free cigarettes.

In mid-March Brigadier Churchill received information from the partisans on Hvar that the Germans were pulling out of that island. Although he had doubts about the accuracy of such information he did, however, decide to mount a full-scale raid to destroy the German garrison in the town of Jelsa on the island. On 22 March 1944 a force consisting of No 43 (RM) Commando, plus detachments from the US Special Operations Group, and a strong contingent of about four hundred partisans, organised into two 'battalions', duly set off from Vis in daylight, though they were well protected by an escort of MTBs. There were no commandos from No 2 on this raid and it was the first raiding operation for No 43. The objective of the raid was that German garrison in Jelsa, which was located in the north of Hvar about four miles from the south coast.

The commandos were aboard LCIs and the partisans on schooners; the marine commandos landed on the south coast unopposed just before last light, but unfortunately the partisans did not land until three hours later. During the late afternoon the RAF had bombed the garrison location at Jelsa and there were subsequent reports received stating that there were signs of the Germans moving out of the area.

During the night both the commandos and the partisans moved towards their respective objectives; as they neared Jesla they were involved in some fierce firefights, but both the commandos and the partisans had the better of these encounters. The commandos killed several of the enemy and captured four prisoners plus a well-laden mule-train loaded with signals equipment, ammunition, and personal luggage, whilst the partisans were engaged in hand-to-hand fighting and accounted for some sixteen of the enemy killed and a 'bag' of over thirty prisoners. The partisans lost four killed, one of whom was a woman soldier. In the final withdrawal to re-embark, the Commando's three-inch mortar unit had the unexpected satisfaction – in the early morning light – of spotting a group of Germans, obviously attempting to escape to the east of the island. They had stopped for a rest and were bunched together: it was too good a target to ignore. They quickly set up their mortars and their prompt and accurate shooting resulted in fifteen Germans killed.

It had been a successful raid and Colonel Simmonds – the commanding officer of No 43, who was also in overall command – was well pleased with the results with fifty Germans killed and eighty brought back as prisoners. As a result of this raid and the previous one on Solta, the Germans no longer felt it safe to move freely around their islands and began to reorganise their island defences, siting strongholds on high ground with wire-fence perimeters and minefields around fortified bunkers. In spite of these changes the commandos and the partisans continued their policy of reconnaissance raids; the partisans began to play a greater part in the raids and with the help of detachments from No 2, Morgan Giles' MTBs, with close support from the RAF, carried out some very successful raids on Korcula and other islands.

However, there was a strong reaction from the Germans as the Luftwaffe, based on the mainland, carried out a series of retaliatory raids on Churchill's defensive positions on Vis, inflicting military and civilian casualties as well as material damage. The ack-ack defences were subsequently bolstered by two batteries of heavy anti-aircraft artillery. That was not all – an airfield was constructed and the commandos were drafted in to help with the labour. A squadron of the RAF regiment also arrived to guard it, so with the arrival of No 40 (RM) Commando in May as well, Vis had become a 'formidable fortress' and its garrison was soon able to boast that they were the 'Malta of the Adriatic'. To cheer the troops up in their off-duty hours a cinema was installed and an island newspaper, *Vis-à-Vis*, was published, whilst other amenities were also introduced to sustain the troops' morale and well-being.

Militarily, there was one disappointing raid on 23 May when a strong commando force of Nos 2 and 43 Commandos plus a detachment from No 40 (RM) Commando raided Mljet, where it had been reported by the partisans that the Germans held three strongpoints on the island, manned by about 150 troops. Unfortunately the raid was unsuccessful for two reasons. Firstly, bad weather upset the timetable and the operation was postponed for two days. Secondly, after landing and a most exhausting approach march over the steepest and precipitous terrain of all the islands, the commandos unfortunately discovered that the partisans' information was inaccurate. There were no Germans in any of the three objective areas – they had been withdrawn to defensive positions on the north coast, which were in range of supporting German guns on the mainland. Brigadier Tom Churchill was not prepared to risk heavy casualties attacking the enemy under these conditions, especially as his men were exhausted after their gruelling and frustrating approach march, so he gave orders to withdraw back to the beaches and re-embark. In the event No 43 did suffer casualties in this withdrawal: one of their parties got caught in an enemy minefield, resulting in one marine being killed and a further eight were captured. Overall the raid was a disappointing failure, although it maintained the pressure on the occupying German forces. Two days later Brigadier Churchill left Vis to fly back to England to report on the general situation.

Meanwhile on the mainland of Yugoslavia the Germans had launched a well-planned airborne operation on Tito's headquarters in Bosnia. Although the Germans failed to capture the marshal he was forced to flee the area; in desperation he sent an urgent request to both the Allied forces headquarters and to the partisan commanders on Vis for an attack to be mounted in Dalmatia to try and relieve the pressure on him and his forces on the mainland. The RAF gave immediate support by bombing and shooting up German targets in Bosnia. Colonel Jack Churchill, now back in charge on Vis, immediately convened a joint British–partisan planning team to prepare a combined operation on the main occupied island of Brac, where some 1,200 troops of the 118 Mountain Division, supported by artillery units, were now garrisoned.

The Germans were located in three main areas, with one garrison in the north of the island and another in the east, although their strongest position was based on three hilltops in the centre of the island near Nerezisce, where the young commando officer, Barton, had carried out his daring assassination of the local commandant earlier in the campaign. There the Germans had established strongpoints, which were well fortified and located to give mutual fire support. These three positions were known by their respective heights in metres as 'Points 542, 622, and 648'.

On the night of 1 June the raiding force set sail from Vis aboard a fleet of some forty-five vessels – local schooners, landing craft, and MTBs. The landing force for Operation '*Flounced*', as it was coded, consisted of No 43 (RM) Commando, plus the heavy-weapons troop from No 40, about 2,500 partisans, a battery of twenty-five-pounders, and some mountain guns from the Raiding Support Squadron, who had recently joined the commandos on the island. No 2 was not committed to this operation, but Colonel Jack Churchill was the overall British commander.

On landing, two partisan battalions set off separately for the garrisons in the north and the east of the island; although they failed to capture their two objectives, their action did prevent the Germans there from dispatching reinforcements to the main enemy positions near Nerezisce.

By dawn on 2 June No 43 was in position to assault its objective on Point 542 and the two partisan battalions were also in place to assault their respective targets. Just after dawn a flight of RAF Hurricanes flew in to attack the three objectives, but the enemy fortifications were so well constructed that the bombing did not cause much material damage, and by the time the commandos and partisans had got to the perimeter defences of wire and minefields the Germans were ready for them with their Spandaus. All three assaults were repulsed and further action was called off. However, Churchill decided to mount an assault on the single position of Point 542 with all three groups – No 43 and the two partisan battalions. Sadly, for a variety of reasons – not least being the problems in communications within the mixed force – the planned support for No 43 by the partisans did not materialise and they were again forced to withdraw and fell back to take up a position of all-round defence for the night of 2–3 June.

During that night reinforcements from Vis were sent to Brac, including the three reserve troops of No 40, under the command of Lieutenant Colonel 'Pop' Manners, two hundred partisans and two more twenty-five-pounders. During the morning Colonel Jack made a personal reconnaissance of the enemy positions and decided to make a major assault on the key stronghold at Point 622, the capture of which would help the fall of the other two enemy positions. Unfortunately his plan did not meet with the approval of the partisans and apparently much time was lost arguing, until at last a compromise was reached whereby the commandos would attack Point 622 and the partisans engage, but not assault, the other two enemy positions. There was a subsequent misunderstanding over the orders to the commandos of No 40: they understood that the assault would be carried out by No 43 alone without their support. As a result, although Point 622 was captured, it could not be held. In the fighting that followed, Colonel Manners was mortally wounded, whilst Colonel Jack – who during a German counter-attack played the tune, 'Will You No Come Back Again', to encourage his troops – was stunned by a German grenade and on regaining consciousness found himself a prisoner.

The raiders could do no more – 'Enough blood had been spilt' – so under the command of Lieutenant Colonel Simmonds the force withdrew to the beach, where a force from No 2 Commando had been landed to provide a beachhead for the raiders to re-embark and return to Vis. So ended the raid on Brac.

In spite of many brave and courageous actions by commandos and partisans alike, the assault on the island was a tactical disappointment, although strategically it achieved its aim, for not only had the Germans been unable to send troops from Brac and the other Dalmatian islands to the mainland to support their hunt for Tito, but now they were so concerned over the security of their forces on the islands that they actually reinforced these garrisons with troops from the mainland.

On a lighter note, Hilary St George Saunders ends his account of the capture of Colonel Churchill and the Brac operation with this snippet: 'Colonel Jack's sword and bagpipes had been taken from him; they were presently on exhibition in a glass case in Vienna.'[6]

Finally, Tito, with the help of the Royal Navy, was evacuated with his staff from the mainland and brought to Vis, where he was greeted by a guard of honour provided by No 2 Commando.

A few days later that Commando was relieved of its duties on the island and returned to Italy for rest and refit; they had done a great job in those six months on Vis, carrying out a role that was truly a Commando one – indeed many of their veterans recall their tour of duty on the island as the most fascinating time of their war. For Stan Buckmaster it was 'something that I suspect few of us would have missed'. Undoubtedly all the commandos involved were glad to have the opportunity to carry out the proper role and intended purpose of Commando raiding operations. What's more, they had the unique experience of operating with the partisans, plus they had freedom of action instead of being tied to formal operations and being misused as 'infantry of the line'. Although the army commandos left Vis towards the end of June, their royal marine comrades continue their raiding operations from Vis until the middle of October.

In Italy No 2 Commando was encamped near Monopoli on the east coast; there they received some reinforcements while some of the officers and other ranks even managed to get away and enjoy the excitement of qualifying as parachutists at a nearby RAF parachute training school. However, Colonel Ted Flynn, who had taken over command of No 2, following the loss of Colonel Jack, did not have to wait long for the call to action.

For on 28 July No 2, plus detachments, left Italy to raid a German garrison sited on a high ridge overlooking the village of Himara, about four miles from the town of Spilje, on the coast of Albania. The raid was part of Allied plans to harass the German occupying forces that were beginning to feel the pressure of the Russian advance into the Balkans, making their continued occupation in Yugoslavia, Albania, and Greece precarious.

The commandos landed unopposed that night and after a tortuous approach march arrived at their forming-up position ready to make a dawn attack on the enemy strongpoint. Bob Bishop records that their approach was 'announced by the incessant barking of local "pro-German dogs" resulting in the enemy on top of the ridge using their technique of searching fire with their MG 42 machine guns every time their furry friends started to bark'.[7]

However, this fire was ineffective: the commandos suffered no casualties and so were able to assault the objective as planned, though they did experience problems with the barbed-wire perimeter and encountered anti-personnel 'S' mines as well. Unfortunately the planned naval gunfire support did not materialise, but nevertheless the attack continued. It was only partially successful because the position was not completely destroyed, although the enemy did suffer heavy losses. The thirty-odd German survivors were overwhelmed two days later by local partisans. The commandos meanwhile disengaged and successfully made their way back to the re-embarkation beach without further problems, thanks to the action of Captain Stilwell's troop, which beat off a German counter-attack. In this action the Commando lost twenty killed and nearly sixty wounded.

During the next two months several operations were planned but all were cancelled, often because of the rapidly changing situation in the region: although the Germans were withdrawing their retreat was slow and their rearguards fought bravely in defensive positions that were well sited on terrain that greatly favoured defence — so a few determined men could hold up much larger forces with comparative ease.

However, the commandos' next major operation on the Albanian coastline was centred on the port of Sarande, opposite the island of Corfu, where the occupying Germans had been forced to relinquish control of the south by the Greek partisans. Confined to the north, the seizure of Sarande would therefore deny the Germans in the north of Corfu the only chance they had of contact and a successful evacuation to the mainland.

Information on the enemy forces in the area of Sarande itself was scanty: it was thought that their numbers were in the order of three hundred, but there were other enemy units stationed further north. The intelligence information was so sketchy that Brigadier Churchill decided to send Captain Parsons and two other officers from No 2 over to the area two days before the operation to find out more about the enemy and to then meet the commando force on the beach when they arrived and update them on the enemy dispositions; it proved to be a very wise decision.

The attacking force, under the command of Brigadier Tom Churchill, consisted of No 2 Commando and attached troops, including some gunners with four 75-mm guns and a detachment from the Raiding Support Squadron with their heavy weapons.

The basic plan was for the commandos to land in a cove, *Sugar Beach*, which was about six miles north of Sarande, then advance up a valley (which has subsequently been named *Commando Valley*) until they met the main road, which they would then take to the port and there with the assistance of the local partisans seize the town.

On the night of 22 September they set sail from a little fishing port just south of Bari. Unfortunately they had not got far when the flotilla ran into a storm and Churchill had doubts about whether they should continue; the winds and the seas settled down, however, and they were able to proceed. Thanks to good navigation they arrived just off the cove and were welcomed by Captain Parson's torchlight flashes. On landing, though, Parsons had bad news for Churchill: he had found out that the Germans had the road to Sarande well covered with field and medium guns that shelled anything using it. More importantly, instead of only three hundred troops in the port area, they numbered four to five hundred at least. As a result of this information Churchill's original plan – which envisaged an operation of about forty-eight hours' duration – had to be scrapped: to carry out the original plan would demand a far greater force. Churchill decided to hold positions on the hills on the south side of 'Commando Valley' and so secure the landing beaches while reinforcements were sought and dispatched. The troops of No 2 set off to advance up the valley and, guided by Captain Parsons, took up positions that he had reconnoitred beforehand. The bad news about the enemy was not the only problem, for soon after landing the heavens opened and down came the rain. By early morning the commandos were in position, although it had taken Captain Webb's troop almost seven hours to reach their hilltop position on Point 586.

Meanwhile Brigadier Churchill had signalled headquarters in Italy for reinforcements including No 40 (RM) Commando and some heavier field guns, needed for support and to engage the enemy positions that were out of range of the guns they presently had.

Having established their base in the valley, secured the landing beach, and organised their programme of patrols, Colonel Fynn's men, already soaked to the skin, had to endure even more rain whilst waiting for reinforcements and supplies – particularly food, as they had landed with only forty-eight hours' worth of rations, enough for the original planned operation.

Two days later No 40 (RM) Commando arrived and they took up positions on the hills to the south of No 2, within a few hundred yards of the enemy outposts. The guns, however, did not arrive for another three days. Throughout this period the commandos had to suffer torrential rain; Tom Churchill, who had served in Burma before the war and experienced the monsoons there, reckoned that he had never seen anything like it, and recorded:

Every valley became a torrent, and the soldiers were wet through all the time. There was no cover to be had for there were no houses, so it was impossible to dry anything. The men had one groundsheet each and one blanket. The blanket was permanently soaking . . . The men's boots were soaking also, and soon began to break open owing to the rockiness of the mountains and the dampness.[8]

Eric Groves of No 2 describes how he and his pal had problems trying to get shelter and make a tent with their groundsheets and gas capes under a ledge just eighteen inches above the ground level. They eventually succeeded and so were able to crouch down and brew up using solid-fuel burners They then tried to get some sleep, but there was 'an increase in rain followed by thunder and lightning. The gas cape flapped and tipped water down my back.' In spite of their efforts to reset their 'tent' they finally had to give in and stick it out until the dawn, when they were relieved and able to make their way down to the beach area to get some cooked food. The rain eventually stopped and the sun even came out. Groves went on: 'This was a great day of recuperation, we swam in the clear waters of the bay, lay in the sun and dried out and watched the landing craft unloading further supplies. All our earlier misery was forgotten, our clothes were dry, we had clean socks and, most important of all, well-shod feet'.[9] (The latter part was thanks to a supply of new boots.)

Nevertheless, in those first nine days in Albania no fewer than 130 of the force had to be evacuated back to Italy with trench foot and other ailments, while nearly 200 were being treated in the beachhead for minor disorders.

Fortunately the weather began to improve and plans were being made for the ultimate attack on Sarande. Brigadier Churchill, under these circumstances, was forced to take his time in his preparations, which included liaison with the local partisans for their full co-operation in the forthcoming operation. This extra time also allowed Churchill to get destroyers of the Royal Navy to provide close-fire support for the attack and he received the added bonus of further reinforcements, including a company of No I Parachute RAF Levies.

On 8 October the two Commandos, Nos 2 and 40 (RM), supported by the partisans and the RAF levies, moved to positions to launch their assault, scheduled to start at 4.30 a.m. next morning (9 October). The final plan was quite simple: No 2 on the left flank was to capture the formidable German battery just outside the town; No 40 was to capture the port; the RAF Levies were to make a landing and mount a diversionary attack on a German position just south of Sarande; and three hundred partisans were to attack the German garrison of Delvine to the north of Sarande, while a smaller party of partisans were to cut off the main road to the north of Sarande and so prevent any enemy reinforcements coming from that direction.

Churchill had established his headquarters on a hilltop overlooking Sarande and subsequently had a grandstand view of the battle. At 4 a.m. the artillery barrage began and it was supplemented by a spectacular display of pyrotechnics, rockets, and lights, organised by an enterprising engineer officer from the New Zealand Army, which was to simulate noises akin to a whole brigade attacking. Apparently it was most successful and Churchill recorded that he had never seen or heard anything like it.

At 4.30 the barrage was lifted and the commandos started on their respective attacks. As dawn broke Churchill heard on his wireless that No 2 had dealt with the enemy outposts en route to the German battery position though the going was proving to be tough and their advance was being slowed down. No 40 had also dealt with the German outposts on their front but were beginning to meet stiff resistance in the town itself. About midday No 2 closed with the battery but, sadly, Captain Parsons – who had done such a splendid reconnaissance prior to the landing of Fynn's original force – was killed in the final assault just twenty yards from the guns. His second-in-command, Lieutenant Jim Coyle, took over but he too was killed a few minutes later. Churchill commented: 'With such leadership there was no stopping the men, and all four guns were in our hands in minutes.'

Meanwhile, No 40, under the leadership of Lieutenant Colonel R. W. Sankey, came under withering machine-gun fire as they were crossing some open ground at the approach to the town itself. It appeared to be coming from a large building that was covered with red crosses, so Colonel Sankey called for artillery and mortar fire on this target. This proved most effective and the marine commandos were able to continue their advance, clearing the town, street by street, until they got to the centre where the German commander surrendered in person and called on his troops to lay down their arms. Churchill recalls: 'By half past five, the place [Sarande] was in our hands and the battle was over.'[10]

It had been eighteen days since Colonel Flynn's original force of just No 2 Commando and those few supporting guns had originally landed on *Sugar Beach* – eighteen days during which they and the subsequent reinforcements had steadfastly – and with typical 'Tommy' good humour – endured the most severe and difficult conditions of the brigade's eighteen months of action in Sicily, Italy, and the Adriatic. Although they had their own losses, the final tally of German losses was considerable: according to Churchill the commandos had taken 650 prisoners in Sarande and the neighbouring hills, while the partisans captured a further 250.

Immediately after the Sarande operation a mixed force from Nos 2 and 40 Commandos was sent to Corfu to assist in the liberation of the island. This operation was most successful, it yielded another 250 prisoners and provided a fitting finale to the commando operations that merited the award of the ADRIATIC battle honour.

Following their exploits at Sarande and Corfu the commandos returned to their base in Italy to prepare ultimately for their involvement at Comacchio.

Meanwhile it is time to relate the activities of No 9 Commando during the period that it was detached from the rest of No 2 Commando Brigade.

Their first major operation after returning from Anzio was what might be called a 'mercy mission', in that it was a raid to bring back some of our prisoners of war who had escaped and were hiding out behind the enemy lines in the coastal area near Ancona. Under the command of Major M. R. H. Allen, MC, they sailed from Manfredonia on 25 May and, overcoming a navigational problem, succeeded in contacting the representative of the organisation handling escaped prisoners; they eventually managed to evacuate some 132 grateful ex-POWs.

No 9 Commando's next operation was 'Gradient 1', where two troops mounted a raid on two small islands in the Adriatic, Chesso and Lussino. They had three tasks: two definite and the other a potential one. The first was the destruction of the bridge that linked the two islands, the second was to destroy any German garrison on the island, and the third, potential, task was the capture of a high-ranking German general who was reported to be on a visit to the island of Chesso.

Embarked on two MTBs and an MGB, the commandos sailed from Ancona for the seventy-five-mile trip to Lussino on the night of 9–10 August. They landed unopposed and once ashore the raiders, having taken folding bicycles, pedalled off for the bridge. Leslie Callf takes up the story:

> The Italians guarding the bridge ran off when they saw this crazy bunch of cyclists and then explosives were laid on the bridge. In bright moonlight we then cycled to the north of Chesso, but could find no garrison and it was said the visiting General had left the previous day. We planted anti-personnel mines near our landing area, found our boats [Goatley boats which had been left there on landing] and waited until we heard the bridge explode, then paddled out to the waiting MGBs.[11]

In addition to demolishing the bridge the commandos destroyed the local telephone exchange and its equipment, and they brought back two Italian prisoners and some locals who wanted to leave the island. On the way back to Ancona they also picked up an American airman who had been drifting for a week in the Adriatic.

No 9 Commando was to be involved in some further potential operations but none materialised until September, when, under the command from headquarters of Land Forces Adriatic, Colonel Tod was ordered to mount a raid to destroy an important radar station on the island of Kythera just off the south-east tip of mainland Greece. A reconnaissance party from No 9 was duly parachuted onto the island on the night of 10–11 September, only to report that the Germans had pulled out of the island on the previous day.

Anticipating the ultimate withdrawal of the Germans from Greece, General Headquarters, Middle East had already started to plan (Operation 'Manna') the sending of troops to Greece to help the liberation and resettlement of that country when the Germans left. Sadly, there were indications that the resistance parties – namely the Communist ELAS (Greek People's Liberation Army) and EAM (National Liberation Front) and the non-Communist EDES (National Republican Greek League) – both on the mainland and on the islands would try to seek power for themselves and possibly provoke civil war. (Indeed it was a situation that the commandos had experienced when they liberated Corfu after the Sarande operation.) With this in mind it was decided to send a force, codenamed 'Foxforce', to occupy Kythera and to be available to act as a vanguard for the troops implementing Operation Manna. So No 9 Commando, supported by 350 men of the Greek Sacred Heart Regiment, with small detachments from the Long Range Desert Group, the Special Boat Section, and the Raiding Support Regiment were assembled under the overall command of Colonel Tod. Incidentally, the Greek Sacred Heart Regiment had been formed by officers of the Royal Hellenic Army who had escaped after the invasion of Greece and had operated with special forces previously in North Africa.

On 17 September Foxforce successfully landed on the island. Initially Tod's main military role was to protect the port of Avlemon on the eastern coastline of the island and assist the local Greeks to work together and adjust peacefully to their liberation. Meanwhile the SBS and the other two detachments from the LRDG and SRR carried out reconnaissance raids on the Aegean Islands and some mainland areas, and the naval forces sought out and destroyed enemy shipping targets in the area. After a few days Tod moved his force to the area around the port of Kapsali on the other side of the island because the port facilities there were better, as were the communication and accommodation conditions. Almost from the outset Tod's main task appeared to be that of maintaining law and order because of the growing hostility between the rival

Communist and non-Communist parties. It was a role for which the commandos were not trained; nevertheless Tod and his men did all in their power to prevent the apparent friction and antagonism between the two opposing factions from developing into civil war – and they succeeded.

Typical of their actions in this role was when they arranged a settlement, with the aid of the Swedish Red Cross – and without bloodshed – between the ELAS and the Greek Security Battalion at Kalamata on the mainland. The latter was a non-Communist force that had been recruited and organised by the Germans and they subsequently took over responsibility for law and order when the Germans retreated. This was a situation that the ELAS were not prepared to accept and were threatening 'to butcher any security battalions left in charge'. Tod arranged for the seventy men of the security battalion at Kalamata to be evacuated to a nearby island, where they were 'apprehended in custody for their own safety'.

While the bulk of No 9 Commando was engaged on these operations – which would later be called 'internal security operations', and in more recent times 'peace-keeping operations' – the detachments of the LRDG and the SBS carried out reconnaissance operations on the offshore islands of the Peloponnese and they reported a general retreat, so Tod decided to move his force from Kythera to Poros. This sudden and bold move caught the Germans by surprise and they then decided to carry out a general retreat from the port of Piraeus as well as from the capital of Greece, Athens. The stage was set for the implementation of Operation *Manna*.

On 14 October Tod's *Foxforce* left Poros for Piraeus and duly arrived to a tumultuous welcome from the local inhabitants: the British were back after their evacuation some three years earlier. On leaving Piraeus No 9 dispatched a troop to secure the nearby airfield at Kalamaki, where the paratroopers from the 4th Battalion of the Parachute Regiment made a descent and joined in the commandos' advance to Athens. There on 15 October the liberators received another tumultuous welcome and much generous hospitality, although it soon became apparent that the Communists were going to make a bid for power. The commandos witnessed noisy demonstrations in Athens by the vocal supporters of the rival political parties, which seemed to herald trouble ahead. Nevertheless, No 9 Commando took part in a memorable liberation parade and Colonel Tod was duly honoured with the freedom of the city of Athens.

There followed a period of reorganisation: *Foxforce* as such was disbanded and No 9 Commando, along with the paratroopers of No 2 Parachute Brigade took over garrison duties, including the guarding of vulnerable and vital installations in the capital.

Meanwhile, back in Albania Brigadier Churchill, after the battle for Sarande, had received orders from the commander of Land Forces Adriatic to carry on and pursue the retreating Germans. For a variety of valid reasons, however, he was not prepared to commit his battle-weary commandos to such a plan without being supplied with the necessary transport, further supplies, and specialist engineer reinforcements with their bridging materials – all of which would be required in a pursuit operation in such terrain as that of coastal Albania. Brigadier Davy, Churchill's immediate superior, would not agree to his request though; there was an obvious clash of personalities and Churchill asked to be relieved of his command, which was granted and Colonel Todd was sent for to take over command of No 2 Commando Brigade, leaving No 9 Commando in Athens under the command of Major M. R. H. Allen, MC. In the end, Davy's original pursuit plan was scrapped.

Towards the end of October No 9 Commando left Athens and moved up to the north of Greece to the town of Salonika, where, together with their red beret comrades of 5th Battalion of the Parachute Regiment, they carried out normal garrison duties, but were also on the alert to support the local authority should the need arise due to civil disturbances or civil war. In early December Lieutenant Colonel J. M. Dunning-White, one of the original volunteers of No 4 Commando and later brigade major of Lord Lovat's Commando Brigade on the D-Day landings, arrived to take over command of No 9.

Meanwhile in Athens the situation had deteriorated and severe fighting had erupted, with the airborne forces there heavily committed and on 18 December a whole British division arrived in the city to take the offensive against the ELAS insurgents. There followed bitter fighting with heavy losses on both sides; fortunately insurrections did not spread to Salonika, although there was an uneasy peace there. Finally, in early February No 9 Commando – after nearly six months of mixed operational actions and garrison duties on the Greek islands and on the mainland in Athens and Salonika – rejoined the fold of No 2 Commando Brigade back in Ravenna in Italy.

Before leaving this account of No 9 Commando's activities during their 'Grecian interlude', one must hasten to add that there were lighter sides to their military experiences. For example, when Captain Mike Long's troop was detached to provide protection for a naval base on the island of Skiathos he decided to hold a display of Highland dancing on the quayside. With the music provided by the troop piper the commandos did eightsome reels and other dances. In addition the captain of HMS *Ajax* ordered the royal marine band to put on a display – not to be outdone, the mayor of Skiathos organised Greek dancing, and apparently everyone enjoyed the occasion. It is also worth mentioning that whilst on the island the troop medical orderly, Lance Corporal 'Doc' Quigley, ran a daily clinic for the locals, which was much appreciated.

Although No 9 Commando had fought no major battles nor carried out any outstanding raids in that six month's deployment, they had, on the other hand, carried out a wide range of difficult and often dangerous, irksome and frustrating operations, so aptly summarised by Hilary St George Saunders when he wrote: 'They had spent difficult weeks and months pouring oil on troubled waters in a land whose natural beauties and incomparable traditions are offset by the apparent inability of its inhabitants to agree among themselves.'[12]

No 9 Commando was deservedly awarded the battle honour of GREECE 1944–45 for their involvement in a successful series of mixed operational and occupational commitments.

CHAPTER 11

NORTH-WEST EUROPE 1944
(Normandy Landing, Dives Crossing, Flushing, and Westkapelle)

FROM THE VERY BEGINNING, in those dark days in 1940 when Britain stood alone and was threatened with an invasion, the newly formed commandos looked forward to that day when they would land on the coast of north-west Europe, not just for a raid, but as part of an invasion force to liberate the peoples of Europe from Nazi occupation. Little did we think at that time it would take some four years for this aspiration to become a reality, although a step towards that ultimate goal was taken when the Allies invaded what Churchill called the 'soft underbelly of Europe', namely Italy, in 1943. Some idea of the pressures put on Winston Churchill by our American and Russian allies to open up a 'second front' in 1942 has already been mentioned, and the disastrous Dieppe raid in August 1942, in particular, clearly demonstrated how unprepared we were to even contemplate such an mighty and demanding amphibious operation. During the next two years, however, plans and preparations ensured that when the day came for such a formidable undertaking – the like of which had never been attempted before – the invasion forces landed with all the means and backing for success and the commandos were in the vanguard of Operation 'Overlord', as the Normandy landings were codenamed. In the autumn of 1943 plans were already at an advance stage: commanders selected, formations earmarked, special equipment – including the building of the components for the Mulberry Harbour and PLUTO (Pipe Line Under The Ocean), plus other innovations such as rocket-firing naval craft and amphibious and bridge-laying tanks – were being tested, and the training of personnel for their deployment was in progress.

Brigadier the Lord Lovat, who commanded No 1 Commando Brigade, consisting of Nos 3, 4, and 6 Army Commandos plus No 45 (RM) Commando, takes up the story:

> In November 1943 I was let into the D-Day picture. The essential needs to establish a Second Front were basic: (1) a port capable of handling large ships should be included in the area, (2) the sea voyage must be as short as possible, and (3) fighter aircraft should be available at all times to cover operations from bases on the South Coast. It was agreed that Normandy offered the best choice. The Caen area was finally selected for the bridgehead.[1]

In the final plan for *Overlord* two Commando Brigades took part, No 1 and No 4. However, No 4 Commando Brigade, commanded by Brigadier 'Jumbo' Leicester, consisted of four Royal Marine Commandos (Nos 41, 46, 47, and 48) and was therefore not eligible for the award of the battle honour of NORMANDY LANDING. The account that follows does not include their actions, although it must be added that they fought with distinction and succeeded in their respective missions, which were to extend and link up the flanks of the British and Canadian divisions landing on 'Sword' and 'Juno' beaches to the west of Lovat's brigade. One must mention here that of the four RM Commandos in Leicester's brigade only one, No 41, had seen action prior to D-Day: their exploits as part of No 2 Commando Brigade in Sicily and Italy have already been mentioned. The other three RM Commandos were raised during 1943–44 from existing RM battalions and they 'graduated' in Commando training at Charlie Vaughan's 'finishing school', the Commando Basic Training Centre at Achnacarry, where I was an instructor at the time. And I might add that we had a really full workload with the extra commitment of these conversion courses, in addition to our regular courses for commando trainees – especially with the urgent demand for reinforcements for Nos 3 and 6 Army Commandos following their losses in North Africa, Sicily, and Italy.

While Nos 3 and 6 Commandos were refitting and retraining with their reinforcements, No 4 Commando – who had not been in a major operation since the Dieppe raid – was selected to participate, with other specialist units of Combined Operations and detachments from No 10 Commando, in a series of cross-Channel raids as reconnaissances for Operation *Overlord* during the winter months of November and December.

From January onwards the training of all units for the invasion was intensified as exercises and dress rehearsals by all involved were carried out over a wide range of landing beaches and other training areas, where battle-simulated exercises using live ammunition were carried out. Added to these obvious preparations was the complicated organisation of the concentration of the Allied invasion forces on the south coast prior to embarkation. It was a huge combined operation, as can be appreciated by a look at just the naval and air forces to be committed to D-Day itself.

The figures for the naval plan, Operation '*Neptune*', were truly impressive – over six thousand vessels, which included four thousand landing craft of various types, plus seven heavy battleships, twenty-three cruisers and over one hundred destroyers. Whilst above this armada, in the sky the Allies planned to deploy twelve thousand aircraft – bombers, fighters, and transport aircraft, the latter to airlift the parachute battalions of the three Allied airborne divisions.

In terms of the specific preparations of Lovat's Commando Brigade, although the commanding officers of his brigade were not informed of the actual destinations and place names of their objectives, they were, however, given sufficient information on which to base their training and obtain any special equipment and stores that may be needed for their respective missions. By May they were all fully prepared: they had trained and trained, carried out exercises and rehearsals in landing craft, under battle inoculation conditions, with live firing on a variety of landing beaches as far apart as Dorset and the Moray Firth in Scotland. They were ready and eager to go.

In his book, *March Past*, Lord Lovat succinctly summarised the 'intention' and 'method' of his brigade's role for D-Day, although for his briefings he had to omit the placenames until his force had actually set sail, such was the need for security:

The Commando Brigade, consisting of Nos 3, 4, and 6 Army Commandos and No 45 Royal Marine Commando, to land on the extreme flank of the Allied Forces on Queen Beach (Sword) and cut inland to join forces with the two Airborne Brigades dropped inland by night by glider and parachute. No 4 to destroy a battery and the garrison at Ouistreham and then later rejoin the Brigade. The rest of the Brigade, landing thirty minutes after No 4, to fight through enemy defences to reach and reinforce Brigades of the 6th Airborne Division, meeting astride bridges spanning the River Orne and the Caen Canal. Further Glider Regiments of the Air Landing Brigades would arrive later the same evening descending in country cleared of the enemy.[2]

For this operation Lovat's Commando Brigade came under the overall command of the airborne division and the object of the paratroopers' and commandos' mission was to secure the left flank of the Allied landings and ensure that any enemy threat to disrupt the build-up of the Allied landings in the following days was repelled. The key to success in this mission was the ability of the commandos to fight their way inland, some five to six miles, to link up with their airborne comrades in three hours. It was, as Lovat confessed, a 'formidable task' and on one of his dress rehearsals on the south coast between Angmering and Littlehampton, near Arundel, his commandos showed a critical and doubting audience of 'top brass' from the planning staff that it could be done – although the realism of the 'mock' landing and assault by the whole brigade, aided by smoke from the two-inch mortars fired from the landing craft, did cause concern and consternation amongst the spectators, and also damaged some of their vehicles. More to the point, however, were Lovat's concluding comments on this most important dress rehearsal: 'The planners were impressed. Everybody else was extremely angry; Southern Command asked for my head and put in a claim for damaged vehicles. No further doubts were expressed over the Brigade's speed off the mark, tactically, the exercise had been completely successfully.'[3]

In April two French troops of commandos from No 10 were placed under the command of Lieutenant Colonel Robert Dawson, No 4 Commando, for the invasion and beyond. Robert Dawson, who had spent most of his early years in Switzerland and was bilingual, had this to say of the French commandos:

> They were tough, self-reliant soldiers, quick in action and very brave indeed. Even before D-Day a measure of mutual respect had developed but after the initial phase (of the invasion) the Commando became so firmly welded together at every level that it seemed entirely natural that we should fight together and live side-by-side till the end of the war, as indeed we did.[4]

By May the detailed training of the brigade was concluded. The morale of Lovat's commandos was high; they were all fit, confident, and ready for that famous date in world history – '6 June, D-Day – the Longest Day'.

It is not intended to dwell on the final preparations, the period of waiting in the camps that had been established for all the troops prior to embarkation, nor paint the picture in any detail of the whole of the south coast of England, from Falmouth in the west to Dover in the east, resembling a vast armed camp, with ports and harbours amassed with naval craft of all sizes, types, and purposes, whilst inland on the airfields bombers, fighters, and transport aircraft awaited Eisenhower's famous clarion call 'Let's Go.' Instead, this narrative will advance to the evening of 5 June when the commandos were all aboard their respective landing craft and ready to set sail, as part of the greatest invasion armada of all time, for the Normandy beaches of Nazi-occupied France.

The commandos' crossing of the Channel that night and their landings next morning has been told in their respective books by Lord Lovat and his piper, Bill Millin. The exploits of Nos 3 and 6 Commandos were narrated by their commanding officers, colonels Peter Young (No 3) and Derek Mills-Roberts (No 6), in their books *Storm from the Sea* and *Clash by Night*, whilst accounts concerning No 4 were chronicled by two officers: Captain Donald Gilchrist, who was the Commando's adjutant on D-Day, and Lieutenant Murdoch McDougall, one of the section officers of F Troop, in their books *Don't Cry for Me* and *Swiftly They Struck*. The account in *The Fighting Fourth* includes contributions from mostly other ranks in No 4, so there is no shortage of material to get the atmosphere of the eve of battle or of the actual run-in, on that morning of 6 June, to the gun-swept beaches of Normandy.

Most of the now Anglo-French No 4 Commando were aboard two LSIs, *Astrid* and *Maid of Orleans*, but the French troops, now under the command of Major Phillipe Kieffer, were aboard LCIs 523 and 527. All of the Commando Brigade sailed from Southampton Docks or the nearby riverside moorings at Warsash, where brigade headquarters along with Nos 3, 6, and 45 Commandos had been transported from their assembly camp in Southampton to embark in their landing craft. Bill Millin, recalls the scene after he had been coaxed into playing as they waited to embark:

> I placed my pipes on my shoulder, blew them up, and strolled around the field visiting the various groups of commandos, and playing request here and there. The pipes were sounding very well. I felt I could have played for hours. The whole scene could have been of a large party of Boy Scouts preparing to go off to camp. The only difference being the presence of so much battle equipment and weapons.[5]

All commandos had been issued rucksacks to replace the traditional large backpacks and certainly were carrying a lot of 'battle equipment'. Each man had spare ammunition for his personal weapon plus spare ammo for his section's Brens, as well as grenades, emergency rations, first-field dressings, and digging tools. Some men had the spare ammunition for the heavy weapons as well, and those who had a specialist role, such as the signallers, medical orderlies, heavy-weapons men (three-inch mortars and K guns), and demolitionists, had to carry all their equipment – wireless sets, heavy weapons plus spares, and ammunition; as the Commandos' jeeps were not due to land until 'D+I'.

As a result each commando soldier had a load that ranged from some 80 to 100 lb (50 to 62.5 kgs) and under all their equipment each man wore an inflatable 'Mae West' life jacket – no wonder Donald Gilchrist aptly commented, 'We were festooned like Christmas trees.' Throughout the training during the previous months the commandos in all their many training exercises carried loads similar in weight. Although they sweated and moaned at these burdens when the 'Day' came they were able to appreciate that the sweat and effort was all worth while. Joe Burnett, one of the three-inch-mortar men in No 4, reckoned that 'all those speed marches with full kit, weapons and ammunition during the build-up for the invasion certainly paid off.'[6]

With embarkation completed, the armada of landing ships and craft, plus their escorts, sailed off; adhering to a carefully timed programme, they headed towards assembly and departure points in the Solent off the eastern coastline of the Isle of Wight.

On board Lovat's landing craft someone suggested to Bill Millin that he should play as they moved ahead. So getting 'his Lordship's approval' he went forward to the bows of the landing craft. He recalls:

> I started to play 'The Road To The Isles'. I felt excited but with a certain amount of apprehension about the journey. The Isle of Wight lay ahead and to the right. Looking around I could see hundreds of ships, a huge armada of large and small ships, all kinds of warships and dozens of various kinds of landing craft. What a wonderful sight it was as we passed these vessels all queuing up to take their turn in line. I was now playing the 'Skye Boat Song'. Someone managed to broadcast the piping over the loudhailer system. This brought a terrific response from the invasion fleet. Troops on board the transports were throwing their hats in the air and cheering. I was feeling very proud that the Commando Brigade was at the forefront of the invasion.[7]

As the armada cleared the Isle of Wight, conditions changed for the worse: the sea became very choppy and a bitter cold wind started to blow, forcing all the troops to go below deck or seek shelter. Many of those on the LCIs in particular became seasick, keeping the medics busy handing out seasickness tablets. With all their last minute preparations completed, the troops heard for the first time, in their final briefings, the real place names for their coastal and inland targets, which hitherto they knew only by codenames. This information was, of course, of much more significance to the French commandos than their British comrades, but what was also much more gratifying to Kieffer and his men was the fact that they were to be the first Free French soldiers to land for the liberation of their *patria*.

For those who were able to get some 'kip' (sleep), reveille was at 3.30 a.m., and for those who had any appetite at that stage the breakfast of eggs, bacon, and lashings of hot sweet tea went down well, although as Bill Bidmead added in his post-war record of his days in the commandos: 'The fish also did well for breakfast.'

Nearing the French coast No 4 transferred from their two LSIs into LCAs for the landings. Dawn was breaking as they came on deck to clamber into their craft; all the heavy equipments, mortars, K guns, stretchers, etc. had been loaded during the previous evening in the allotted craft as rehearsed so many times during the training. Conditions were still unkind: it was cold and very unpleasant. As the troops started clambering into their craft there was a loud explosion on their port bow and 'in a lurid orange glow, one of the escorting destroyers broke in two . . . It was the most depressing sight imaginable . . . The two halves of the stricken ship reared up out of the water like an inverted V and slowly, slowly sank into the leaden waves,' wrote Murdoch McDougall,[8] while Bidmead also recalled the tragedy and the fate of the sailors, as he moved to his LCA, with these words: 'Poor blighters, they didn't have a chance.'[9]

There was a heavy sea swell running as the LCAs started their run-in and several of the craft took in water: the one carrying Captain Porteous, VC, and his troop was swamped. He recalled:

There was a hand pump to pump out the bilges, but it wasn't working very well, so we started baling out like mad. We managed to keep the water down but every time a big wave came along we took in a bit more water. So we were baling all the way in . . . I thought that the thing [LCA] was going down when we were still miles from the beach.[10]

Fortunately it did not sink on the run-in, although it did eventually sink about sixty yards out from the beach in three feet of water so Pat Porteous and his men had to wade ashore. On the whole, however, the Commando's run-in went well with only a few casualties, which was surprising considering the amount of hostile gunfire at the time.

Recalling that historic run in, McDougall continued:

On the run in it was impossible not to be thrilled by all the happenings round about. Aircraft scurried to and fro in the lightening sky above, all with a mission, all independent and all beautifully ours. Shells from the *Warspite* and *Romillies* were screaming overhead, destroyers fired salvo after salvo, and soon we heard a new sound – the roaring swish of the missiles from the rocket ships. The whole coastline was under a thick pall of black heavy smoke.[11]

Then as the commandos, many top heavy under their rucksacks' load, dashed off the ramps of the landing craft onto the beach – which was under enemy mortar and machine-gun fire – casualties began to mount. Among the early victims was the popular intelligence corporal, Brian Mullen, the Commando's 'official war artist'. But a worse scene awaited them as they stormed up the beach – it was not what they expected. In the overall plan troops of the 3rd Infantry Division, supported by tanks with special equipment, had been allotted the task of clearing the beaches' anti-invasion devices and the infantrymen were to clear a bridgehead so that the commandos could dash ashore and speedily make for their objectives in Ouistreham and Pegasus Bridge. Instead they found the obstacles only partially cleared – worse still was the sight of scores of infantrymen dead and wounded, 'just swilling around in the water,' as Porteous recalled.

The commandos, right from those early days in the autumn of 1940 when they first started to carry out their training for beach assaults, had been drilled to get out of the craft and go 'split-arse' up and off the beach – regardless of anyone or anything, including hostile fire. Survival depended on adhering to this basic drill: it was fatal, quite literally, to go to ground to become a 'sitting target' or try to dig in. This fundamental principle of an assault landing was drummed into all commando trainees at Achnacarry in their final spectacular exercise, the famous 'opposed landing', which none of them ever forgot, nor its purpose.

The commandos on Sword Beach that morning saw the consequences of not following this basic drill for opposed landings in the numbers of fallen infantrymen dead or wounded in the water just lapping around their feet. In direct contrast the commandos kept going and, in spite of a few casualties, they cleared the beach and got to their first assembly area just beyond the barbed-wire fences, which fortuitously had been breached and a gap opened up by the naval gunfire during the preliminary bombardment. There, beyond the beach dunes, amid some half-demolished buildings, No 4 Commando regrouped and reorganised for the next phase of their mission – the twin assaults into Ouistreham. The first part of the assault was to be the two French troops' destruction of a German stronghold based on the site of an old casino; the second, but separate, operation was to be the destruction of an enemy battery located at the eastern flank of the invasion beaches, near the entrance to the

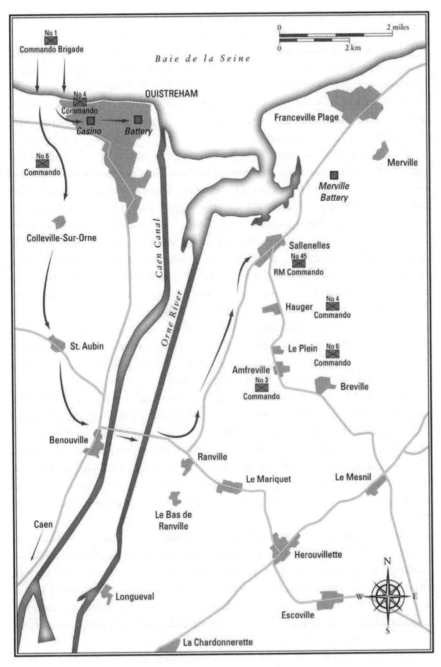

MAP 17. Normandy Landings

port. Of course, en route both groups had to deal with enemy posts and pillboxes forming part of the coastal defences of the 'western wall'.

There is a full account of these two actions, which were hard-fought but completely successful, in *The Fighting Fourth* and it makes gripping reading. Furthermore the story of the Anglo-French No 4 Commando's action at Ouistreham and subsequently up to VE Day is told in film, pictures, recordings and models in the unique No 4 Commando Museum, located almost opposite the old casino.[12]

On the way to their objectives the commandos had dumped their loaded rucksacks, as planned, in the area around a couple of empty houses on the main inland road leading to the centre of the town. There the Commando medical officer, 'Doc' Patterson, had established the regimental aid post (RAP) and was soon in business as the walking wounded and other casualties were brought in, among them the commanding officer, Colonel Robert Dawson. So for a while Major Menday took over command until Dawson had been treated and, refusing to give in, rejoined the fray. The area of the RAP also became the collecting point, under the supervision of the regimental sergeant major, Bill Morris, for enemy prisoners captured en route to the two objectives, as well as from the stronghold at the casino and the battery area.

Having completed the first phase of their D-Day missions, No 4 started on the next: the link-up with the airborne troops and the rest of Lovat's brigade on the far side of the Orne, about six miles away.

The rest of Lovat's Commando Brigade were scheduled to land from their LCIs after No 4 Commando, which they did, starting with No 6 at 8.30 a.m., right on time. They too were shocked to see the men of the East Yorkshire Regiment still on the beach. 'The beach was littered with equipment and dead. One poor devil floated in the shallow water supported by his Mae West; he was dead but the swell gave him grotesque lifelike movements – he was only one of many,' recalled Colonel Mills-Roberts, who was leading his men from the front.[13]

There are some very vivid pictures of the commandos' landings at this stage – taken by photographers specially trained and assigned to various units in the landing – and it is pertinent to highlight the fact that this was the first time in history that the news of a military action was conveyed to a listening public almost as soon as it was actually happening. Those BBC reports from the Normandy beaches on D-Day were vivid, dramatic, and immediate. They represented an important milestone in war reporting.

Like their comrades in No 4, those commandos landing from the LCIs in their dash up the beach suffered casualties, but they still kept going – they knew the drill! No 6 Commando, on clearing the beach, regrouped in a prearranged area on the side of the main road and got ready to 'cut through the German defences'. Instead of a linear coastal defence the Germans had built a belt of pillboxes, often mutually supporting and usually covering the roads, so Mills-Roberts had – from his study of photographs and maps overlaid with the positions of the German defences – based his plan for advancing to the Orne as quickly as possible on the following simple aim: 'to blaze a trail to the bridges and not to get involved with any enemy who were not directly barring our way'.[14]

With this aim in mind No 6 Commando set off and, avoiding the main road for obvious reasons, initially took a cross-country route, across a flat salt marsh that had a couple of deep drainage ditches barring the way. Prepared for these hazards, the commandos had brought bamboo scaling ladders, which were put to good use. At this point they came under enemy fire from the first pillbox, but Captain Pyman's troop, already earmarked for this possible task, was dispatched to deal with it. The next troop, following up, pushed on towards the next objective – the by-passing of the inland village of Colville-sur-Orne. As they successfully outflanked the village Mills-Roberts received a signal from Pyman stating that, with the aid of a flame-thrower – which they had been dying to use – they had destroyed the enemy strongpoint.

The commandos pressed on towards their next objective, the village of St Aubin-d'Arquenay; at this point No 6 was still on time, but behind the village there was an enemy four-gun battery, still bringing fire on to the landing beaches. Having dealt with some enemy soldiers in the village itself, Mills-Roberts detached a troop to attack them in the rear, whilst his main body, with Lord Lovat now following closely behind, continued on with their advance. The battery was manned by Italians, and Mills-Roberts explained: 'Isolated in the midst of the shrub there was no real fight in them . . . [They] surrendered without much fuss; to be quite honest, they were well and truly taken aback and had not much option . . . We left a spiking party to spike their guns, whilst they joined our motley column of prisoners.'[15]

Beyond the village the road swung left and led to the two vital bridges, about two thousand yards away. No 6 Commando continued to advance 'with all possible speed'. Although they came under some sniper and rifle fire they made good progress, enabling them to join up with their red beret comrades almost on time, although Lord Lovat did apologise to his airborne counterpart for being 'two and a half minutes late'. Following up were the other two Commandos, No 3 under Colonel Peter Young and No 45 (RM) Commando under Colonel Ries, and they too got across the bridges and onto the open ground on the east bank. From here, together with the paratroopers, the commandos were to advance to the east and take up a defensive position on the ridge to secure the left flank of the Allied bridgehead. Although most of the commandos got across the bridges unscathed, they did suffer casualties from snipers, one of whom was Colonel Ries who was wounded and his second-in-command Major Nicol had to take over. This sniping continued for some time – indeed it was still going on when No 4 Commando, coming up to join their comrades some four hours later, after their successes in Oustreham, crossed the bridges. Unfortunately, among their casualties on the canal bridge was the popular section officer, Lieutenant Peter Mercer-Wilson, who was fatally wounded.

Once on the far bank of the Orne the original plan had to be amended because of mounting enemy counter-attacks on the paratroopers' positions around the bridges. So General Gale, commanding 6 Airborne Division, and Brigadier Lovat agreed to hold a smaller defensive position than originally planned, with the area allotted to Nos 3, 4, and 6 Commandos taking in the villages of Amfreville, Le Plein, and Hauger; No 45 (RM) Commando had an area down towards Salenelles on the way to the coast.

Under this amended plan Lovat's four Commandos set off for their respective localities to take up all-round defensive positions ready to repulse the inevitable enemy counter-attacks. We follow No 4 Commando as they, still carrying those heavy rucksacks, trudged off to their allotted area on the ridge, which surrounded the impressive château at Hauger, about two and a half miles to the east of the river Orne. Having reached the grounds of the château, Major Menday, still 'holding the fort' for the wounded Dawson who had returned to the RAP for further treatment, allotted troop areas, with the specific overall order 'not to yield an inch'.

The area was typical bocage country: close countryside of small fields marked with hedgerows and sunken tracks, orchards, and farm outbuildings. Linear defence was out of the question, the only solution was a system of little islands (subsequently referred to as 'blobs') of all-round defence, with extremely limited fields of fire and later backed up by active patrolling.

In the early evening, as they were digging in, the commandos were greatly encouraged to see the spectacular arrival of glider-borne airborne reinforcements descending on the ground behind them in the paratroopers' close perimeter around the bridges.

Bill Bidmead had this to say about his troop (A) position:

We arrived at our allotted area well in front of the rest of the Commando . . . it seemed to be a death trap of a place . . . a corner of a wood with a cornfield on our right flank ... practically no field of fire because of the woods. We could be approached by the Germans with little difficulty and no warning, if we didn't watch it ... After a little 'thanksgiving' get-together by Ted Lewis, our Troop Sergeant Major, we started to dig the best positions for ourselves and our 'K' guns.[16]

In the preparations for the invasion the commandos had rejected the usual infantryman's 'entrenching tool' and instead had acquired proper digging spades and picks – although these added to their loads they knew that with them they could prepare decent 'slit trenches' and defence posts far quicker than with the entrenching tools. It was a decision that was most successful. Initially the commandos worked in pairs to dig, but as good progress was made one of them started on that all-important chore of 'brewing up' and getting something to eat. Each man had forty-eight hours' ration packs plus a little 'Tommy' cooker for boiling water and heating tinned foods.

As darkness fell and the trenches were being completed there was general quiet on the commandos' front on that ridge, though enemy shells did continue to whistle overhead on their way to the airborne perimeter and further on to the landing beaches. With the trenches dug and some food consumed the commandos settled down in their slit trenches to watch and wait, expecting attacks from any quarter at any time during the night.

However, that night was quiet, according to Murdoch McDougall: 'not just quiet, but menacingly quiet', and although there were some suspicious sounds of the enemy nearby, it had been laid down – as Commando policy – not to fire or try to make contact with the enemy that night unless directly attacked, because by lying 'doggo' the Germans would get no idea of their strength or their positions.

Thus it was that by midnight Lovat's commandos were all firmly dug in their respective 'blobs' on the ridge beyond the Orne, having achieved all that had been demanded of them on that historic day. Captain Knyvet Carr, who commanded the heavy-weapons troop of No 4, later wrote:

I was one of the luckier ones [although he had been wounded on the wrist and hand by some shrapnel on the beach] to be around at the end of D-Day ... So ended the greatest day of my army career, a day on which I am proud to have been of service to my country, a day for which I give thanks to God for my survival, and to my wonderfully brave comrades who fought with me.[17]

Those sentiments, so aptly expressed by Knyvet Carr, are a fitting place to conclude the narrative of the commandos' actions that earned for them the battle honour of NORMANDY LANDINGS, an honour awarded only for those units that took part on 'The Longest Day': 6 June 1944.

In the days that followed, the commandos held their ground against repeated enemy counter-attacks, although the greatest problem was probably the incessant enemy fire on the commandos' positions by artillery, mortar, self-propelled guns, and, on some rare occasions, by enemy fighter aircraft. It was during one such bombardment on 10 June that Brigadier Lord Lovat was badly wounded and had to be evacuated – his wounds were so bad that for him the war was ended. Before being evacuated, however, he called for Colonel Mills-Roberts and handed over command to him; Mills-Roberts was subsequently to lead the Brigade across the Rhine and into Germany for the final victory and VE Day.

There are many accounts of the battles fought and the privations suffered by the commandos during the period 6 June to 17 August, and although their daily routine did not vary much – the aim being to hold fast on that ridge beyond the Orne – they did move to different positions within the general area of that original perimeter on the extreme left flank of the Allies' bridgehead. In the early days they were repeatedly attacked by the Germans attempting to dislodge them, as well as being under sustained enemy artillery and mortar bombardments, which inflicted substantial casualties. But they held fast, and as time went by the commandos' defence became decidedly more offensive with daily programmes of fighting patrols and sniping forays. Each Commando had its team of 'star snipers', many of whom were well-deservedly awarded the Military Medal – in particular, two names readily spring to mind: Paddy Byrne of No 4 and 'Ossie' Osborne of No 3.

From D-Day onwards the national daily newspapers contained regular reports of the fighting in Normandy. One such report in the *Daily Mail* was particularly graphic and in a feature headlined 'Battle of the Orchard' described the battle on D+2 when a fierce German counter-attack was launched on No 3 Commando's position, during which the popular Lieutenant George Herbert, DCM, MM, was killed. Mention has been made earlier of this outstanding commando who rose from the rank of corporal to lieutenant in the same unit – a rare achievement – and who had seen action in all No 3 Commando's raids and campaigns. With an obvious feeling of personal loss, for he had recruited George for his own troop back in July 1940, Peter Young wrote:

We were all deeply distressed. Nobody in my old Troop had given me more wholehearted support . . . George's body was brought in by Donald Hopson and some of 6 Troop, and at about 5.30 we buried him in the Garden of Amfreville. Lord Lovat arrived to visit us just as the brief ceremony was about to begin and stood with us at his graveside.[18]

Notwithstanding this long period of continuous – day in, day out – action, there was no specific battle honour for the commandos so we move on to the next honour, that of the DIVES CROSSING.

On 16 August there were indications that the enemy on the whole of the Commando Brigade front were withdrawing and so preparations were made to pursue them. No 4 Commando was chosen to lead the breakout on the morning of 18 August. They were glad to be on the move at last and advanced some three miles, unopposed, to the village of Bavant, which had been evacuated by the Germans only that morning. It was quickly occupied by Captain Lofi and his French troop who were warmly welcomed by the local villagers. From information received from these folk it was clear that the Germans were retreating across the river Dives and beyond to the high ground – 'the heights of Angouville' – to take up a naturally strong defensive position.

Following the capture of Bavant and the acquisition of this information, Brigadier Mills-Roberts received orders in the mid-afternoon to attack and seize the 'heights' during that night, 18–19 August. On his way back in his jeep to issue orders to the COs of his four Commandos he decided not to carry out a conventional night attack with artillery support, but rather attempt a more daring surprise attack – by avoiding the main road axis of advance, moving cross-country to outflank the enemy positions, and attacking them from the rear. It was a bold plan and was dependent on well-trained troops being able to move rapidly and stealthily in the dark.

At his subsequent 'O' group Mills-Roberts received the full support of his four Commando leaders for his unorthodox plan. There followed a desperate rush to give out orders and prepare to cross the start line at midnight.

The plan was for the whole brigade, some fifteen hundred strong, led by No 3 Commando, to advance, one behind the other, on the track alongside the railway, but away from the main road. After crossing the river, they would strike across country to skirt the hills and outflank the enemy.

Progress along the railway track was good until they got to the railway bridge over one of the tributaries of the Dives, and found that the bridge had been blown. However, with the aid of an improvised bridge, using kapok floats, they all crossed over; quite a few men fell into the water, but were all successfully pulled out. Thereafter the advance continued without any further hitches, as the leading troops of No 3 paid out white tape to mark the route – 'rather like a paper-chase' recorded Mills-Roberts. During this stage the commandos had the consolation of hearing heavy German gunfire on the main road away to their flank: obviously the enemy knew something was afoot and, suspecting activity on the road, were shelling it, not appreciating, nor imagining, an advance other than astride the main road.

As they neared the hills the brigade split up to tackle four different objectives. No 4 was the first to leave the brigade, peeling off to attack an enemy located in the area of a château that was occupied by personnel from various units. The commandos took the enemy completely by surprise. After a short exchange of fire the commandos had forty-three prisoners, several enemy were killed, and among the enemy guns captured was one 75-mm and two 81-mm artillery pieces, together with ammunition that Captain Knyvet Carr added to his heavy-weapons troop's armoury.

No 3 Commando attained their objective with complete surprise too; Lieutenant Alan Pollock, at the head of his leading section, shot and killed the sentry outside the enemy headquarters, and the rest of the enemy were quickly accounted for. No 6 Commando, following up behind No 3, passed through their comrades' position to continue on to the top of the hill. On their way they surprised and killed the crews of two horse-drawn field guns, but as they reached their objective they met stiffer opposition, as the enemy was by now alerted. Nevertheless, after a short battle, in which they killed seven of the enemy, including the local commander, and captured thirteen prisoners, they started to consolidate on their position. The tactical handling of the brigade had been perfect: they had slipped past the enemy's lines, listening posts, and patrols and reached their objectives undetected, even though the river crossing, after leaving the railway track, was but a few hundred yards away from an enemy machine-gun position.

With their objectives secured the brigade began to consolidate and prepare for the enemy's inevitable counter-attacks, which started from midday onwards. There were four main attacks and the brunt of these fell on No 6 Commando's position; all were preceded by heavy artillery and mortar fire, as was expected, and as Mills-Roberts recalls: 'Everyone had to dig in and dig well and fast and our defensive perimeter had to remain intact at all costs.'[19]

The little souvenir history of No 6 Commando, produced for all members of that Commando on disbandment in 1945, provides a brief and apt summary of the operation that was to form the basis of the battle honour of DIVES CROSSING:

The Heights of Angouville were a naturally strong defensive position and it was known that the enemy meant to defend the heights and he was dug in there in large numbers. However the Commando Brigade, after marching all night in silent single file, outflanked the German defences and in the morning the Germans woke up to find us in their rear. A fierce battle ensued – it was found that the Germans included S.S. troops – and finally at about 1500 hours the last German counter-attack was broken up by No 6 Commando. Throughout the day we were subjected to the most intense bombardment we had yet met.

The enemy had retreated and No 1 Commando Brigade had fought its last battle in Normandy, for although they continued to carry on in pursuit of the Germans to the Seine there were no further major actions. On their way they liberated a number of small towns and villages, including Le Haye Tordue, Pont L'Eveque (home of the famous cheese), and finally Beuzeville. The war diary of No 4 for this period captures the atmosphere of that part of the pursuit: 'We entered a part of France which had not been a battlefield and for the first time we were among undamaged houses and a habitable area. The French people everywhere accorded us an enthusiastic welcome with cries of 'Vive L'Angleterre' and the odd bottle of wine.'[20]

It was at Beuzeville that the commandos' advance was halted and they were given the welcome news that they were to return to the United Kingdom – by this time they were just seven miles from the Seine. After a few days enjoying the sunshine and generally relaxing they were transported back to the beaches and, boarding various landing ships and landing craft, sailed back to 'Blighty' in early September. Mills-Roberts has the last word to say on his Brigade's long stint in Normandy: 'So we came home. The Brigade had been in the fight for eighty-three days without being rested. Of the 146 officers and 2,252 other ranks who had taken part 77 officers and 890 other ranks had become casualties.'[21]

Back in England once more, the commandos of Mills-Roberts's brigade were sent off on fourteen days' leave. Some of them, returning to their families in the Home Counties, had a taste of the dangers and trials that were assailing the civilians living in that region during those summer months of 1944 when Hitler responded to the Allied invasion with his latest weapons: the V-1 ('Doodlebugs') and the V-2 rockets, taking their daily toll of lives and property.

Returning from leave, the following weeks were spent in reorganising, absorbing the intakes of reinforcements from Achnacarry, and training to get back to 'battle fitness'. The brigade received warning orders to prepare for service in the Far East where they were to join No 3 Commando Brigade, which was already on active service in that theatre. However, at the beginning of October it was decided that No 4 Commando was to leave Mills-Roberts's command and replace No 46 (RM) Commando in Brigadier Leicester's No 4 Commando

Brigade, stationed in Belgium, which had up until that point been composed solely of Royal Marine Commandos. The Belgian and Norwegian troops from No 10 Commando also joined the brigade at that point.

When No 4 Commando and the two troops from No 10 arrived in the Den Haan area they found that the rest of No 4 Commando Brigade was already training for a 'combined operation of considerable magnitude', codenamed 'Infatuate'.

Here it is necessary to outline the background to this projected operation. By September 1944 the Allies had swept up through Belgium and into Holland, capturing the port of Antwerp, reckoned to be one of the finest in Europe – most importantly, they had seized it with all the docks' facilities intact. This meant that the Allies had an ideal port to use as a supply base to further their intended deep thrust into the heart of Germany. However, there was a major problem: Antwerp lies some forty miles from the mouth of the Scheldt and all the water approaches to the port were covered by enemy coastal defences, thus denying its use to the Allies.

Nevertheless Montgomery had declared that 'the Allies' need to use Antwerp was imperative' and Admiral Ramsey, Eisenhower's naval chief, was convinced that the opening up of Antwerp could only be achieved by an amphibious assault to seize Walcheren. Accordingly Monty appreciated that his forces needed to clear the enemy on the western banks of the Scheldt before an amphibious operation could be mounted on Walcheren and by the end October this had been successfully concluded thus providing a launch pad for Operation Infatuate.

The basic plan for Leicester's Commando Brigade was that No 4 Commando would land and capture the port and old town of Flushing and the other three Royal Marine Commandos, with the two troops from No 10, would capture and secure the port and area of Westkapelle. After securing Flushing No 4 were to join the rest of the brigade in the Westkapelle area and together the brigade were to destroy the enemy in the locations of Domburg and Vrouwenpolder on the north coast of the island. Units of the 52 Lowland Division were to pass through No 4 Commando in Flushing and destroy the German forces in the centre of the island around Middelburg and also those to the east in North Beveland. The successful conclusion of this operation would enable the Allies to use and exploit the advantages of the port of Antwerp.

In their training preparations for their role in Infatuate, Dawson's Commando had concentrated on street fighting and house clearing; fortunately they were able to use a war-damaged built-up area near Ostend for this type of training. Also in the preparations the commandos were introduced to amphibious LVTs, already mentioned in connection with the operation at Comacchio in Italy. Some

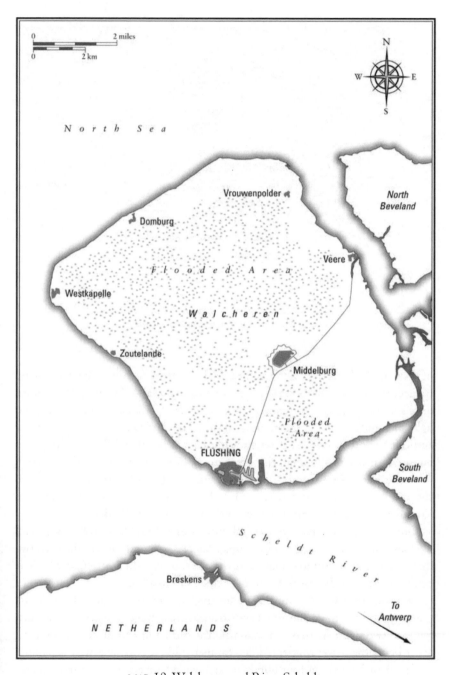

MAP 18. Walcheren and River Scheldt

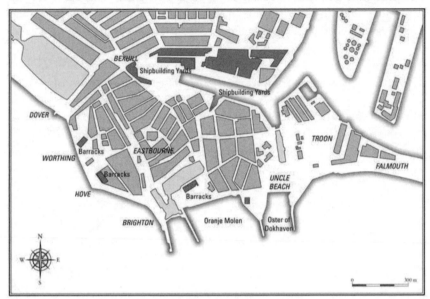

MAP 19. Flushing: Operation *Infatuate*

of No 4's MT section were trained as LVT drivers. Bill Bidmead, having transferred to the MT Section after Normandy, recalls: 'We were learning to drive some amphibious "tin cans" called "Weasels" . . . they were tracked vehicles, light and amphibious . . . the training consisted of driving into a nearby reservoir and out the other side . . . it resembled a lake at Southend. I expected at any minute someone to shout out through a megaphone, "Come in number seven."[22]

In the event No 4 Commando did not use the LVTs but stormed ashore in the more familiar – and preferred – LCAs, although the Royal Marine Commandos did use these 'tin cans' in their landings at Westkapelle.

Once again, as the relevant battle honours of FLUSHING and WESTKAPELLE were awarded solely to the army commandos of No 4 and No 10, the narrative that follows concentrates mainly on their actions and not those of their comrades in the other three Royal Marines Commandos.

Dawson's plan for the capture of Flushing was governed, quite obviously, by the layout of the town and the disposition of the defending enemy. The town fell into two distinct parts: one covering the old town and dock area, and the other being the newer residential development. These two areas were separated by a neck of land about four hundred yards wide with a main road in each area connecting the 'old' with the 'new'. These two crossroads were bottlenecks –

seize and hold them and one would have complete control of the old town and dock area, as well as denying the enemy access to be able to reinforce troops in the old town, where the main defences were located; these roads were the key to success.

In making his plan for the operation Dawson wisely chose – considering the tongue-twisting nature of most of the Dutch place names and street – to give all the salient features, tactical bounds, and objectives codenames, designated after the towns where the commandos had been stationed in Britain. It was a nice little 'billets honours' list and, of course, these names were easy to remember. Using this system, those two vital bottlenecks were named *Dover* for the western one and *Bexhill* for the other.

Dawson's basic plan was simple enough: land on a little beach on the southern promontory just to the east of a prominent windmill and secure a bridgehead, through which the main force of four troops, plus the two French troops, would pass to assault the town itself, with the overall aim of getting up to *Dover* and *Bexhill* and establishing control of these two defiles as quickly as possible.

The major problem facing him was the question of choosing a suitable landing beach. All the likely beaches were well covered by enemy gun positions and strongpoints, and the waterfront was mined and wired. In addition the beaches were further screened with anti-landing stakes, some with shells attached. However, Dawson eventually based his selection of the landing beach on the advice of the Dutchman, van Nahuijs, who had been the police inspector in Flushing up until September, before escaping to join the Dutch resistance and work with the Allies. In fact he joined No 4 and went into action with them at Flushing, staying with them subsequently until the end of that campaign. It was he who recommended to Dawson that a promontory of rubble and rubbish on the south bank of the old town alongside the Ooster of Dokhaven was a favourable possibility.

For this operation No 4 was supplemented with various supporting arms including a detachment of cliff-climbing and small-boat (dories) experts from the commando training centre at St Ives who had been attached to the Commando Brigade for D-Day and subsequent operations. As Dawson later admitted, the most difficult part of the operation was finding a suitable place to land so he decided to send in the 'St Ives' experts', together with Captain Rewcastle and a section of I Troop, ahead of the main flotilla to try out Nahuijs's landing beach, codenamed 'Uncle Beach', or to find an alternative nearby. They would then signal back to the main force and guide them in to the chosen beach. This initial reconnaissance landing was phase one of the operation and a suitable amount of time was allotted to it.

Phase two would follow: the bridgehead force under the command of Major Bill Boucher-Myers, one of the original volunteers for No 4 and a veteran of the Lofoten and Dieppe raids, would land with Captain Thorburn's No 1 Troop and also Captain 'Tug' Wilson's No 3 Troop. Disembarking on the selected beach, they would clear the area and establish a firm perimeter beachhead for the rest of the Commando to land and push on to their respective objectives in the old town (phase three) with the major two objectives, *Dover* and *Bexhill*, being priorities. Once the main body had passed through the bridgehead, Boucher-Myers's party of Nos 1 and 2 Troops would then thin out and tackle their further objectives – the barracks at *Brighton* and the old dockside defences at *Troon* and *Falmouth*. One of the French troops, No 5, under the command of Captain Alec Lofi, was to capture and secure *Dover*; the other French Troop, No 6, under the command of Captain Guy Vourch, had the objective of *Bexhill*. Both these two troops were allocated the Vickers machine guns from Captain Knyvet Carr's heavy-weapons troop.

This was the basic plan for the Commando, and at the end of October they moved up to the newly liberated port of Breskens ready to attack Flushing in the early hours of 1 November. During the previous weeks the RAF had carried out heavy bombing attacks on Walcheren, which had resulted in many of the dykes being breached, thereby causing widespread flooding. This ultimately hampered the commandos in their advance after they had captured the main ports of Flushing and Westkapelle, though this is where the amphibious LVTs subsequently came into their own. The RAF was also scheduled to carry out a bombing raid on Flushing just prior to the landings of No 4; a detailed programme of artillery support was also arranged, with forward observation officers (FOOs) attached to Dawson's headquarters to call for supporting fire from their gun positions in the area should it be required.

It was after midnight in the early morning of 1 November when the commandos left their make-shift billets in the war-damaged port of Breskens and trekked down to the quayside to board their LCAs. At 1.15 a.m. they slipped anchor and set off to cross the short stretch of water of the river Scheldt to Flushing. The weather was bad – so bad that the RAF had to cancel their planned bombing attack and it was left to the artillery to take on the job of softening up the enemy defences. Donald Gilchrist takes up the story:

A hellish bombardment started at 4.45 a.m. Big guns thundered and flashed and fires were soon blazing in the town of Flushing, while craft cruised in the darkness keeping an eye open for mines and one-man torpedoes. Suddenly, the silhouette of the windmill, the Oranje Molem, was thrown into relief against the glare of burning buildings, giving an unmistakeable guide to the landing area.[23]

At about 5.45 a.m. the SBS/Rewcastle group got ashore – after a couple of minor mishaps – on the tip of the promontory by the side of the windmill. They were able to winkle out an outpost of Germans, who were still sheltering from the bombardment, and so had the first bag of prisoners before a shot had been fired. They then cut the wire on 'Uncle Beach', marking the gap with white tape before sending the lamp signal for Boucher-Myers's group to come in to land.

It was at this stage that some of the other enemy posts on the waterfront began to fire and the LCAs came under attack – luckily it was too high and all of Boucher-Myers's men landed without any casualties. Meanwhile, Rewcastle had carried on clearing the enemy in the area and by the time the beachhead party was ashore and taking up their positions Rewcastle had twenty very scared German prisoners kneeling on the ground near one of their own pillboxes. Leaving them under guard Rewcastle went off again and rounded up another batch of Germans from a large underground shelter towards the back of the promontory. Dawson later used this underground shelter for his own Commando headquarters.

Once ashore, with the beachhead established, Boucher-Myers's men started clearing the enemy that were manning defences along the promontory. They were successful, capturing twenty-five prisoners and two guns – a 75-mm and dual-purpose 20-mm – which they added to their armoury and subsequently used to assault further pillboxes in the areas of the barracks at *Brighton* and *Hove.*

The stage was set now for the landing of the rest of No 4 Commando, along with elements of the follow up and support troops. By now the enemy was thoroughly alerted and opened up with machine guns and 20-mm guns. Fortunately few casualties were suffered, although one landing craft, which had the Commando's three-inch mortars aboard, was a victim. Les Lilley was in that craft and remembers:

> The run up to the actual landing was very noisy indeed . . . our landing craft took God knows how many small arms hits as it was approaching the touch-down point, we were under fire from the Hotel Britannia complex [on the coast in the new town beyond *Dover*] . . . just as the ramp went down we either got a direct hit low down or ran over one of the steel defences.[24]

As their LCA started to sink they scrambled ashore, but one of the mortars and other equipment was left on board – Lilley and all but one of his comrades reached the windmill. Lilley records: 'My long term friend, Gunner Hill was shot dead on the beach.'[24]

However, Captain Carr, assisted by his two of his men, waded out to the sinking LCA and, while under fire, salvaged one mortar and four cases of bombs. The other mortar had, fortunately, already been carried ashore.

With all his Commando now ashore Dawson's men set off on their various tasks in the old town and dockside. Full descriptions of the day's fighting are given in both *The Fighting Fourth* and *Swiftly They Struck*. As expected, practically all the action in Flushing involved the most difficult and deadly type of infantry fighting, namely street fighting/house clearing, but Dawson had prepared his men for this – they had trained hard and long in the Den Haag and Ostend areas for just this eventuality – and that training paid off.

In the accounts of the street fighting in Flushing there is one particularly sad episode when one of No 4's most popular characters, Private Donkin, was killed. An ex-miner and an army reservist of the Loyal Regiment, he had joined No 4 way back in July 1940 with his great pal, McVeigh. At the time of Flushing, Donkin was forty-one years old, married, and had nine children. McDougall's first-hand accounts of the street fighting includes the story of Donkin's final moments:

[He] jumped into the doorway and stood there framed, with both feet planted firm, stocky body balanced on slightly bandied legs, and methodically started to tommy-gun from left to right among fifteen or so Germans visible to him. He reached the right-hand end of his swing and was starting the return, when one man on the left, whom he had missed at the start, got in a quick shot. It took him straight through the throat, killing him at once. McVeigh, who was beside him with a rifle, made no mistake with his return shot.[25]

By the late afternoon most of the old town and dockside were in the Commando's hands, although among the areas not completely cleared was the crossroads at Dover. It was not until next morning, with the aid of an air strike from six Typhoons on the enemy strongpoint just beyond Dover, that the commandos completely secured the vital crossroads and eliminated all the enemy in the area, thus making it available as a launch pad for 155 Infantry Brigade's advance towards the centre of the island. Elsewhere in the town and on the dockside mopping operations continued throughout 'D+2' and it was not until the next day that No 4 Commando could successfully hand over to battalions of the relieving brigade, withdraw from Flushing, and rejoin the rest of Leicester's Commando Brigade to carry on with the elimination of the Germans in the north of Walcheren.

In the late afternoon of 3 November No 4 Commando completed its mission and could claim that they had successfully carried out the first direct assault on the waterfront of a strongly defended enemy port since the Dieppe raid. It had been a major success, resulting in the well-deserved battle honour of FLUSHING.

The award of the next battle honour, WESTKAPELLE, was made to just two troops – the Belgian and Norwegian troops from No 10 Commando – for their part in the Walcheren operation. It was a unique honour inasmuch as it was the only specific Commando battle honour, as opposed to a campaign honour, awarded to sub-units (troops) – all the others were awarded to a Commando as a unit.

These two troops, under the overall command of Lieutenant Colonel Peter Laycock, joined Brigadier Leicester's Brigade in the Den Haan area at the end of September and were attached to No 41 Commando. On arrival they immediately started training for their part in the forthcoming operation, '*Infuriate*', although as Ian Dear records:

> There was time for the Belgian Troop to snatch a few days' leave to return to their homes, a brief but joyous reunion, but for some it was also a time of additional anxiety. One man found that his father was in prison for collaborating with the Germans and that the rest of the family had fled to Germany. Another discovered that his wife had left him for a Luftwaffe pilot.[26]

Brigadier Leicester's outline plan for the Westkapelle operation was as follows. His entire force would sail from Ostend during the night of 30 October–1 November and land in the early hours on the dunes of either side of the partially mined and flooded beaches of the village of Westkapelle. After clearing the village the commandos would separate to advance to the north and the south of the village to subsequently clear the banks of the Scheldt of the Germans' coastal batteries and other defences.

No 41, along with the detachment of Belgians and Norwegians from No 10, were to strike northwards towards Domburg, while the other two Commandos were to advance southwards along the coast from Westkapelle towards Flushing. The Belgians and Norwegians had two roles: one section of the Belgian troop was to provide close infantry protection to the tanks of 1st Lothians, who were supporting the Commandos' assault; the other section of this troop, plus the whole of the Norwegian troop, after helping No 41 to clear the village were to provide flank protection for No 41 in their advance to Domburg.

With all the coastal defences on the banks of the Scheldt cleared, the whole Commando Brigade was then to carry on and destroy the German units located in the north of the island and thus complete the seizure of Walcheren.

The three RM Commandos and their supporting troops left Ostend in the early hours of 1 November in a mixed armada of 182 vessels, including those of the Royal Navy Support Force, supplemented by the battleship *Warspite*. There were about one hundred tank-landing craft – such a large number was required to put ashore all the Weasels, Buffaloes, tanks, guns and, of course, two thousand men. This formidable naval force weighed anchor at 3.30 a.m. and sailed towards Westkapelle. Raymond Mitchell, who was in No 41, records:

> As the Task Force moved unhurriedly towards its objective, more and more of the Westkapelle tower was revealed, seeming to grow out of the ocean. The German look-outs at the top would have had ample time to count the precise number of vessels approaching Westkapelle, while the gun crews in their concrete emplacements could afford to eat a leisurely breakfast before the first ships would have come within range of even the heaviest artillery pieces.[27]

At 8.20 a.m. the naval support fire opened up on the enemy coastal batteries and defences, which were mostly well prepared with reinforced concrete bunkers and, in some cases, barbed-wire perimeters – although many of these were destroyed in the naval bombardment.

As a result of this fire support, which was intense and included the fifteen-inch guns of HMS *Warspite*, the landing flotilla had a comparatively easy passage towards the landing beaches. The majority of the casualties were suffered by the close-support naval monitors, nine of which were sunk by the enemy's counter-fire.

There were some casualties among the ships and landing craft of the landing force as well, however, and these included the craft carrying some of the tanks of the Lothians and their protection party from the Belgian troop. Their landing craft received three direct hits, damaging all the tanks and inflicting casualties among the tank crews and commandos. So serious were these that the skipper decided to abandon his mission and limp back to Ostend.

On the whole, though, the landing on the Westkapelle beaches went well and by 11.50 a.m. the Inter-Allied Commandos were all ashore and in action supporting their marine comrades.

The Belgian commandos supported No 41 in mopping-up operations in the northern part of Westkapelle whilst the Norwegians supported two troops of No 41 in an assault on a prominent enemy strongpoint. The Norwegians suffered some initial casualties but succeeded in getting into suitable firing positions, from a flank across open ground, to give covering fire to the marine commandos that was so effective that it forced the enemy to withdraw to underground cover. As a result No 41 was able to close on the battery emplacement and – with the support of an AVRE (Assault Vehicle Royal Engineers), which fired a 'dustbin' filled with high explosives instead of the conventional tank armament – successfully 'make the kill'.

Following this success Colonel Laycock brought his party, reduced to a total of fifteen altogether, to the battery area to set up his headquarters there; his two inter-allied troops from No 10 also reverted back to his command. With this reorganisation completed, Laycock was given the tasks of establishing a defensive position to secure Westkapelle, along with its landing beaches, and also beating off any enemy counter-attacks.

With his rear thus protected Leicester ordered the rest of No 41, with armoured support from those tanks of 1st Lothians that had successfully managed to land, plus artillery support from the Canadian gunners in the Breskens area, to press on to capture Domburg, destroying another major coastal battery en route.

The aim was to take the town before nightfall. However, although No 41 had nearly succeeded in this mission, Leicester had to change his plan because the joint advance by Nos 47 and 48 to the south towards Flushing was not progressing fast enough, and so he decided to transfer some of No 41 to speed up this southern advance. As a result, Laycock, with his two troops, was sent up to take over from No 41 on the outskirts of Domburg, where there were already two troops from No 41, which were placed under his command. The time was now about 4.30 p.m.

As Domburg was only partially captured there were enemy still in the town, dispensing sniper and machine-gun fire. Lieutenant Roman of the Belgian troop took out a fighting patrol and returned with some useful information that was put to use later when tanks from 1st Lothians and two AVREs arrived. Under Laycock's command, with Roman's information, they soon put an end to the snipers' and other small-arms fire, although Laycock's commandos still had to endure enemy mortar and shell fire throughout the night.

Next day Laycock decided to launch a co-ordinated attack on the enemy position from where the hostile fire of the previous night had probably originated. During the morning he sent out a reconnaissance patrol, followed in the afternoon by an assault by the Norwegian troop – supported by two tanks and a rolling barrage from the gunners in Breskens. The enemy position was well prepared with a wire perimeter and mines, but the Norwegian commandos, led by Captain Rolf Hauge, successfully advanced and got to the perimeter. Using a scaling ladder, Hauge attempted to breach the wire, but was hit by enemy fire and wounded in the arm. However, in spite of this setback they did manage to find a way through the obstacle, losing one killed and one wounded in the process. Nearing the concrete emplacement Lieutenant Gausland got close enough to lob a grenade through the entrance – this quickly brought a surrender of the occupants.

Hauge then reorganised and finding the way ahead clear, he decided to press on across the dunes to tackle two smaller outposts. Again they were successful; bolstered by these successes, Hauge then ordered Gausland to take his section on further and the latter found the large fortified enemy battery (W. 18) partially hidden in a dip in the ground. It was decided that this target was, without further reinforcements and planning, beyond the scope of Hauge's troop, so they withdrew back to Domburg. During the course of the Norwegians' actions that afternoon they had captured some 175 prisoners. On his return Captain Hauge was examined by the medical officer and his wound warranted him being evacuated back to Ostend, but he was later awarded the Military Cross for his leadership in this most successful skirmish.

This action was the last in the period covered by the WESTKAPELLE battle honour – 1 to 3 November – but No 4 Commando and the troops from No 10 continued, with the rest of the Commando Brigade, to clear the enemy from the north of the island. The concluding action took place near Vrouwenpolder on 7 November when the local German commander formally surrendered to Colonel Dawson and all the fighting there and across the rest of the island came to an end. Over nine hundred German prisoners marched into No 4 Commando's cage that day. Dawson in his report commented: 'No 4 Commando, the first to land on Operation *Infatuate*, had the unique distinction of being also the last troops in action and the recipients of the final surrender.'[28]

During the whole operation No 4's casualties amounted to one officer and twelve other ranks killed and one officer and twenty other ranks wounded. On the other hand the Commando had taken, in all, no less than twelve hundred prisoners and inflicted probably two hundred casualties, besides capturing and destroying large quantities of weapons and equipment of all sorts and sizes.

Little wonder that Dawson ended his report with: 'It had been a perfect little campaign', and No 4 and their Allied commando comrades from No 10 had added the battle honours of FLUSHING and WESTKAPELLE to the other thirty-six.

CHAPTER 12

NORTH-WEST EUROPE 1945
(The Rhine, Leese, and the Aller)

As MENTIONED EARLIER Mills-Roberts's Commando Brigade returned to England in September 1944 to be reinforced, reorganise, and prepare for active service in the Far East. However, during the late autumn the Allies' advance in north-west Europe suffered serious setbacks, especially when the Germans mounted a concerted counter-attack in the Ardennes with the ultimate aim of pushing the Allies back to Antwerp and Brussels. Initially they were successful, but by Christmas the German advance had been halted and sealed off.

Nevertheless it was decided that the Commando Brigade should return to Europe to reinforce the British Liberation Army (BLA) in their thrust towards Germany instead of joining their comrades in No 3 Commando Brigade in the Far East. So January 1945 saw them deployed in a defensive role on the line of the river Maas in Holland. However, it was not long before they were called upon to carry out offensive patrols. These were the first of a series of operations involving river crossings – five in all: the Maas, the Rhine, the Weser, the Aller, and the Elbe – that were carried out by the brigade as they pursued the enemy to the Baltic and final victory in May 1945.

Shortly afterwards, while the memories were still fresh in his mind, Brigadier Mills-Roberts compiled an account of these operations entitled, 'Five Rivers –

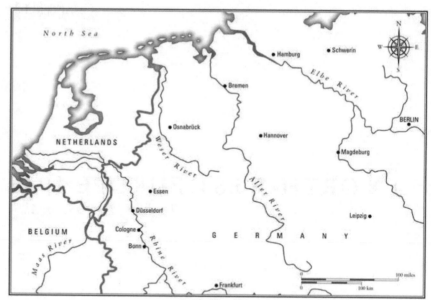

MAP 20. Five Rivers

First Commando Brigade, Germany 1945'. He later incorporated details from this account into his book, *Clash By Night*.

I have a rather battered copy of that original typed account. It was given to me in 1988 by the late Bert Draper, who had served in No 3 Commando, and he had received it from Colonel P. T. Bartholomew, DSO, who commanded No 3 during these operations. The following narrative has extracts from this unique account.

Of those five river crossings, only two, those over the Rhine and the Aller, qualified for the awards of battle honours; the other battle honour of this campaign was for Leese, an important German town, following the crossing of the river Weser. Therefore emphasis here will focus on these three honours, namely RHINE, LEESE, and ALLER in that order, although brief mentions will be made of a couple of other notable actions in the campaign.

The first of these actions took place towards the end of January when the brigade was involved in operations crossing a canal and capturing the town of Linne in the Allied drive to clear the enemy between the rivers Maas and Rhine.

Under the command of the 7 Armoured Division the commandos launched their advance on the bitterly cold night of 22 January when No 6 Commando successfully crossed the Juliana Canal, which was iced over. No 45 took over the lead and quickly captured the village of Brachterbeek without casualties. But then, when advancing towards the next village of Montefortebeek, the leading troop, under the command of Captain Dudley Coventry, came under heavy machine-gun fire, which inflicted several casualties.

Totally disregarding the danger, however, Lance Corporal Henry Harden (a pre-war butcher from Northfleet, Kent, who had enlisted in the Royal Army Medical Corps and subsequently trained for the commandos) attached to No 45 as a medical orderly boldly took immediate action to rescue three of his wounded marine comrades. Firstly, he ran across one hundred yards of open ground to the first casualty, gave him first aid, and, carrying him on his back, brought him back to safety. Although slightly wounded, and against all advice, he insisted on going back with two volunteer stretcher bearers to rescue another casualty, though the second wounded commando was hit and killed whilst on the stretcher. Undeterred, Harden went back for the third time to collect the section officer – but during the attempt Harden was hit in the head and killed.

Harden's supreme self sacrifice was rated as being in the highest traditions of the Commandos and the RAMC and he was later awarded a posthumous Victoria Cross. Buried in the Nederweert War Cemetery, his heroism is remembered and recorded on a plaque installed on the bridge at Brachterbeek.

Just after Harden's gallant rescue attempts the enemy counter-attacked but they were beaten off and the advance continued; with No 3 Commando leading, the town of Linne was captured on 24 January. On leaving that town the Commando Brigade, under the command of 7 Armoured Division, advanced towards the Allies' next major objective, the crossing of the Rhine.

Although Operation 'Plunder' (the crossing of the Rhine) did not take place until 23 March, Brigadier Mills-Roberts was briefed for his brigade's possible role whilst being involved in the actions just outlined on their way to the Rhine. Therefore they had two whole weeks to prepare and train for their formidable task in this special operation, which was rated as the most important and biggest single Allied operation after D-Day in the north-west Europe campaign.

The overall plan involved both the British Second Army and the US First Army, plus two airborne divisions. The latter were to drop on the eastern bank of the Rhine and link up with the Allied forces after they had crossed the river. The specific task of the Commando Brigade was to secure the right flank of the Allied (British) crossing by seizing the riverside town of Wesel following a heavy air attack on the town by Lancaster bombers on the evening of 23 March. This task allotted to the Commando Brigade was of vital importance because the town of Wesel was to become the most important communications centre on the British front.

A key factor in the overall plan was the bombing programme – Mills-Roberts reckoned that it was the cornerstone of the operation, on which was built the whole

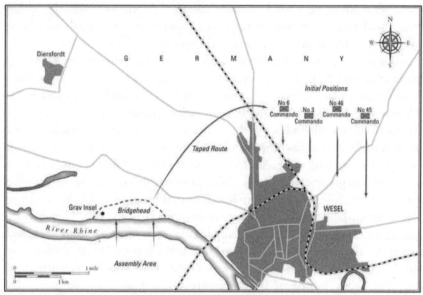

MAP 2I. Rhine Crossing

plan, with all the timings of the various phases and the tactical considerations linked to it. Furthermore, it was generally agreed that unless the bombing was successful the whole brigade operation would be extremely hazardous.

The town of Wesel had a population of about 24,000 and the river at this point was about three hundred yards wide with quite high flood banks. Fortunately Mills-Roberts was able to carry out a thorough reconnaissance of the area during that fortnight's period of preparations – as a result he was able to draw the following conclusions, on which he based his ultimate plan for the brigade.

Firstly, in order to gain the full effect of the intense bombing programme the commandos must be ready to enter the town almost on the heels of the Lancasters, and therefore they had to accept the risk of crossing the river during the bombing and to advance up to the town, ready to enter it as soon as possible after the bombing – 'while the defenders were still punch-drunk.'

Secondly, he decided for several tactical reasons that a frontal attack across the river on Wesel was out of the question, so once again he planned an outflanking attack on the town, employing those key principles of surprise and speed.

His plan, therefore, was based on landing two miles downstream from the town on a flat marshy area known as 'Grav Insel', and establishing a secure bridgehead there with one of his Commandos (No 46). The other three Commandos would then pass through the bridgehead and advance in 'Indian file' to the north-western outskirts of the town, using his tested 'white-tape marking' technique that had proved so successful in Normandy.

At the last stage of the planning it was decided that the RAF would mount a second bombing raid on Wesel while the commandos were crossing the river and assembling in the bridgehead. So to take advantage of this bonus Mills-Roberts allotted areas in the northern suburbs for his commandos to make for on arrival at the outskirts. But although they would send out patrols from their respective areas, no attempt would be made to actually clear the town before daylight or before any counter-attacks from the enemy outside the town had been dealt with.

Mills-Roberts also wanted all traces of his bridgehead cleared before daylight, so leaving the enemy in complete ignorance as to the strength of his force and its whereabouts. With this in mind No 46 (RM) Commando was to follow up in the rear of the rest of the brigade and join their comrades in Wesel.

Finally, the enemy tank threat was assessed as 'slight'; it was reckoned that the rubble and damage in the town resulting from the devastating bombing raids would preclude the use of tanks – any attempt to employ tanks could be coped with by using captured German 'Panzerfausts' and the brigade's own anti-tank weapons, along with artillery support.

For two weeks prior to Operation *Plunder* the brigade was able to concentrate on boat training in the Venray area where a small creek, soon to become known as 'Commando Creek', provided ideal facilities for both boat and LVT (Buffaloes and Weasels) training, which was co-ordinated by a specialist, Major Reid, from Commando group headquarters. This period of training was most successful and impressed several high-ranking officers visiting the commandos. By the end of the fortnight Mills-Roberts was able to report that 'no man in the Brigade felt any river was an obstacle to him' and he was also able to later quip, 'Hannibal crossed the Alps using elephants, my commandos crossed the Rhine using Buffaloes.' It is also interesting to mention that in this period some dories – motor-driven craft eighteen feet long and used by the commandos in their training for rocky landings – together with their instructors were brought over from St Ives in Cornwall, for use on the crossing as 'rescue boats'. On 20 March the brigade moved into the concentration area – a few miles back from the crossing area opposite Wesel – for those last-minute preparations, which in this case proved to be considerable, especially the organising of the boats and LVTs.

The plan was finalised as follows: No 46, together with Mills-Roberts's small tactical headquarters, were to cross in Buffaloes to Grav Insel at 10 p.m. on the night of 23 March to destroy the enemy in the area and establish the bridgehead.

No 6 Commando were to follow in stormboats, then No 45 (also in stormboats – some forty in all of these craft were used), and finally No 3, crossing in the Buffaloes. In this last wave a number of Weasels were also to be ferried across in the Buffaloes. The Weasels carried medical and engineer teams.

No 6 was to lead the advance from the bridgehead to the northern outskirts of Wesel and on arrival there establish a firm base for the rest of the brigade to pass through to their allotted areas. No 45 had the important task of holding the area around a large factory that was considered to be a key defensive position. At daylight it was hoped to start clearing the town – a priority that morning would be clearing a route down the west side of the town down to the river bank and railway bridge so that a Buffalo ferry could be set up to enable the 1st Battalion of the Cheshire Regiment to cross over and start to relieve the Commando Brigade of the occupation of the town.

At 10 a.m. the 17th US Airborne Division was due to drop in the area north-west of Wesel and they too were to link up with the Commandos. So much for the outline plan.

The morning of 23 March was spent on the final preparations, including last-minute briefings, checking of weapons and equipment, issue of ammunition, and the priming of grenades, as well as collecting 'Mae Wests' and emergency rations. Nonetheless, the commandos did have a treat for their midday meal – not out of a tin, but half of a chicken! – after which they were dismissed to rest before the night operation.

In the late afternoon they heard the approaching Lancasters, nearly one hundred of them, heading towards Wesel; at 5.30 p.m. precisely their bombs began to fall on the German town. The bombing lasted about fifteen minutes and was followed at 6 p.m. by a programme of artillery barrages on enemy targets – including Grav Insel – on the far bank of the river; this continued on selective targets well after H hour. The continuous noise of all the gunfire, on top of the bombing, prompted Colonel Bartholomew, who was now commanding No 3 Commando in the wake of Colonel Komrower's departure to join us at Achnacarry as Chief Instructor, to write in his diary: 'It seemed as if more than mortal powers had been unleashed.'

At 9 p.m. No 46 Commando and Mills-Roberts's headquarters party embarked in their Buffaloes about one mile inland from the Rhine and started on their way. Their crossing went well and they landed just before 10 p.m.; they found that the gunners' bombardment had been very effective. Though one enemy position did put up some stubborn resistance, this was quelled and within half an hour the commandos had cleared the area and were establishing their bridgehead – although they had casualties, they had also captured over seventy prisoners. It was a good start.

Next to cross was No 6 in their stormboats. They, of course, had to march down from the concentration area to the river bank to embark on their craft – no 'cushy' ride in the Buffaloes for them!

Bill Sadler, a signaller in No 6 takes up the story:

> En-route to the river, our column passed through a number of heavily engaged artillery positions, and from then on the march was to the accompaniment of the crash and thunder of the guns and the sound of the shells continually passing overhead, the packs and equipment began to assume twice their original proportions and weight, but shortly before reaching the river a halt was called to supply the column with some unexpected and welcome refreshments, the packs and equipment being left in a position to move off again, while each man collected his issue of tea, rum and sandwiches – the last bread we would see until after the war.[1]

Sandler goes on to compare the noise of the artillery fire 'to the opening movement of Beethoven's Fifth Symphony or the more impressive parts of the 1812 Overture'.

No 6 Commando's crossing, on the whole, went well although some boats had problems. It was later claimed that RSM Woodcock had three stormboats shot out from under him during the crossing; fortuitously those four dory 'life boats' manned by the commando instructors from St Ives did sterling work picking up survivors from the water. In spite of these problems the crossings of the other two Commandos went as well as could be expected and the brigade was able to reorganise in the bridgehead as planned – and on time. A few minutes before 10.30 p.m. the leading RAF Pathfinder flew low over the town of Wesel and dropped its marking flares. The bombs followed – Mills-Roberts wrote: 'for fifteen minutes nothing could be heard but the shriek of the descending bombs and the terrible explosions around the glare of the Pathfinders' flares.'[2]

Meanwhile a troop of No 6, led by Major C. E .J. Leaphard, had started its advance out of the bridgehead – followed by the rest – and was making steady progress, although it did meet opposition from a strongly defended flak position soon after starting. The men were able to quickly deal with it and the advance was only delayed for a short while, albeit they had some casualties: seven wounded, who were evacuated back to the bridgehead. By midnight Leaphard's men had reached the outskirts of the town. Meeting only weak opposition they quickly were able to establish their allocated troop position, thus enabling the rest of their Commando, led by Colonel Tony Lewis, to take up their positions according to plan.

After the two heavy air raids, the commandos found the town a complete shambles, 'resembling the surface of the moon, with huge craters and the air full of smoke and dust'. Nevertheless the two Commandos that were following, Nos 3 and 45, who had made good progress along the taped route, reached their comrades without any problems, whilst back in the bridgehead No 46 had reorganised and were also on their way to Wesel. Some of the Weasels had returned to the 'home' bank of the Rhine with wounded commandos and the German prisoners.

By 3 a.m. the brigade was established in the north-west suburbs of the town, although No 45 did meet some opposition on their way to the factory area with a few casualties – including their commanding officer, Colonel W. N. Gray, but he kept going for the next forty-eight hours before being evacuated for further treatment.

From their respective areas the Commandos sent patrols out with limited objectives – though one of these from No 6 had great success. Led by RSM Woodcock, his patrol discovered the local overall commander, General van Deutsch, and his staff in an underground shelter. The general was killed by a burst of machine-gun fire while attempting to resist; the rest of the staff were captured. The patrol also found a haul of maps showing details and dispositions of all the enemy units in the area – the relevant details were quickly sent back to corps headquarters where plans were promptly effected to bombard some of the flak positions in advance of the fly-in of the US airborne division due at 10 a.m. that morning.

At about 5.30 a.m. an enemy patrol of cyclists approached the positions held by two troops of No 45 in the factory area. They seemed to be completely ignorant of the commandos' whereabouts and so they were, in the words of Mills-Roberts, 'well and truly punctured, leaving ten dead and the rest fled in disorder'.[3]

A little later another patrol from No 6 Commando, moving down the western side of the town, got to the railway bridge over the Rhine to find that it was only partially blown, so a party from the brigade's signal troop under Lieutenant Christie was able, with great difficulty, to lay a telephone line across. 'It was quite a daring feat as they moved from girder to girder high above the river, under spasmodic machine-gun fire from some isolated enemy in the southern corner of the town.'[3]

As the morning wore on several counter-attacks were made on the Commandos' position, including a particularly strong one on No 45's position. Although it was repulsed Mills-Roberts decided to send Captain Alan Milne's troop from No 3 to reinforce the marines. A self-propelled gun also appeared and started to shell the commandos' positions. At about 1.30 p.m. it was observed that a strong enemy force appeared to be assembling, ready to launch an attack – the SP gun had also moved up to within four hundred yards of the factory, obviously ready to provide supporting fire. Fortunately, Major Rushton, the gunner officer at brigade headquarters, was able to arrange a devastating fire programme that broke up this enemy concentration and they apparently 'withdrew in disorder'.

However, through the night and the next day (24 March) and until the link up with the American airborne division could be made secure sporadic counter-attacks from outside the town continued. The commandos held on, though, and during the afternoon the Buffalo ferry was established to the railway bridge so that by 7 p.m. that evening the men of the relieving Cheshire Regiment had crossed over and were in positions to keep the route through the town clear.

The brigade remained in their positions throughout the night of 24–25 March, during which the enemy made some counter-attacks. Again these were mostly against the commandos in the factory area, but they were beaten off by 'aggressive defence and some superbly accurate supporting fire' from the brigade's gunners; the 1st Mountain Regiment, RA, inflicting very heavy casualties on the enemy.

Early next morning (25 March) the link up with the American airborne was completed and the brigade came under their command. Operations were started to mop up those isolated groups of enemy still in the town. The Commandos, the Cheshires, and the Americans were all involved in these operations: No 3 Commando successfully cleared the centre of the town, whilst by evening No 46 had patrolled right to the east of the town, down to a tributary of the Rhine, and made contact with the American Ninth Army.

By nightfall the capture of the town was completed and the Commandos' job was done. In all nearly nine hundred prisoners were captured and hundreds of enemy lay dead, particularly in their slit trenches at Grav Insel, in the streets of Wesel, and on the approaches to the factory in the north of the town. It must, of course, be remembered that many of the enemy casualties and the demoralisation that led to the Germans surrendering must be attributed to the devastating combined bombing and fire power of the RAF and the artillery. Nevertheless, it was a great and important Commando victory. In striking contrast to the enemy casualty figures, those of the Commando Brigade were relatively light: eight killed, seventy-one wounded, and seventeen missing.

The task completed, Mills-Roberts received many messages of congratulations to pass on to his men from the army commander, General Ritchie, downwards. The general wrote:

> A very fine show and I would like to congratulate you all on your success. You will have realised how much importance was attached to your mission, without Wesel it would be impossible adequately to develop the operation of the Second Army. We are very proud to have you with us and are delighted that such resounding success has been yours.[4]

On a lighter note, Mills-Roberts recalls, in his account, 'that night the large barrel of excellent hock which had been captured at the enemy Headquarters was slaking many thirsty throats as the stories of the battle were recounted.'[5]

There is no doubt that the battle honour of the RHINE is a most worthy one and the account of the whole operation is aptly summed up by Mills-Roberts with these words: 'The battle had gone exactly as planned, at no time did we lose the initiative, and the timetable had been religiously adhered to even by the enemy himself. The Brigade was in tremendous heart, and eager to leave the dust of Wesel and pursue the beaten enemy to the Baltic.'[6]

The brigade spent the next few days under the command of the American airborne division, but on 29 March they came under the command of their old friends, the 6th Airborne Division. They were in reserve for a few days then were involved in the operation to seize Osnabruck. The initial assault on the city by the paratroopers had been held up in the western outskirts, so the Commando Brigade was ordered to attack and capture the centre of the city. After a reconnaissance on the afternoon of 3 April, Mills-Roberts decided that, as the paras were held up in the southern outskirts, any further assault from that quarter would be fiercely contested. So he decided to carry out an outflanking night advance and approach the city via the north to mount a dawn attack from this, hopefully, unexpected quarter.

The night march led by a troop from No 3 went well in spite of some short delays and the attack went in at dawn. Although the commandos met spirited opposition they made steady, if slow, progress towards the centre of the city. One particular success occurred when Captain John Clapton, with his troop from No 6, with great flair stormed a stubbornly defended enemy position in the factory area, killing six Germans and capturing a further twenty, for the loss of just three wounded. However, it was not until next morning when No 3 cleared an area by the canal that the city – the largest yet occupied on German soil by British forces – was finally cleared by the brigade, with a total of 450 prisoners and fifty enemy killed and wounded. Among those killed was the local chief of the Gestapo who had been tracked down by Captain Arthur de Jonghe, the brigade field intelligence officer and a colourful Belgian viscount who had volunteered for the Commandos early on, and at one time was a fellow instructor of mine at Achnacarry.

Bill Sadler, who had been the troop signaller with Captain Cruden of No 6 Commando, recalls his amusing experiences at the conclusion of this successful operation:

> 2 Troop established Troop Headquarters and its signal station in the library of one of the larger houses, which also contained an extensive collection of classical, dance and military band records, together with (Nazi) rally songs including '*We March Against England*'. Some of these records accompanied us further into Germany, together with an excellent gramophone, carried for us in the Troop jeep, which always arrived after a position had been taken. The jeep driver was also the Troop cook, so his arrival was always welcomed.[7]

The next major operation was the battle for Leese: a town on the far bank of the third of the five rivers, namely the Weser. After leaving Osnabruck the Commando Brigade had been placed under the command of the 11 Armoured Division to assist in the crossing of the Weser, a fairly fast-flowing river about eighty yards wide.

On arrival at the river the commandos found that a company of the Rifle Brigade had successfully made a crossing in assault boats during the previous night and had established a small bridgehead on the far bank, but they were coming under counter-attacks that threatened any further building-up of the bridgehead and subsequent pursuit of the enemy. These attacks seemed to be mounted by German troops stationed in Leese itself. As a result the divisional commander ordered Mills-Roberts to capture the town.

No 45 (RM) Commando was rushed up to cross the river and assault the town; the crossing in stormboats, which had by now been brought up, was completely successful and Major Alf Blake, RM, who was commanding in the place of Colonel Gray (still receiving treatment for the wounds he had received at Wesel) decided to mount an immediate frontal attack – across open ground

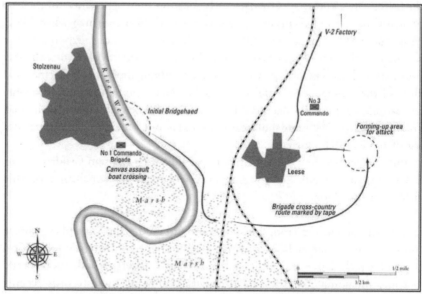

MAP 22. Leese (courtesy of Mrs J Mills-Roberts)

— on the town, which was barely a mile away.

However, the leading troop soon met stiff opposition from the enemy in prepared positions – although the marine commandos did have some successes in the initial firefight it soon became apparent to Major Blake that the enemy were in much greater numbers than originally appreciated and their defences were deep and strong. Furthermore, it was learnt from one of the prisoners captured in the initial skirmish that the enemy were mostly young fanatical recruits from the 12th SS Training Regiment, and even Mills-Roberts later admitted that 'their sniping was first class.' As a result it was decided that the whole brigade would be required to assault and capture the town of Leese, although this meant that the operation could not be mounted until all of the brigade had crossed the Weser, as sufficient craft were not readily available, there was a delay whilst more boats could be brought up.

The situation also suffered another setback when, during the afternoon, the Luftwaffe made one of its rare but really determined appearances; it was estimated that about forty planes took part in the raids. A bridge under construction was damaged, and nearly fifty royal engineers employed on the task were wounded. The air raids also disrupted the other river crossings that were possible, and as a result only No 3 got across that night and took over the bridgehead from the riflemen. During the night an enemy patrol tried to rush one of No 45's outposts but were repulsed, leaving seven dead on the ground.

Next day the enemy shelled the commandos in the bridgehead, inflicting some casualties. However, more boats arrived and so the rest of the brigade was able to cross over during the hours of darkness; by midnight all of the Commando Brigade was concentrated on the far bank and ready to attack Leese. Once more Mills-Roberts shunned the idea of a frontal attack and favoured another outflanking advance across some marshy ground to attack the town from the rear. No 6 was chosen to lead the brigade – Captain Cruden's No 2 Troop blazing the trail, with the rest of the commandos following in single file along a marked tape route.

This time, though, the going was tough, especially crossing the marshy area as many of the ditches were full of water. Mills-Roberts reckoned it was 'the most arduous march of the campaign'. Fortunately the enemy seemed to have no idea of the commandos' presence, probably because the commandos' supporting artillery fire during the night was concentrated on those enemy positions between the river and the southern outskirts of the town, suggesting to the enemy a frontal attack. However, there were one or two 'hairy' moments as the commandos advanced. Bill Sandier wrote: 'We were not immune to surprises ourselves, Captain Cruden later confessed to a few moments of unease when he had to resort to a torch in a barn to check his position on a map.'[8]

The advance eventually got to a metalled road near the railway embankment and there Captain Cruden's men had their first success when the leading section, nearing the end of the approach march, came across a flak position where the dual-purpose guns were actually firing on the original bridgehead positions, unaware of the commandos' nearby presence!

Captain Peter Cruden and his men rushed the position and captured four 20-mm guns and two German officers – the rest of the crews 'disappeared into the darkness'. Other enemy in the area were all caught completely by surprise and by 7 a.m. on 8 April the town was completely in the commandos' hands, having killed about thirty Germans and captured some fifty prisoners in the action, while the commandos lost four killed and twenty-two wounded. The brigade intelligence officer later learned from his interrogation of prisoners that the main force had evacuated the town in the early hours of darkness during the previous evening.

However, there was a further unexpected prize from this operation when a patrol from Colonel Bartholomew's No 3 Commando later that morning went off to investigate a factory location about one mile north of Leese. After Mills-

Roberts had signalled their early morning success, tanks were pushed over the repaired bridge to provide support. The leading commando troop, whilst crossing open ground en route to the factory, came under small-arms fire and the troop Leader, Captain John Alderson, was killed. Colonel Bartholomew was following up and he jumped on to one of the tanks and directed its fire at the enemy position at close range. This prompt action saved the situation and the commandos pressed on to the factory. By 1 p.m. the factory had been captured and the commandos, much to their surprise, discovered that it was evidently connected with the manufacture of the V-2 weapon, for there on the railway siding they found a long train of low wagons and on each one was a V-2 rocket. As well as capturing this important factory intact, they rounded up its complete staff of scientists. It was a fitting climax to a very successful operation and the subsequent battle honour of LEESE.

Following this success the brigade left the Leese area, still under the command of II Armoured Division, and advanced towards the next river obstacle, the Aller. By nightfall on 9 April they were at Helsdorf, available to assist in the crossing of the river. The following day the leading elements of the armoured division got within a mile of the river before being held up by enemy still holding positions that covered the only road leading to the bridge. Consequently Mills-Roberts was ordered to force a crossing of the river that night and if possible capture the bridge intact so that the armour could cross over and continue the pursuit.

After his reconnaissance Mills-Roberts decided to try and cross over the river by a railway bridge that was about a mile further downstream. Late that night the brigade set off with No 3 as vanguard and the leading troop laying white tape down to the railway bridge, which they reached just before midnight. As the troop, under Captain Guernsey, neared the bridge there was a loud explosion. However, following a quick 'recce' of the bridge, Guernsey discovered that only the first span of the bridge had been blown and fortunately this was over flat ground before reaching the water, so it did not really present a major problem.

Captain Guernsey decided to send one of his sections, led by Lieutenant Arthur Wardle (a Mancunian shopkeeper before the war) to dash over – in their stockinged feet – in a quick surprise assault. They acted with such speed that the bridge was successfully rushed and the small enemy post defending it destroyed, although Wardle did have five of his men wounded. Fortunately there were no further explosions, although a detachment of the royal marine engineer troop that was attached to No 3 Commando did discover some charges laid under the bridge. They quickly defused these, enabling the rest of the Commando Brigade to cross over the bridge in safety and follow No 3, albeit they did have to run the gauntlet of some sporadic enemy gunfire.

On the far bank the commandos took up defensive positions in front of a wooded area; whilst plans were then being made to attack the enemy guarding the road bridge, the Germans started to launch counter-attacks. In one of these, directed at the area occupied by No 3 and tactical brigade headquarters, the enemy using a covered approach through the wood, got within fifty yards of the commandos' position, and the firefight went on for nearly three hours. At one stage a German even got within yards of the brigadier himself, but fortunately he was warned and fired his Garand rifle (a souvenir from his days in North Africa with No 6) just in time. He later wrote: 'I had the safety catch off my Garand and let him have it . . . I hit him. A yell, a sob and a moan and no more.'[9]

Unfortunately in this particular attack Captain James Griffiths, a German-speaking officer from No 10 Commando serving in Mills-Roberts's headquarters, was killed. Captain Rushton, the FOO, was once again able to call up artillery support and this proved to be so effective that the counter-attacks petered out following heavy enemy losses. Among the dead later identified were the bodies of the German commanding officer, his adjutant, and two company commanders.

Nevertheless, the situation was such that Mills-Roberts had to amend his original plans for the capture of the road bridge. He decided to use No 6 Commando, who were uncommitted at this stage, for the assault. Due to the proximity of the other Commandos, close artillery support for their attack was ruled out — instead No 6's Vickers machine guns, skilfully placed on the right flank and firing almost non-stop for thirty minutes on the enemy positions, provided covering fire right up to the start of the final charge. Sadler sets the scene:

> The moment they [the machine gunners] stopped firing, each man knew what he had to do. Lying there with bayonets fixed, nine rounds in the magazine and one up the spout, safety catches off. The commandos just waited for the bullets to stop. The moment they did so, No 6 Commando rose to its feet as one man, and with the second-in-command sounding a 'tally ho!' on his hunting horn, they charged forward.[10]

The chronicler of the souvenir No 6 brochure rated this action to be 'No 6 Commando's finest hour' and goes on to describe that bayonet charge through the woods of Essler: 'and like one man the unit rose to its feet and raced through 500 yards of wood towards the bridge with the men shouting at the top of their voices. The enemy, terrified at such a spectacle, got up and ran, but were immediately shot down before they had a chance to escape.'[11]

Shortly after 11.30 a.m. the road bridge, which had been blown some two hours before, was captured by No 6 – led by Colonel Lewis himself – and the unit consolidated on the line of the road. Over fifty enemy dead were later counted in the path of the commandos' bayonet charge through the wood and over seventy-five prisoners were captured, thirty of whom were wounded.

Just as the commandos were completing their consolidation at the bridge a strong counter-attack was mounted by two fresh companies of the enemy's Marine Fusilier Battalion. Although the commandos were running short of ammunition, this attack was repulsed, with heavy losses to the enemy. Later that afternoon No 46 arrived to reinforce and help their comrades of No 6 to establish a secure bridgehead; when this was achieved the ferrying and bridging operations were able to go ahead. The ferrying also included the dispatch of the wounded back to field hospitals for treatment.

At the end of the day the Commando Brigade had fulfilled its initial mission, although the action in and beyond the bridge continued for another two days – during which time they were engaged in some fierce fighting to expand the bridgehead and in particular to capture the village of Hadenstorf, which dominated the new bridge that the engineers had constructed to replace the blown road bridge. However, by the evening of 13 April, following the capture of the village by No 45 (RM) Commando, the battle to secure the crossing over the Aller came to an end.

In his summary Mills-Roberts wrote: 'Much had been achieved. The river Aller had been crossed, a bridge had been built, two Marine Fusilier Battalions, one S.S. Training Battalion and an anti-tank Battalion had been severely mauled. The Brigade's casualties had not been light . . .'[12]

The losses in all four Commandos amounted to a total of twenty-nine all ranks killed and nearly one hundred all ranks wounded; however, the enemy losses as already indicated were much heavier, in addition to those killed the enemy prisoners totalled nearly two hundred.

Among the messages of congratulation subsequently received by Mills-Roberts was one from General B. H. Barker, CB, CBB, DSO, MC, the corps commander, which says it all and provides a pertinent footnote to the battle honour of the ALLER: '. . . I must congratulate you most heartily on the really excellent show your Brigade has put up in the Aller bridgehead. Your crossing must have been well planned and executed, and the way you defeated all the counter-attacks the following day with such heavy casualties to the marine opposition was quite splendid . . .'[13]

Although the Aller operation was the last battle honour for the Commandos' participation in the north-west Europe campaign it was not their last action because there was still that final fifth river, the Elbe.

After the Aller they moved forward with the armoured division to Luneburg, where for nine days they had a 'well-earned rest' and the chance to reorganise for further action. This shortly followed when they were placed under the command of the 15th (Scottish) Division to support them in their crossing of the Elbe by protecting their right flank with the capture of the town of Lauenburg and then seizing two bridges over the Elbe–Trave Canal that was just beyond the town.

The river at the proposed crossing site was about as wide as the Rhine, and unfortunately, its banks were major obstacles themselves as they were steep and up to one hundred feet high. On this crossing the whole brigade was to be ferried across in Buffaloes and they were also to have the support for the later stages of the operation from a battalion of the Seaforth Highlanders and a squadron of DD tanks (which stood for 'Duplex Drive' – these were amphibious tanks that could 'swim' across rivers) from the Staffordshire Yeomanry.

A co-ordinated programme of 'softening-up' support was planned from both the RAF and the artillery, although because of bad weather the immediate pre-crossing bombing had to be cancelled, so that the actual river crossings went ahead with just artillery support.

At 2 a.m. on 29 April the commandos in their Buffaloes commenced their crossing; No 6 in the first wave had responsibility for storming the enemy positioned on those steep banks and then establishing a bridgehead on the far side for the brigade to pass through. Once again Mills-Roberts had selected a crossing place downstream from the actual objective and an outflanking advance to attack the town of Lauenburg from the rear.

In spite of the artillery's supporting fire, No 6 in their Buffaloes did come under some small-arms fire from the enemy occupying the bank, however their first two troops – under the leadership of the Commando's 'heavenly twins', captains John Clapton and Peter Cruden – showing lots of guts and determination, scrambled up the bank in the dark, 'under a hail of grenades', and dashed on to successfully deal with the enemy in the outposts and then cleared the immediate area. The rest of the Commando followed up and soon a secure bridgehead was established to allow the rest of the brigade to pass through.

Leading the brigade's advance was Captain Norman Easton's troop of No 46

(RM) Commando and they were followed by Mills-Roberts with his small headquarters and the rest of No 46; next came No 3 Commando following close behind on the tape. All was going well when a lucky shell from the enemy fell on the tape line and caused half a dozen casualties to the marine commandos of No 46 – but apart from this incident the advance towards Lauenburg went according to plan. By 4 a.m. the leading troop of No 46 had seized the high ground in the northern outskirts that had been selected as the start line for the brigade's assault on the town, but they soon found – much to their surprise – the enemy also digging in in the same area.

Charles Messenger in his book quotes an account from No 46 (RM) Commando's history of this bizarre situation: 'As night turned into day, some confusion and amusement was caused when it was found that British and German troops were digging side by side. No fight was left in the Boche, who were promptly disarmed and then made to adjust their position to suit our requirements.'[14]

Meanwhile the other three Commandos, followed by the Seaforth Highlanders, were approaching the town and by 5.30 a.m. all the Commandos were ready in their respective areas to start the clearing of the town, whilst a patrol from No 3 Commando had already pushed forward and captured the main bridge over the Elbe–Trave Canal. The end quickly followed: by 8 a.m. the town was virtually cleared and the enemy had clearly lost the will to fight on, as the haul of some 650 prisoners suggests. With the town taken and the enemy eliminated, bridging operations over the Elbe got underway. Meanwhile the DD tanks had arrived; together with the Seaforth Highlanders they began to exploit the situation and push on beyond the town. Their mission completed, the Commando Brigade consolidated in Lauenburg and became the division's reserve. So ended the last of the Brigade's five river crossings.

The commandos' next task was simple enough – to go as hard as they could for Neustadt on the Baltic as part of the general advance of the Allied forces in the wake of the collapse of German resistance. As they advanced the commandos found the countryside filled with masses of refugees, disorganised German soldiery, escaped Allied prisoners, and lots of pitiful escapees from concentration camps in the area, including the notorious Belsen.

In the context of stories of the Allied prisoners of war, who were escaping from their Stalags in the wake of the Russian advance from the east, one of No 6's men, D. Blackburn, relates a most remarkable incident. He starts his story by recalling that when No 6 Commando had to withdraw from Green Hill in North Africa (see Chapter 6) they had to leave some of their wounded in the care of the troop medical orderly/stretcher bearer, who had volunteered to stay behind with them knowing full well he would be taken prisoner. Blackburn then goes on to relate how No 6 had taken up a temporary position during their advance towards the Baltic and continues:

> Having posted a look-out, the rest of the section stood down. After a while the look-out shouted, 'Movement ahead to immediate front!' and we saw two figures. One was in RAF uniform and the other wore khaki . . . We were very cautious . . . It was full sunlight and we lay very low as the two figures unsuspectingly approached . . . when they were in shouting distance, we hailed them, 'Halt, who goes there?' The reply came, 'British prisoners of war.' We replied, 'Advance slowly' and as they came towards me I could not believe my eyes. 'Good God! It's Garth!' The stretcher bearer who had stayed behind two years before on that hilltop in Africa had walked straight into his own section in the middle of Germany. Out of, I suppose, one million British, American, French and Canadian troops, he had walked into his own unit – incredible![15]

The brigade continued its advance to the Baltic town of Neustadt. On arrival there Mills-Roberts's men found plenty of evidence of atrocities perpetrated by the Germans including 'many corpses of displaced persons . . . who had been butchered by their S.S. captors.'

It was in Neustadt on 4 May that Brigadier Mills-Roberts took the surrender of all the German forces in the area under the command of Field Marshal Erhard Milch. It has been reputed that Mills-Roberts had been so disgusted with the sights and reports of atrocities that, on receiving the Field Marshal's baton as the token of his surrender, he hit Milch on the head with it!

Notwithstanding, this surrender provided a fitting climax to the Commando Brigade's trail of successes in their six-week campaign in Germany, during which they had won the three battle honours of the RHINE, LEESE, and the ALLER as a legacy of their gallant actions – and their sacrifices – in the fight for the liberation of occupied Europe.

Although the war in Europe came to an end with VE Day, it was not the end of the Second World War – our forces, including commandos, were still fighting against the Japanese in the Far East, for as Mills-Roberts wrote at the time, in the conclusions of his account: 'The story of the First Commando Brigade in Europe ends here, the Pacific lies ahead.'

CHAPTER 13

BURMA 1943–1945
(Alethangyaw, Myebon, and Kangaw)

ON 15 NOVEMBER 1943 No 3 Commando Brigade, commanded by Brigadier
W. I. Nonweiller, RM, and consisting of two army Commandos (Nos 1 and
5) and two Royal Marines Commandos (Nos 42 and 44) had left Gourock on
the Clyde in two troopships for India and subsequent action against the Japanese
in Burma.

A detachment of commando officers and NCOs had been sent out to India
in March 1942 to help in the training of Wingate's Chindits for their long-
range jungle operations and these commando officers and NCOs stayed on and
took part in the subsequent Chindit operations. One of them, Lieutenant
Jeffery Lockett, from my old troop in No 4, not only won promotion to
lieutenant colonel, but was also decorated with the Military Cross. Detachments
of the Special Boat Section also took part in operations in Burma during
1943–44. Apart from these particular commandos, however, the men of No 3
Commando Brigade were the only 'green berets' to fight alongside the British
and Commonwealth forces – often referred to euphemistically as the 'Forgotten
Army' – in this theatre of war. Certainly public interest and media cover right
up to VE Day was almost exclusively centred on the Allies' fighting in North
Africa and Europe and very little coverage was afforded to the forces fighting
in the Far East.

However, that was not all: the forces in the Far East also suffered from shortages in weapons, equipment, and the other requisites of war. This was particularly frustrating for Admiral Mountbatten, who took over as supreme commander for South-East Asia in 1943, and was keen to carry out offensive amphibious operations on the coasts of Burma, but was denied sufficient landing craft for any large-scale amphibious operations.

The Commandos' two troopships en route to India in November 1943 were part of a larger convoy and their journey from Britain was going well until, as they were sailing through the Mediterranean, they were twice attacked by German bombers. The first attack, just off Algiers, resulted in the loss of one merchant ship; in the second attack on 29 November the *Ranchi*, the troopship carrying Nos 1 and 42 Commandos, was hit – there were casualties, though none were commandos. There was, however, severe damage to one side of the ship, and the *Ranchi* had to put into Alexandria for repairs. The other troopship with the rest of the brigade onboard continued on its passage to India, reaching Bombay on 10 December 1943.

As a result Nos 1 and 42 Commandos had to disembark at Alexandria and encamp at Amyria, some fifteen miles away in the desert. Although these two Commandos had the bonus of spending Christmas Day on dry land, it was not until early January that alternative shipping became available to transport them to India. At Amyria their time was spent on training, though this was confined to basic and fitness training and not specifically applicable to jungle warfare. Eventually they disembarked in Bombay in early January 1944, but surprisingly it was not until September that year that the brigade was reunited, when they joined forces in Ceylon (Sri Lanka).

In the meanwhile Nos 5 and 44 Commandos, after a brief spell of jungle training, took part in operations in the Arakan. The other two Commandos underwent a more lengthy and thorough spell of jungle and amphibious training, but all had to learn how to adapt to the vastly different climatic and health conditions of this theatre of war.

Describing this training, 'Tag' Barnes of No 1 provides an apt introduction:

The jungle was exactly as one had seen on films at the cinema (pre-war), except the high tree canopy proved to be so dense it blotted out most of the sun's rays, thus creating a twilight effect throughout the day. However the rest was all there, the towering trees hanging with vines, the whistling and screeching of birds and animals, day and night, the monsoon beetles which whined through the trees in their thousands.[1]

There was only one way to prepare to fight ruthless, cunning, and experienced jungle warriors, such as the Japanese, in this type of terrain and that was to live and train in the densest parts of the jungle for days and nights on end, and to adapt the predominantly European tactics and battle techniques to the vastly different jungle environment. Nos 5 and 44 Commandos did not get the same opportunities to train and prepare for this type of warfare as did their comrades in the other two Commandos – they had to learn 'on the job' as we shall see.

Nos 1 and 42 started their jungle training in the Belguam area in central India and later underwent some amphibious training at a 'horrible place', Cocanada, on the Bay of Bengal, where conditions were terrible and malaria and dysentery were rife. Fortunately, by the time the commandos had arrived in the Far East medical resources for fighting these diseases had greatly improved and the commandos normally received a daily ration of three essential tablets: mepacrine (anti-malaria), vitamin 'C', and salt. Henry Brown of No 1 Commando reckoned that 'the mepacrine tablets were a boon against the dreaded malaria – in fact many of us after a month were almost as brown as the tablets, but they did the trick.'

Finally, on this subject of training and preparing for jungle warfare, mention must be made of a tactical innovation developed by the commandos, aptly known as the 'commando box'. This was really based on the principle of 'all-round defence' but adapted to meet the demands of jungle warfare. Although known as a 'box' it did not always have four sides, sometimes it was triangular or even circular.

While corresponding with me on the subject of commando training, Colonel Ken Trevor, DSO, who commanded No 1 in Burma, referred to the circular version: 'The concentrated camouflage defensive circle was about 100 to 150 yards in diameter, depending on the thickness of the jungle or the type of terrain. The fighting Troops occupied the perimeter, the arcs of fire were co-ordinated so as to overlap. In the centre was located the reserve Troop and Headquarters.'

Tag Barnes in his book remembers an alternative layout, though it employed the same principles of all-round defence with close mutual fire support. This time he describes a triangular layout with just three fighting troops occupying the three sides. At each point of the triangle was sited one of the Commando's medium machine guns and along the sides were sited the rest of the troop's men with their personal weapons. Some of the riflemen still had their US Garand automatic rifles from their North Africa campaign. Outside the box the commandos placed various devices, obstacles, and booby traps to warn them of any enemy advances, as well as hindering them. Many of these devices were 'home-made': for example, in the absence of more sophisticated devices the commandos prepared 'panjis', lengths of bamboo, cut and sharpened at each end, that were stuck into the ground, concealed or camouflaged, on approaches to the commando's position.

Colonel Shaw's No 5 Commando and Colonel Horton's No 44 Commando did not have much time to train and prepare for their first operation before they went into action on 11 March 1944, just six weeks after their arrival in India. Although No 5 had seen action in Madagascar, for No 44 it was to be their 'baptism of fire'. The two Commandos were to take part in an amphibious operation, codenamed '*Screwdriver*', landing on the Arakan coastal strip of Burma.

The Arakan is the area between the inland mountains and the Bay of Bengal, which consists mostly of swamps and jungle interspersed with rivers – the largest being the Irrawaddy in the east – and streams ('chaungs'). The object of *Screwdriver* was to exploit the successful action of the Fourteenth Army in beating off the Japanese offensive operation '*Ha Go*' during the period from 6 February to 3 March, with a limited offensive behind the enemy's front line astride the Maungdaw–Buthidaung road.

Frank Atter, who was with No 5 aptly summarises the commandos' mission: 'Alethangyaw was an operation where both Commandos went into action very much on their own without any close support. The object was to take the strain off the main corps' battle on the Maungdaw–Buthidaung road and attract attention so as to divert Japanese troops who might have been used there.'[2]

The two Commandos were to land on two separate beaches: No 44 near the village of Alethangyaw and No 5 on the coast to the north of the village towards Maungdaw. Although No 44 had problems during their run-in to the beach, both Commandos landed unopposed during the night, reportedly in 'mostly old and leaking LCAs'.

Horton's men moved inland without any difficulties but as they entered the village they met stiff opposition, followed by much confused fighting in the dark. However, by dawn most of the village was in the commandos' hands. After resting and a daylight reconnaissance of the area Colonel Horton decided to move during the following night to establish his commando box on a hill to the north of the village. However, the route to the hill was through dense jungle and the commandos soon discovered the problems of movement on such terrain, especially, as in this case, the ground was swampy marshland. There was only one solution – wading waist-deep up a chaung for most of the way. Having reached the hill, they quickly established their box, from which they were able to send out their patrols to seek out and harass the enemy. Horton's commandos stayed in the area for several days before leaving to join their comrades further north in the Maungdaw area.

Here it must be pointed out that the subsequent award of the battle honour of ALETHANGYAW was not like most of the other Commando battle honours, inasmuch as it was not for one specific action. On the contrary, it was for a series of small, usually troop-size, patrol engagements behind enemy lines, over a relatively long period, from 13 March to 28 April. For this reason one can only provide a general picture, with one or two highlights, of the Commandos' part in Operation *Screwdriver*.

John Wall, a veteran of Madagascar and who served with No 5 throughout the Burma campaign, sets the scene, recalling that after the landing: 'We made a box from which make our forays on the Japanese communications . . .' and goes on to relate a most unusual encounter during one of their early forays into the jungle.[2]

They had adopted a 'T' formation; while moving through the jungle one of Wall's comrades, at the extreme end of the horizontal top of the 'T', suddenly came face to face with a solitary Japanese soldier. Wall goes on to tell the story of how the commando concerned, 'Titch' Shoreman, being the EY-grenade rifleman in the troop, had the discharger already fixed on his rifle – though it was only loaded with a cartridge – ready for action. Titch was in an obvious quandary, but by some clever miming he apparently persuaded the solitary soldier, who probably assumed that Shoreman was also Japanese, as they were of similar height and build, to move a few steps to his left where he came towards and opposite the next man in the line who promptly shot the unsuspecting Japanese soldier.[3]

Moving on they ran into a party of Japanese and the troop had to take cover and quickly form a defensive triangular box. Unfortunately their Bren fire, which had tracers mixed with the ordinary ball rounds, gave away their exact position and 'we automatically became a target for almost every enemy gun in the area.'[3]

This was but one of the many lessons they were to learn in the early actions. Wall also mentions that they 'quickly learned how the Japs would shout in English something they had heard. One of our chaps, very badly wounded, was calling for his Troop commander and the Japs would repeat the same shout in an effort to confuse and attract an approach towards them.'[4]

Some idea of the smaller-scale actions undertaken by the commandos during the 'Alethangyaw period' can be gleaned from a summary of an entry in No 5 Commando war diary in Messenger's book. It starts at 4.45 p.m. when No 5 Troop, under the command of Captain Kerr, was attacking an enemy machine-gun position sited on a hill. The attacking sub-section under Lieutenant Pammenter was under fire as it moved up the hill, although it did receive covering fire from the other sub-section of the troop. This greatly helped

Pammenter's men to capture the gun, killing three Japanese soldiers in the process. The assaulting sub-section, having cleared the enemy post, destroyed and hid the parts of the gun. They moved on but were fired upon at close range by five more Japanese. Under the leadership of Sergeant Burnett they closed with the enemy and killed three of them while the other two fled down the hill – a grenade was thrown at them but there was no confirmation of its effect, although a scream was heard.

Throughout the rest of March and into April the two Commandos – No 44 having moved up from Alethangyaw to join No 5 – were fully occupied on further patrolling, until they were rushed up to Silchar, a few miles south-west of Imphal, where they mounted three–four day patrols into the Assam hills. This was a very difficult and gruelling time, with the commandos having to endure the monsoon with its continuous rain and mud. However, in August the two Commandos left Burma and moved by train to Bangalore, via Calcutta, where they were able to enjoy fourteen days' leave before going on in September to join up with Nos 1 and 42 Commandos in Ceylon.

Their stay in Ceylon did not last long though as the beginning of November saw the brigade back in the battle zone in Teknaf, a prominent peninsula-like strip on the Arakan coastline. There was also a change of command: Brigadier Nonweiller had fallen ill and been sent back to Britain to recover, and Lieutenant Colonel Peter Young – who needs no introduction – had arrived from Britain to take up the appointment of deputy commander of the brigade, and so he took over temporary command whilst awaiting the arrival of the new brigade commander, Brigadier Campbell Hardy, DSO.

In Teknaf the Commando Brigade came under the command of General Christison's 15 Indian Corps, but because of the lack of landing craft and no immediate prospects of any amphibious raiding, the brigade, at Young's request, took over a section of the corps' front line for three weeks to get – in Young's words – 'battle experience'. There is no doubt that the three weeks' stay there was of considerable value – especially for Nos 1 and 42 Commandos who, unlike the other two Commandos, had not been in the Alethangyaw engagements, as well as for the reinforcements from Britain who had joined the other two Commandos in Ceylon.

One feature of the commandos' brief stay in the line was the capture of a Japanese prisoner. Apparently the formation whose sector the commandos took over for that short time had been in action in the Arakan for some eight months, and such had been the fanatical conduct in battle of the Japanese soldiers that they had not been able to take a single enemy prisoner alive. This presented a challenge to the likes of Peter Young. He decided to make this challenge into a competition, offering the prize of a 'fiver' (a lot of money in those days, over twice the weekly pay of a sergeant) to the first commando who captured a Japanese prisoner. No I Commando won the prize, when a patrol under the command of Captain Garner-Jones attacked and overran an enemy position and in the close-quarter fighting that followed a commando's grenade stunned one of the enemy – before he could recover, two other commandos grabbed him and made him captive. Bound and gagged he was brought back to the Commando's lines. All-in-all this was a most significant and successful patrol, recognised by the award of the Military Cross for Garner-Jones and also Military Medals for the two men who took the prisoner. It was a morale-boosting achievement.

In December Brigadier Campbell Hardy arrived and took over command. A Royal Marine commando, he had served throughout the Normandy campaign in charge of No 46 (RM) Commando with considerable distinction, winning two Distinguished Service Orders in three months.

The brigade spent the Christmas period waiting for their next operation. Being 'out of the line' they were able to make the best of the limited festive 'treats', which included a film show. Tag Barnes tells of how the film, entitled *This is the Army*, was spoilt somewhat because there was only one projector and every fifteen minutes the show had to be stopped while a new reel was fitted.

On New Year's Eve the brigade was given forty-eight hours' notice to prepare for an operation, which was to capture the offshore island of Akyab, about sixty miles to the south of their location at Teknaf. This was part of a general advance to pursue the Japanese forces, who were retreating following a series of successful operations by the Fourteenth Army; hopes were even being expressed of pushing on towards Rangoon.

The enemy strength on Akyab was uncertain but the planning for the landings included full air and naval support – this was to be the largest amphibious operation to date in Burma. On 2 January the brigade embarked on a mixed fleet that included cruisers, destroyers, sloops, landing craft, and an odd collection of local boats. On the same day, the day before the planned landing, an artillery observation officer flying over the island on a reconnaissance trip saw no signs of the Japanese. He even landed and contacted some locals, who informed him that the Japanese had evacuated the island.

As a result of this unexpected information the softening-up programme of air and naval support was cancelled. The commandos, supported by some tanks, subsequently landed unopposed at midday on 3 January 1945. Having cleared the beaches the commandos set off in the intense midday heat to occupy the rest of the island, followed by troops of the 26 Indian Division.

Although the commandos met no opposition it was a 'hard slog', as they were carrying full loads. Unlike their comrades fighting in the north-west Europe campaign, men of No 3 Commando Brigade did not have the luxury of rucksacks to carry all their ammunition and rations, etc. – they still had the large pre-war backpack and the small side haversack. Tag Barnes describes his load for this particular operation:

> As well as my rifle, I carried two hundred rounds of ammunition, two spare Bren magazines, three hand grenades and a short handle spade. My large back pack contained a gas cape (useful in the wet weather), a forty-eight hours ration pack, a cap comforter, spare socks, boot laces, mess tin, a mug and odds and ends that included water sterilization tablets and a first field dressing.[5]

He did not mention the little 'Tommy' cooker usually shared between two men, on the 'me and my pal' basis, for that all-important brew-up of char.

There was one airfield on the island and it was in this area that the Commando Brigade was based for the rest of their time on the island. Apart from one skirmish – when a patrol from No 5 was sent in a landing craft to one of the small neighbouring islands, where they surprised an isolated party of ten Japanese soldiers, six of whom they killed without loss – there was no other action.

For the next few days the commandos played what Barnes referred to as the 'waiting game', during which time he and his troop, living in a large disused house in a wood close to the airport, were able to buy some chicken and eggs from the locals 'to supplement our frugal diet'.

However, plans were already being made for the next operation, the objective of which was to be the Myebon peninsula to the south of Akyab, where the enemy had established a staging post to send reinforcements to the north, evacuate casualties to the south, and use as a base for stores and supplies.

Following a reconnaissance, from a naval sloop, of the southern tip of the peninsula, looking for suitable landing places, Brigadier Campbell Hardy devised a simple plan for the brigade's landing on two beaches on the tip, just to the west of the enemy's strongpoint at Agnu. The landings were to be preceded by heavy air attacks and a naval bombardment centred on Agnu, then at high tide the commandos were to land and ultimately, after mopping up the enemy in this area, to push north to Kantha, via Myebon on the east coast of the peninsula. See Map 23 on page 252.

The Commando Brigade was also to be supported by units of 50 Infantry Brigade, a number of tanks, and a troop of twenty-five-pounders. This whole operation was part – albeit an important part – of General Christison's overall corps plan to destroy the retreating 28 Japanese Army before it could reach the mountains, to the east of the Arakan, and the Irrawaddy valley.

By capturing and clearing the Myebon peninsula the two main waterways on the western flank of the retreat would be denied to the Japanese. The operation was planned for 12 January and the previous night a team from the specialist Combined Operations Pilotage Party (COPP) – a sub-unit similar to the SBS – was sent out to make a gap in the anti-landing obstacles, which were made of stakes, on the planned run-in to the landing beach. The raiders successfully fitted delayed-action fuses to charges placed on the stakes and these were time-set to detonate just before H hour at 8.30 a.m.

Prior to H hour the RAF pounded the area of Agnu and other known enemy positions on the southern part of the peninsula – so successful was this that the first wave of the commando landing force, No 42, got ashore with hardly a shot fired at them. There were no enemy strongpoints covering the beaches, although there were a couple of Japanese field guns in dugout emplacements slightly inland, which fired on the craft as they came inshore, but their fire was sporadic and did little damage. However, the landing was still far from ideal as the commandos had to wade ashore through water up to their armpits with, in places, glutinous mud underfoot.

Once ashore No 42 quickly established a beachhead for No 5 to pass through. The tide was beginning to ebb, but their landing went reasonably well, although they did suffer a few casualties on some 'mines' that had been improvised from artillery shells.

No 5 advanced through the inland mangrove vegetation and were making good progress when they came under fire from a Japanese machine-gun position sited on a shrub-covered hill. The leading troop prepared to attack with one section while the other, with a solitary tank (the only one to get ashore that day), provided covering fire. Although the troop commander was wounded in the assault, the position was taken, with all the Japanese killed.

Next to land was No 1 Commando, which had difficulty landing as by now the tide was well on the ebb. Although they had to wade ashore, taking much longer than planned, the men had no other problems and were soon off to seek out those enemy field guns and destroy them, which they duly did. Tag Barnes ends his description of the capture of one of the 75-mm guns: '. . . killing half-a dozen Japanese in the process'.[6] The Commando then established themselves on some nearby hillocks and started to dig in.

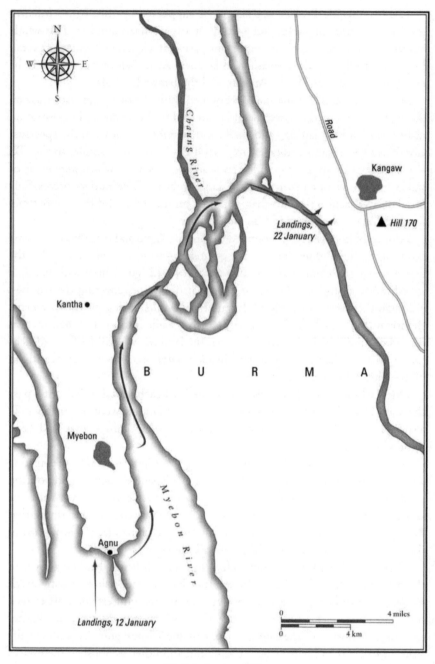

MAP 23. Myebon and Kangaw

By the time the last wave of landing craft started its run-in the tide was well and truly out and No 44 Commando had nearly four hundred yards of deep mud – in some cases up to their armpits – to cross. It took nearly three hours before all the commandos had made it to the beach; fortunately for them there was no opposition nor enemy fire at this time. Recalling No 44's landing, Young later wrote: 'Under fire it would have been murder.'[7] It took time for No 44 to sort themselves out, clean their weapons, and reorganise after this experience, but then they moved off to clear the area around Agnu, though the village itself had already been badly damaged in the RAF strike.

Nightfall saw the brigade firmly established on the southern tip of the Myebon peninsula, with No 1 on the extreme left, and next to them, on a hill christened 'Pagoda Hill', was No 42 (where they incidentally found a stock of food, blankets, and clothing in the bunkers on the hill). No 44 consolidated in the Agnu area; No 5 stayed on the hills they had occupied earlier, positions that were slightly ahead of the rest of the brigade, but this was convenient as they were due to lead the advance next day. Much to the surprise of everyone in the brigade the night was peaceful, although some machine-gun fire was heard from the area of Myebon.

On D+1 the advance continued: No 5 was in the vanguard with the mission of capturing an enemy position on a subsequent hill, which had been christened 'Rose'. Their assault had the support of a 'softening up' air strike and naval fire, plus two more tanks that had managed to get ashore on the early morning tide to join the one Sherman already supporting the brigade. Also supporting No 5 were their comrades of No 1: they had two main tasks, firstly to provide fire from their three-inch mortars and secondly to take up positions to ambush any Japanese who might 'bolt' from Rose. The assault by No 5 was completely successful, though once again there were no prisoners as the Japanese all preferred to fight on until killed.

No 42 then passed through to push on and capture Myebon itself, which was about a mile further on from Rose, on the banks of the chaung. They had no difficulty in clearing the village, but when pressing on beyond Myebon they came under heavy fire from an enemy position situated on yet another hill, which they attacked with success, but had casualties – four of their officers, including the CO, Colonel David Fellowes, and a number of the marine commandos were wounded.

Meanwhile No 1 Commando, which was advancing along a tree-covered ridge, encountered another enemy post; with the support of their own heavy weapons they stormed and cleared it with only a few minor casualties. Tag Barnes recalls a first-hand experience of a typical Japanese tactic following this successful action:

Trouble was experienced from one fanatical fellow who decided to hang back and snipe us from a tree top hide. As we carefully advanced, scanning the foliage, I saw Danny moving forward on my right. He presented a picture of calculated coolness that has always lived in my memory . . . He was good on the move with his Bren. Suddenly he let loose a burst of fire, probably a quarter of a magazine, [about six to eight rounds], and from the top of a tree forty yards away there came a crash as a body plummeted through.[8]

Apparently when Barnes and his mates reached 'the lifeless body' they discovered that he was very big, the largest Japanese soldier they ever encountered, at least six feet tall – a fact that prompted one of Barnes' mates, with a sense of humour, to suggest that this particular soldier must have been a guardsman in the Emperor's Imperial Guard!

Next day as the advance continued towards the final objective, Kantha, they met a series of isolated enemy posts on the hills and Campbell Hardy decided to call a halt and plan a brigade attack for the next day, as by now his commandos needed to rest and replenish with food and other supplies. So the Commandos – by now No 44 had been brought up from the beachhead to reinforce and support No 42 – took up their defensive 'boxed positions' and just sent out patrols during that day and the following night.

On 15 January No 1 Commando, supported by tanks, went into action to clear the enemy on Point 200 as well as another hill that dominated the approach to Kantha. The planned air strike did not materialise, but with the support of the tanks, which was both daring and decisive, by midday the way was clear for No 42 (RM) Commando to take Kantha. This they did with ease as the Japanese had abandoned the village – apparently in haste, as they left behind arms and documents.

The Commando Brigade consolidated in and around Kantha; with their mission concluded, they were relieved by troops of 74 Infantry Brigade and two days later returned to the original beachhead area at Agnu.

It was estimated that the commandos had killed some 150 Japanese in this small, but important, campaign, for the loss of four killed and thirty-eight wounded. The Myebon peninsula had been cleared of all enemy and the waterway was denied to them. The brigade had won its first big battle for which they were later awarded the battle honour of MYEBON.

Back at Agnu the brigade rested and reorganised and it was here that they received reinforcements from Britain. Included in this party was a newly commissioned officer, Lieutenant George Knowland, who, like a lot of us, had been commissioned from the ranks of the commandos. He had served with distinction in No 3, but was then posted to No 1. It was normal to post the newly commissioned commando officer to a Commando other than his original one, although this was not a hard-and-fast rule and there were exceptions: for example, George Herbert in No 3 Commando.

Now that the Myebon waterway was denied to the enemy there was only one main alternative for the Japanese retreat and that was down the inland Myobaung–Tamandu road. As a result General Christison decided to cut this route at a critical bend where the road left the plains and started to swing eastwards, where this point of the road was dominated by 'Hill 170' – a name that would become immortalised in Commando history – and was near the little inland 'port' of Kangaw.

One immediate problem was that of getting the forces required to Kangaw as quickly as possible, especially as the overland route was bedevilled with water obstacles. So Christison decided, using Campbell Hardy's Commando Brigade, which was immediately and conveniently available at Agnu, to mount an amphibious operation with the mixed armada that had landed the commandos on Akyab.

There was one major snag to the proposed waterborne approach to Kangaw, which was that the final part of the passage was up a five-mile stretch of the Daungbon chaung that was barely one hundred yards wide – the risk of being caught by an enemy with troops posted on both, or even one bank, could be disastrous. However, both Christison and Campbell Hardy thought, on the information available, that such an adverse situation was unlikely and so decided to take the risk – and it paid off. The outline plan briefly was that No 1 Commando would land at noon on 22 January and advance to capture Hill 170, which was about one and a half miles from the proposed landing point. No 42 (RM) Commando would land on both banks of the chaung, bearing in mind that the chaung was barely one hundred yards wide, to provide all-round protection to the landing point.

Next to land would be No 5 Commando, which was to reinforce No 1 on the southern slope of Hill 170, whilst No 44 (RM) Commando would initially be held in reserve in the beachhead area, ready to advance past Hill 170 to Kangaw on D+1.

The embarkation and the waterborne approach went well so that the late morning of D-Day saw the flotilla progressing up the narrow stages of the chaung, subject only to some 'desultory shelling', which did no harm.

No 1 Commando landed at 1 p.m. without any problems and started their approach, firstly across a mangrove swamp and later across paddy fields, towards Hill 170. As they advanced RAF Mitchell bombers carried out strikes on identified enemy positions in the Kangaw area.

At about 4.30 p.m. No I Commando launched their assault on Hill 170 from the southern side and there followed a short, but intense fight, in which they succeeded in clearing most of the hill, with the loss of three killed and nine wounded.

During the afternoon No 5 had moved up and taken up positions south of Hill 170; brigade headquarters had also moved up to a position in the same area, while three troops of No 44 had made a successful assault on a little ridge east of No I. Having established a defensive position there, they were able to support their comrades on Hill 170. All the commandos spent the last hours of daylight digging in and preparing for the inevitable counter-attack – it was launched at about 11 p.m. on the forward two troops of No I, but the Japanese were repulsed with heavy casualties.

Barnes, who was in one of those forward troops, described what happened and how, as they were waiting, they could just hear the Japanese quietly approaching, but they held their fire, allowing the enemy to advance closer. They just waited, each man with a primed grenade in his hand, ready and waiting for the order 'Throw'. When it came the result was conclusive – 'explosions that shattered the silence of the night, followed by rapid small-arms fire, then all quiet except for the moans of the wounded.'[9] The first counter-attack had failed.

Two hours later a second attempt was launched by the enemy and this time it took longer to force them to withdraw. Even this failure did not deter the Japanese – at 3 a.m. they made yet another attempt to dislodge the two forward troops of No I.

In this third attack they quietly got within close range before opening up with their automatics and throwing grenades. The commandos held their ground, forcing the enemy once again to withdraw, leaving their dead and wounded behind. Among the commando casualties was Barnes's 'number two' on the Bren gun, who was killed by a burst of enemy automatic fire, and Barnes provided a poignant account of how his mate died in his arms. He was not the only one to be killed in the attacks that night: in Barnes's troop position alone some ten of his comrades were wounded, though they were successfully evacuated for treatment back at the beachhead.

When daylight came the commandos took stock of their position and strengthened their defences. One of the two forward troops of No I, which had borne the brunt of the night attacks, counted eighteen dead Japanese in front of their position. During D+I No 44 advanced, seized, and occupied, without any difficulty, a further hill towards Kangaw. Here, for some unknown reason, they failed to dig in and later when they came under heavy shelling they paid the price – sixteen men killed and forty-five wounded. However, they did repel an enemy attack and were then relieved by troops from 25 Infantry Division.

Back at the original landing point further reinforcements and supplies were arriving. Stores of ammunition and food were carried forward to the Commando Brigade headquarters area by Ghurka porters (who were very brave and hard working), from whence they were collected by parties from the four Commandos. Casualties were also evacuated back to beachhead where they were ferried back to Akyab for further treatment.

In the ensuing days no more counter-attacks were made, instead the Japanese kept the brigade's area under constant shell-fire, though apart from the shelling the situation was 'remarkably quiet'. The commandos spent this time improving their defences and preparing for the inevitable storm that would follow this 'calm'.

One consoling feature of the Japanese shelling was the fact that some of the shells failed to explode for one reason or another; in fact one officer in No 5 Commando is on record as saying: 'One night we had a stream of twenty-one shells land on the hill, nineteen of which were duds'. His men, being more laconic, added, 'Ya, yer never touch me' – a phrase that became familiar as the salvoes hissed harmlessly to earth.[10]

During this period the follow-up units of the 25 Infantry Division were able to advance south of Hill 170 towards Kangaw, and consequently on 28 January 51 Infantry Brigade captured the two hills that dominated the vital Myobaung–Tamandu road at the Kangaw bend. No 5 Commando also supported this operation by providing patrols in the area of Kangaw, but they encountered no enemy.

It became obvious to the Japanese, now denied free use of the 'escape' road, that the key to removing this threat to their continued retreat was Hill 170 – if they could recapture this feature and subsequently eliminate the beachhead at Daungbon then 51 Infantry Brigade would be isolated and could be dealt with.

Ironically, following the successful occupation of those two hills by 51 Infantry Brigade, Brigadier Campbell Hardy received orders that the commandos were to be relieved, but the Japanese quickly put paid to that plan.

Just before dawn on 31 January, as the commandos 'stood to' in their slit trenches, the enemy opened up a heavy bombardment of artillery, mortar, and machine-gun fire on the Commando Brigade's positions, particularly on those forward positions held by the men of No 4 Troop of No 1 Commando, at the northern end of Hill 170. When the barrage lifted, the enemy, who had been advancing under cover of the wooded lower slopes of the hill, launched a very determined mass attack on No 4 Troop, which was under the command of Lieutenant Roy Semple (another of my old instructor mates at Achnacarry);

also in this position was Lieutenant George Knowland, in charge of one of the troop's two sections.

The Japanese were also attacking on the western side of the commando box, where Captain Merriam, who was commanding the three tanks of the 19 Lancers that were supporting the commandos, had leagued his tanks in a saddle there overnight. Merriam provides an apt introduction to what was to be the epic battle of Hill 170:

> We were rudely awakened by some very fast and accurate shell-fire at about 0545 which continued until about 0620 when a babble of voices in the nearby bushes west of our position followed by the noise of machine guns indicated that we were being attacked. The first twenty minutes were confused as it was definitely a case of the queen getting into line inasmuch as the Japs got into our perimeter.[11]

A few minutes later a Japanese suicide raider blew up one of Merriam's tanks, killing the entire crew, but the other two tanks managed to get out.

However, the full force of the Japanese assault fell on No 4 Troop. It was estimated that up to three hundred Japanese were committed in this attack, but Semple's and Knowland's men – supported by the Commando's heavy machine guns firing from a flanking position on a feature nick-named 'The Fingers' – held on as they repelled wave after wave of the enemy. It was George Knowland, the relative newcomer to No 1 Commando, who was the undoubted hero and inspiration for the commandos' stoic stand that morning. One can do no better than refer to the text of the citation[12] for the award of the Victoria Cross awarded posthumously to Lieutenant Knowland to describe the action that followed.

It starts before the actual enemy assault, when the commandos were coming under heavy mortar and machine-gun fire: 'He moved about his men keeping them alert and encouraging them, though under fire himself at the time.' When the first wave of enemy came in he moved from trench to trench distributing ammunition, firing his rifle, and throwing grenades, personally accounting for several of the enemy. Later when the men of one of his Bren teams had been put out of action, wounded, he sent a runner back to troop headquarters for a new team and ran forward to take over the gun himself until the relief team arrived.

At this stage there were some enemy just ten yards away, but below him, so he stood on the parapet of the slit trench and, firing from the hip, kept them at bay while a medical orderly gave first aid to the wounded Bren gunners in the trench below him. Unfortunately the two relief Bren gunners became casualties themselves on their way to join Knowland, so he kept firing the gun until a further team managed to take over.

There was then a short lull in the enemy attack, during which time more replacements came forward to reinforce No 4 Troop, but the enemy attacked once more and during this assault Knowland took over a two-inch mortar when their crew went forward as riflemen to replace casualties in a forward trench. Firing the mortar from the hip – no easy feat – he killed six of the enemy with his first bomb. Having used all his bombs he then went back to his original trench; picking up a rifle, he stood and started to fire at the enemy. By this time the enemy had closed to within ten yards of him. His rifle magazine was empty and he had no time to reload, so he snatched up the Tommy gun of a casualty and started to spray the advancing enemy, but was struck and mortally wounded, though he still managed to kill or wound an additional ten Japanese in his final action.

It was an extraordinary act of selfless heroism, which undoubtedly inspired the survivors of his troop and the rest of the Commando to cling on to their positions resolutely for the rest of that day, as reinforcements were brought up to the northern end of the Hill. Colonel Ken Trevor had come forward to see the situation for himself and he organised reinforcements from No 42 (RM) Commando to help No 4 Troop by putting in a counter-attack, though it was beaten back. Trevor also ordered a section from No 3 Troop forward and they were sent by Lieutenant Semple to clear the enemy off the east side of his position. This little group met stiff opposition from the enemy at the foot of the hill and suffered several casualties, but they in turn accounted for a number of the Japanese before returning to the top of the Hill and their original trenches.

Joe Edmans recalls what happened:

> We got into our trenches and waited, while at the northern end, 2 Section of 6 Troop under Captain Evill, were given the job of clearing the Japs off that end of the hill. Suddenly the Japs charged up the hill, yelling and shouting, we waited and let them come up so far and then we gave them everything we had. We used Bren gun, Tommy gun, American semi-automatic rifle, Colt. 45, and tossed a few grenades. After several attempts they gave up.[13]

By now it was late morning and Brigadier Campbell Hardy came forward to assess the situation. As a result he decided to send in a troop of No 42 to recover some of the lost ground and at 12.30 p.m. the marine commandos, supported by the only surviving tank, attacked, but they were unable to make any progress and so joined No 4 Troop in their position. Undeterred, another effort to dislodge the enemy established at the northern end of the hill was made by No 6 Troop of No 1, but they too failed, suffering 50 per cent casualties – the survivors also withdrew to No 4 Troop's position. The commandos' main concern throughout the battle on Hill 170 was their determination to keep their Brens firing. Indeed the determination of the section officers and NCOs to keep this weapon manned and in action was undoubtedly a major factor contributing to their ultimate survival and success. Section officers and NCOs were ever watchful to replace the 'number one' (firer) with a rifleman who was equally 'at home' on this weapon. Captain Dashwood of No 5 had this to say: 'Twelve men, one after the other, were hit behind one vital Bren gun, each accounting for a number of Japs. Today I am proud to think that I was beside such gallant fellows.'

During the early afternoon Colonel Trevor began to 'tidy up' his defences because by now he had sub-units of three Commandos in his forward location. These reinforcements included the bulk of No 5, now under the command of Major Robin Stuart following the evacuation of their CO, Colonel Pollitt, who had been wounded.

As evening fell reports were received that the Japanese were pulling back and that night was 'quiet enough'. Next morning No 5 Commando went forward but found no live Japanese soldiers – only dead ones. Peter Young, who followed them, wrote: 'The Japs had gone, leaving the hillside carpeted with their dead. When it was light enough I went forward to look at the ground where 4 Troop of No 1 Commando had fought. I could hardly move a step without treading on a dead Jap. There were nearly three hundred of them . . .'[14]

Further down the northern slope, as well as on the western slope, there were hundreds more. The Japanese losses had been very high, although Nos 1, 5, and 42 Commandos had suffered too – five officers and forty other ranks killed and six officers and eighty-four other ranks wounded. Later, on 1 February, the Commando Brigade were relieved by Indian troops of 25 Infantry Division and General Sir Phillip Christison issued a 'Special Order of the Day to the Commandos in Burma', in which he said:

> Having been placed under the command of the 15th Indian Corps to lead assaults in particularly hazardous and important amphibious operations, you have successfully completed the tasks which were assigned to you.
>
> Your courage and determination in assault and attack, your tenacity and aggressiveness in defence and counter-attack have won the praise and

admiration of the Commanders and troops, British, Indian and Ghurka, of all the other formations engaged in the operations and who fought beside you.

The battle of Kangaw has been the decisive battle of the whole Arakan campaign, and that it was won was largely due to your magnificent defence of Hill 170.

I am very proud of you, and thank you all for the decisive contribution you have made to the success of the campaign, and the rout of the Japanese in this theatre.[15]

The official 15 Indian Corps' history of the Arakan campaign clearly acknowledges the significance of the Commandos heroic stand on Hill 170, stating that 'if the Japanese had seized Hill 170 the whole of the Kangaw operation would have been doomed to failure.'[16]

For his inspiring leadership at both Myebon and Kangaw Brigadier Campbell Hardy received a second bar to his DSO, while another well-deserved DSO went to Colonel Ken Trevor, much to the delight of his men. Other awards included Military Crosses and Military Medals, though topping the list was the award of the Victoria Cross to George Knowland.

Later, in 1957, long after the Army Commandos had been disbanded, the Commando Association received the final battle honour of KANGAW for their defence of Hill 170, which also happened to be the last commando action of the Second World War and so provides a fitting finale to this account of the battle honours of the Army Commandos in the Second World War.

After leaving the battle area of Kangaw the Commando Brigade moved back to Akyab and then to India to prepare for further action in Malaya. However, on 6 August the first atomic bomb fell on Hiroshima, followed three days later by a second bomb dropped on Nagasaki. On 14 August 1945 Japan surrendered unconditionally and the Second World War was over.

Victory at long last was complete and the Commandos had fought in every theatre of that war, as those thirty-eight battle honours emblazoned on the Commando flag in St George's Chapel in Westminster Abbey testify, and will continue to do so in the years ahead.

Notes

CHAPTER 1

1. Winston S. Churchill, *The Second World War, Volume II: Their Finest Hour*, The Reprint Society, London, 1949, p. 146.
2. James Dunning, *It Had To Be Tough*, Pentland Press, Bishop Auckland, 2000, p. 50.
3. J. E. A., *Geoffrey*, Blandford Press Ltd, London, 1946, p. 50.
4. Brigadier John Durnford-Slater, *Commando*, William Kimber, London, 1953, p. 32.
5. Elizabeth Keyes, *Geoffrey Keyes, VC*, George Newnes Ltd, London, 1956, p. 136.
6. Donald Gilchrist, *Castle Commando*, Oliver & Boyd, Edinburgh and London, 1960. Foreword by Admiral of the Fleet Earl Mountbatten of Burma.

CHAPTER 2

1. Durnford-Slater, p. 46.
2. James Dunning, *The Fighting Fourth*, Sutton Publishing Ltd, Stroud, 2003, p. 40.
3. Bernard Ferguson, *The Watery Maze*, Collins, London, 1961, p. 87.
4. Durnford-Slater, p. 69.

5 Peter Young, *Storm From The Sea*, Greenhill Books, London, 1989, p. 37.

6. Extracts from a letter, with photographs, from Mrs D. Roderick of the memorial service at Sachsenhausen in July 2001.

7. Stephen Schofield, *Musketoon*, Jonathan Cape Ltd., London 1964, republished by Corgi Books, London 1974.

CHAPTER 3

1. Charles Messenger, *The Commandos, 1940–1946*, William Kimber, London, 1985, p. 95.

2. W. E. Parker, *The Unwilling Volunteer*. Published privately and a copy given to the author in 2001. 'Bill' Parker joined the Commandos (No 4) in Weymouth in July 1940 and served in that Commando until December when plans were being made for Operation '*Workshop*'. He then volunteered to transfer to No 7 because they were calling for volunteers to make them up to strength for operations in the Middle East. In the Introduction, Bill explained that he had written the book 'in the interest of my ten grandchildren, scattered world wide, to answer their question, "What did Grandad do in the War?"'

3. Parker, p. 22.

4. Parker, p. 23.

5. Charles Messenger, *Storm from the Sea*, William Kimber, London, 1988, p. 146.

6. Messenger, *The Middle East Commandos*, p. 87.

7. William Seymour, *British Special Forces*, Jonathan Cape Ltd., London, 1986, p. 145.

8. Messenger, *The Middle East Commandos*, p. 89.

9. Seymour, p. 146.

10. John Keegan, *Second World War*, Hutchinson, London, 1989, p. 326.

11. After the war a British feature film titled *The Desert Fox* was made starring James Mason as Field Marshal Rommel. Interestingly the introduction to the film was a graphic re-enactment of the Commando raid by Colonel Keyes on Rommel's headquarters outlined in this chapter.

12. Seymour, p. 154.

13. Letter to author from Geoff Riley, ex-Commandos, dated 14 May 1988. Later Geoff sent a copy to Robin Neillands and it is quoted in his book *The Raiders*, a book that is based mainly on contributions from ex-commandos of the Second World War, following an appeal by Robin for their wartime experiences that was published in our Commando Association newsletter.

14. Ibid., p. 2.
15. Letter to author from John Wall (sergeant, No 5 Commando in Madagascar and later in Burma), dated 24 November 2009. The technique of 'crash landing' troops on to the quays of docksides was also practised by us in No 4 Commando from the deck of HMS *Royal Scotsman* at Kirkwall in the Orkneys, when we were preparing for Operation *Puma*, a plan to capture ports in the Canary Islands in 1941, which was later cancelled. See Dunning, *The Fighting Fourth*, pp. 46–9, for further details.

CHAPTER 4

1. Messenger, *The Commandos, 1940–1946*, p. 130.
2. Max Arthur, *Forgotten Voices*, Ebury Press, London, 2004, pp. 182–3.
3. Arthur, p. 185.
4. Arthur, p. 185.
5. Ken Ford, *St Nazaire 1942: The Great Commando Raid*, Osprey Publishing Ltd, Oxford, 2001, pp. 46–51. My good friend and fellow military historian Ken Ford kindly gave me permission to summarise his account of the fate of the motor launches (MLs) in the raid as narrated in his book.
6. Ford, p. 85.

CHAPTER 5

1. Lord Lovat, *March Past*, Weidenfeld & Nicolson, London, 1978, p. 241.
2. Young, p. 61.
3. Young, p. 67.
4. Robin Neillands, *The Dieppe Raid*, Aurum Press Ltd, London, 2005, p. 147
5. Dunning, *The Fighting Fourth*, p. 79.
6. Arthur, p. 189.
7. Dunning, *The Fighting Fourth*, p. 81.
8. Dunning, *The Fighting Fourth*, p. 82.
9. The War Office, *Notes From Theatre of War No 11*, London, February 1943. The Introduction to this training booklet pays a handsome tribute to No 4 Commando with these words: 'Operation *Cauldron* is an outstanding example of what can be achieved by troops only armed with infantry weapons and by gallantry, sound planning and thorough training.' This operation is still studied by special forces and other army units that visit Dieppe and follow the action by walking the routes taken by the commandos from the beaches to the location of Hess battery and back to the re-embarkation beach.

CHAPTER 6

1. Keegan, *The Second World War,* Hutchinson, London, 1989, pp. 316–19.
2. Messenger, *The Commandos, 1940–1946,* p. 166.
3. Tag Barnes, MM, *Commando Diary,* Spellmount Ltd, Tunbridge Wells, Kent, 1991, p. 23.
4. Barnes, p. 23
5. Barnes, p. 23.
6. Hilary St George Saunders, *The Green Beret,* Michael Joseph, London, 1949, p. 137.
7. Brigadier Derek Mills-Roberts, *Clash By Night,* William Kimber, London, 1956, p. 52.
8. Barnes, p. 26.
9. Messenger, *The Commandos, 1940–1946,* p. 186.
10. Mills-Roberts, p. 67.
11. Robin Neillands, *The Raiders,* Weidenfeld & Nicolson, London, 1989, p. 105.
12. Mills-Roberts, p. 78.
13. War diary, No I Commando. Entry for 0730 hrs 28 March 1943.
14. Ibid. Entry for 1600 hrs 28 March 1943.
15. Ibid. Appendix I and entry for 22 April 1943.

CHAPTER 7

1. In the context of the Sicily and Italy campaigns it is pertinent to mention the excellent book written by Raymond Mitchell who served with No 41 (RM) Commando from its beginnings in 1941 to final victory in 1945: *They Did What Was Asked of Them,* Firebird Books, Poole, Dorset, 1996, p. 199.
2. Durnford-Slater, p. 135.
3. Young, p. 84.
4. Young, pp. 100–1.
5. Young, p. 109.
6. Bob Bishop, *History of No 2 Commando,* a privately published account originally written for the Commando Veterans Association by Bob Bishop, who served in No 2 in Sicily, Italy, and the Adriatic. Bob gave me full permission to quote from his account, for which I am most grateful, particularly as it provides an insight of action as seen and experienced by a commando soldier.
7. Neillands, *The Raiders,* p. 115.

CHAPTER 8

1. Saunders, p. 179.
2. Major-General T. Churchill, *Commando Crusade*, William Kimber, London, 1987, p. 106.
3. Bishop, p. 1.
4. Mitchell, p. 51.
5. Mitchell, p. 51.
6. Bishop, p. 1.
7. Bishop, p. 1.
8. T. Churchill, p. 117.
9. T. Churchill, p. 118.
10. Saunders, p. 199.
11. Durnford-Slater, p. 169.

CHAPTER 9

1. Messenger, *The Commandos, 1940–1946*, p. 234.
2. Messenger, *The Commandos, 1940–1946*, p. 236.
3. T. Churchill, p. 152.
4. Neillands, *The Raiders*, p. 129.
5. Neillands, *The Raiders*, p. 132.
6. Neillands, *The Raiders*, p. 135.
7. T. Churchill, p. 166.
8. Neillands, *The Raiders*, p. 143.
9. Neillands, *The Raiders*, p. 145.
10. Neillands, *The Raiders*, p. 169.
11. W. G. Jenkins, *Commando Subaltern At War*, Greenhill Books, London, 1996, p. 127.
12. Messenger, *The Commandos, 1940–1946*, p. 374
13. Neillands, *The Raiders*, p. 171.
14. Neillands, *The Raiders*, p. 174.
15. Saunders, p. 318.
16. Saunders, p. 318.

CHAPTER 10

1. Neillands, *The Raiders*, p. 151.
2. Neillands, *The Raiders*, p. 153.
3. Bishop, p. 5.
4. Messenger, *The Commandos, 1940–1946*, p. 339.
5. Bishop, p. 6.

6. Saunders, p. 259.
7. Bishop, p. 6.
8. T. Churchill, p. 252.
9. Neillands, *The Raiders*, p. 161.
10. T. Churchill, p. 257.
11 Neillands, *The Raiders*, p. 149.
12. Saunders, p. 293.

CHAPTER 11
1. Lovat, p. 287.
2. Lovat, p. 293.
3. Lovat, p. 295.
4. Dunning, *The Fighting Fourth*, p. 120.
5. Piper Bill Millin, *Invasion*, The Book Guild Ltd, Lewes, Sussex, 1991, p. 62.
6. Dunning, *The Fighting Fourth*, p. 131.
7. Millin, p. 63.
8. Murdoch McDougall, *Swiftly They Struck*, Grafton Books, London, 1954, p. 72.
9. Dunning, *The Fighting Fourth*, p. 127.
10. Dunning, *The Fighting Fourth*, p. 128.
11. McDougall, p. 73.
12. No 4 Commando Museum – Musée Franco-Britannique. This unique museum in Ouistreham, Normandy, is the only museum in Europe dedicated entirely to a single Commando. It is opened daily from March to the end of October – and well worth a visit.
13. Mills-Roberts, p. 94.
14. Mills-Roberts, p. 95.
15. Mills-Roberts, p. 98.
16. Dunning, *The Fighting Fourth*, p. 144. K guns were originally made to arm fighter aircraft, but were used – with great success – by the SAS in North Africa. The Commandos managed to get some for the Normandy landings.
17. Dunning, *The Fighting Fourth*, p. 145.
18. Young, p. 161.
19. Mills-Roberts, p. 133.
20. Dunning, *The Fighting Fourth*, p. 164.
21. Mills-Roberts, p. 141.
22. Dunning, *The Fighting Fourth*, p. 170.
23. Donald Gilchrist, *Don't Cry For Me*, Robert Hale, London, 1982, p. 172.

24. Dunning, *The Fighting Fourth*, p. 177.
25. McDougall, p. 223.
26. Ian Dear, *Ten Commando, 1942–45*, Leo Cooper, London, 1987, p. 163.
27. Mitchell, p. 140.
28. Dunning, *The Fighting Fourth*, p. 187.

CHAPTER 12
1. In 1987 whilst collecting material for my book, *It Had To Be Tough*, Bill
   Sadler sent to me a lengthy and comprehensive account of his experiences
   in No 6 Commando and extracts from his account are included in this
   chapter. Bill later sent a copy to Robin Neillands who included extracts in
   his book, *The Raiders*. I subsequently deposited my copy of Bill's
   reminiscences in the archives of the National Army Museum, London.
2. Mills-Roberts, p. 163.
3. Mills-Roberts, p. 167.
4. 'History of No 6 Commando' under the section headed, 'Appreciation'.
   Incidentally the copy I have of this little history booklet was given to me
   by the late George Bower, who was born in Vienna of Jewish parents. When
   Hitler took over Austria, George was evacuated to England. Later when
   war was declared George was interned on the Isle of Man. However, in
   1942 he was allowed to volunteer to serve in the British Army and
   subsequently after training joined No 6 Commando in their intelligence
   section and served in that Commando from D-Day to VE Day.
5. *Five Rivers*, p. 12.
6. *Five Rivers*, p. 13.
7. Bill Sadler's account, in Neillands, *The Raiders*, p. 209.
8. Neillands, *The Raiders*, p. 209.
9. Mills-Roberts, p. 186.
10. Bill Sadler's account, in Neillands, *The Raiders*, p. 211.
11. 'VI Commando', History of No 6 Commando, p. 10.
12. *Five Rivers*, p. 23.
13. 'VI Commando', History of No 6 Commando, p. 10.
14. Messenger, *The Commandos, 1940–1946*, p. 311.
15. Neillands, *The Raiders*, p. 212.

CHAPTER 13
1. Barnes, *Commando Diary*, p. 55.
2. Neillands, *The Raiders*, p. 218.
3. Neillands, *The Raiders*, p. 219.

4. Neillands, *The Raiders*, p. 219
5. Barnes, p. 84.
6. Barnes, p. 88.
7. Young, *Storm from the Sea*, p. 209.
8. Barnes, p. 88.
9. Barnes, p. 98.
10. Saunders, *The Green Beret*, p. 346.
11. Messenger, *The Commandos, 1940–1946*, pp. 399–400.
12. Barnes, p. 106–107.
13. Neillands, *The Raiders*, p. 234.
14. Young, *Storm from the Sea*, p. 219.
15. Barnes, p. 105.
16. *Messenger, The Commandos, 1940–1946*, p. 403.

ACKNOWLEDGEMENTS

I am glad to have this opportunity to acknowledge and thank all those who have helped with the writing of this book. They comprise of a wide range of people and include old comrades, authors, publishers, organisations and friends.

In particular I would like to thank those authors and publishers who have kindly allowed me to quote from their works and I have included full details of these sources in the Footnotes and the Selective Bibliography.

In the case of other contributions and illustrations I have, over the years – thanks to the comradeship of the Commando Association and subsequently the Commando Veterans Association – received contributions from commando veterans who took part in the actions of the Battle Honours and these have given the accounts a personal touch of involvement. Sadly many of these comrades are no longer with us, but nevertheless I have included their names below as if they were.

I must also record my special thanks to the Imperial War Museum for their very generous help with the illustrations.

So without further ado, my thanks are due to Max Arthur, Tim Balchin, George Bower, Eric Buckmaster, Bob Bishop, Gwyn Bowen, Michael Burn, Bill Bidmead, Elsevier – re George Newnes Ltd, Ken Ford, Will Fowler, Greenhill Books, Donald Gilchrist, Emyr Jones, Idris Jones, Brigadier Lord Lovat, Charles

Messenger, Mrs Jean Mills-Roberts, Alex Morris, Murdoch McDougal, Colonel Bob Montgomery, Geoff Murray, Roland Oliver, Orion Publications, Bill Parker, Ernest Reid, Geoff Riley, Mrs Desiree Roderick, Colonel John Reynolds, Peter Rogers, Vic Ralph, John Southworth, Spellmount Publications, Bill Sadler, Joe Spicer, Alistair Thorburn, Ron Youngman, John Wall, Freddie Walker and John White.

My special thanks are also due to Michael Leventhal and Deborah Hercun of Frontline Books for their editorial guidance, help and patience in the preparation of this book.

Finally, I must acknowledge and pay tribute to my dear wife, Jane, for her help, encouragement and support – she has also done more than her fair share of proofreading too.

I consider myself fortunate to have had the help and support of all these people and am most grateful to them. They have my special thanks.

JAMES DUNNING
ROMSEY

SELECT BIBLIOGRAPHY

A great number of books have been published over the years narrating the exploits of the Commandos (Army and Royal Marines) in the Second World War as well as those dealing with separate Commando sub-units such as Small Scale Raiding Force, also known as No 62 Commando, and the Special Boat Section (SBS), but none is devoted entirely to the battle honours of the Army Commandos.

However, as this book does not pretend to provide a full account of each action that merited the award of a specific battle honour it is recommended that readers seek out those books in the following list that deal in greater depth with the particular battle or action. In several cases the books have been written by commandos who took part in the actions.

Barnes, Tag, *Commando Diary*, Spellmount Ltd, 1991. A personal account of the author's service in No I Commando from October 1942 to March 1946 and so includes NORTH AFRICA 1941–1943, SEDJENANE, BURMA 1943–1945, ALETHANGYAW, MYEBON, and KANGAW.

Churchill, Thomas, *Commando Crusade*, William Kimber Ltd, 1987. Brigadier T. Churchill was at the LANDING IN SICILY and subsequently, after the battle of SALERNO, took over command of No 2 Commando Brigade in Italy and was involved in ANZIO, MONTE ORNITO, and ADRIATIC operations.

Dear, Ian, *Ten Commando, 1942–45*, Leo Cooper Ltd, 1987. A well-researched book on No 10 Commando, which was composed entirely of men who originated from countries that were under Nazi occupation – French, Dutch, Polish, or even Germans. It was the small detachment from this Commando that took part in the action that led to the award of the battle honour of WESTKAPELLE. Later republished by Pen & Sword Ltd.

Dorrian, James, *Storming of St Nazaire*, Leo Cooper Ltd, 1998. The most comprehensive and detailed history of this famous raid. Essential reading for the full story.

Dunning, James, *The Fighting Fourth*, Sutton Publishing Ltd, 2003. The story of No 4 Commando from 1940 to 1945, including full descriptions of that Commando's part in the Lofoten raid (NORWAY 1941) and in the battle honour actions of DIEPPE, NORMANDY LANDING, DIVES CROSSING and FLUSHING. Republished by The History Press, 2010.

Durnford-Slater, John, *Commando*, William Kimber & Co Ltd, 1985. First-hand account by the original commanding officer of No 3 Commando and as such provides details of the Lofoten (NORWAY 1941), VAAGSO and DIEPPE raids, LANDING IN SICILY, SICILY 1943, LANDING AT PORTE VENERE, and TERMOLI. The original book was later reprinted by Greenhill Books, London.

Ford, Ken, *St Nazaire 1942*, Osprey Publishing, 2001. Excellent summary of the raid with coloured artwork, three-dimensional maps, and photographs.

Fowler, Will, *The Commandos at Dieppe*, HarperCollins Publishing, 2002. A well-researched book that deals exclusively with No 4 Commando's part in the ill-fated raid. One of the interesting aspect of the book is the German commanders' comments on the raid.

Gilchrist, Donald, *Don't Cry For Me*, Robert Hale Ltd, 1982. Gilchrist served in No 4 Commando and in this book, full of amusing anecdotes, he recalls his experiences on the Dieppe raid and in Normandy.

Jenkins, W.G., *Commando Subaltern at War*, Greenhill Books, 1996. No 43 (RM) Commando's operations as part of 2 Commando Brigade in Italy and the Adriatic. Includes descriptions of the actions VALLI DI COMACCHIO and ARGENTA GAP.

Keyes, Elizabeth, *Geoffrey Keyes, VC*. George Newnes Ltd, 1956. Elizabeth wrote the biography of her brother, who became the Commandos' first VC recipient. The book also covers the formation and early training of No 11 Commando and their brief campaign in SYRIA, LITANI, and the story of Keyes's raid on Rommel's headquarters in North Africa.

Lovat, Lord, *March Past*, Weidenfeld & Nicholson, 1978. The autobiography of one of the Commandos' most outstanding leaders and his service in the Commandos from 1941 until he was badly wounded in Normandy in June 1944. Includes details of Lofoten, Boulogne, and DIEPPE raids, as well as D-Day and the early days of the invasion of Normandy.

Messenger, Charles, *The Commandos 1940–1946*, William Kimber Ltd, 1985. This is undoubtedly the most comprehensive and definitive history of the Commandos of the Second World War and includes details of the exploits of those smaller commando units whose actions were not specifically recognised in the awards of battle honours.

Messenger, Charles, *The Middle East Commandos*, William Kimber Ltd, 1988. Deals exclusively with the three Commandos (Nos 50, 51, and 52) raised in the Middle East in 1940. It recalls their actions from 1941, which includes operations in Eritrea and Abyssinia. However, importantly in the context of this book, it covers their part, together with No 7 Commando, in the tragic story of CRETE.

McDougall, Murdoch, *Swiftly They Struck*, Grafton Books, 1954. 'Big Mac', as McDougall was affectionately known in No 4 Commando, wrote this first-hand account of his experiences in the Commando during the Normandy and Walcheren campaigns. After VE Day, he and other German-speaking commandos formed a team to interrogate Nazis prisoners in the POW camps in efforts to find those SS, Gestapo, and concentration camp personnel who had to answer for their misdeeds during the war.

Mills-Roberts, Derek, *Clash By Night*, William Kimber Ltd, 1956. Mills-Roberts was another outstanding Commando leader and in his book he recalls his part with No 4 Commando in the DIEPPE raid, his campaign in North Africa, commanding No 6, where his Commando won the battle honour of STEAMROLLER FARM and then later in Normandy, still commanding No 6, stormed the beaches on D-Day; he took over command of No 1 Commando Brigade, when Lord Lovat was badly wounded, to subsequently lead them in the DIVES CROSSING, RHINE, LEESE, and ALLER operations in the north-west Europe campaign of 1944–45. He was highly decorated with the CBE, DSO and bar, MC, Legion d'Honneur, and Croix de Guerre.

Ministry of Information, *Combined Operations*, 1943. The very first book published during the Second World War on the Commandos. It deals with the raising of the Commandos and commando operations, up to and including the DIEPPE raid. As such it covers the great raids of Lofoten,

VAAGSO, ST NAZAIRE, and DIEPPE as well as the MADAGASCAR campaign.

Neillands, Robin, *The Raiders*, George Weidenfeld & Nicholson, 1989. This book was the result of an appeal way back in the early eighties by Robin Neillands to the secretary of the Commando Association, Henry Brown, calling for contributions from members recalling their wartime experiences in the Army Commandos. As such it does contain some stories relating to the battle honours, which are mentioned in the narrative, but there are many other fascinating stories as well.

Saunders, Hilary St George, *The Green Beret*, Michael Joseph, 1949. The first post-war book on the Commandos and an excellent one too. It covers all the major battles and actions of the Commandos in the Second World War.

Scott, Stan, *Fighting With The Commandos*, Pen and Sword Ltd, 2008. The most recent addition to commando books is that written by Stan Scott (edited by Neil Barber), who vividly describes his experiences with No 3 Commando in the Normandy campaign and subsequently in the crossing of the Rhine and on to the Baltic and VE Day.

Young, Peter, *Storm from the Sea*, Greenhill Books, 1989. This is a reprint of an earlier book written by Peter Young, he arguably saw more action in commando raids and campaigns in Sicily, Italy, north-west Europe, and Burma than any other commando leader – during the course of which he rose in rank from lieutenant to brigadier in five years. His accounts of the actions are always enhanced by personal recollections and amusing stories.

INDEX